Praise for *Global Brand Strategy*

"*Global Brand Strategy* strongly resonated with my own experience managing brands on a global basis. It is packed with examples from around the world and includes many actionable frameworks and tools. A must-read for any global brand manager and business leader wanting to take their brands overseas."
– Global President of Sales at a leading CPG company
(name witheld due to company policy)

"While many marketeers ignore globalization, and some pretend that it means that customers everywhere want the same thing, Steenkamp provides a much more granular—and practical—discussion about how much and how to standardize different elements of the marketing mix within an integrated framework."
– Pankaj Ghemawat, Professor of Global Strategy at IESE and New York University, and author of *World 3.0: Global Prosperity and How to Achieve It*

"*Global Brand Strategy* offers a refreshing and comprehensive exploration of global marketing that addresses 'what, so what, and now what.' It addresses 'what' with substantive foundational global marketing insight that benefits both experienced and new global marketers. 'So what' or why should you care is made clear with relevant and intriguing examples.

'Now what' drives practical action with valuable tools and managerial takeaways."

> – **Mary Garrett**, former vice-president of marketing and communications at IBM, Director of Ethan Allen Global Inc., and chairperson-elect of the American Marketing Association

"Drawing on his 25 years of international experience, Jan-Benedict Steenkamp's *Global Brand Strategy* provides extraordinary insight, and useful, practical guidance on how to build and maintain strong global brands. This work is particularly helpful for attorneys dedicated to protecting the intellectual property of clients around the world, as it details how and why trademarks, geographical indications, and other forms of intellectual property create value for global companies and their consumers, including through the use of insightful examples of corporate successes and failures."

> – **Partner at a top international law firm**
> (name withheld due to company policy)

"Jan-Benedict Steenkamp takes us in this book into a very profound knowledge adventure, showcasing his extraordinary wisdom and experience in global brands and global marketing. With vivid and practical examples, he is capable of teaching and demonstrating how global brands have emerged in the global scenario, their trends, characteristics, features and future in digital challenge. With figures, tables, grids, matrices, and guiding scorecards in all the chapters, he offers a very practical guide for decision makers to facilitate their tasks."

> – **Mauricio Graciano Palacios**, Corporate Affairs Director Coca-Cola/FEMSA Group

"Jan-Benedict Steenkamp's *Global Brand Strategy* achieves one milestone that most business books miss these days—it encourages you to think and draw your own conclusions, this time about the journey of building and nurturing global brands. And to help you in this challenging journey, Steenkamp provides you with very pragmatic frameworks, tools, and real examples of brands that have successfully become global."

> – **Jorge Meszaros**, former Vice President Hair Care, Procter & Gamble China

"At a time when globalization is the name of the game at corporate head offices, and we are all witnessing the expansion of global brands, this book is a must-read for anyone who would like to pursue a career in global marketing or in managing global brands. After a thorough analysis about the current trends, based on his renowned expertise in branding, the author has crafted probably the best toolkit a global brand manager can have today, including the COMET Scorecard and different assessment tools for both one's organization and for the customers served. Last but not least, the author makes an effort in identifying managerial implications and take-aways for global brand managers."

– **Josep Franch**, Dean of ESADE Business School (Spain)

"Few would argue with the idea that we live and do business in a branded world. Yet, traditional notions of brand building and brand value today are in flux due to globalization, the rise of the emerging markets, and the advent of the digital age. Amidst these changes, Steenkamp's work is a welcome re-interpretation of how to build value through brands that will be very useful for any organization operating in today's global, digitized markets."

– **Victor Fung**, Group Chairman of Fung Group (Hong Kong)

"Building and keeping a successful global brand in a world in disarray leads us to the perennial paradox of motivation arising from fear or aspiration. Jan-Benedict Steenkamp's masterpiece *Global Brand Strategy* shines a light of brilliance on your aspirations."

– **Luis Niño de Rivera**, Vice Chairman of
Banco Azteca (Latin America)

"This is a remarkable book on global brand strategy, not only written skillfully but with a rare mix of knowledge, passion, and practical wisdom. A must-read for managers and executives in all industries facing a dynamic marketplace and branding challenges."

– **Zhao Ping**, Chairman of the Marketing Department,
Tsinghua University (China)

"This book takes you into a journey of great intellectual perception and holistic understanding of the term 'brand' and its intricate ubiquitousness in our daily lives. It fundamentally paves the way to a better appre-

ciation and comprehension on the cruciality of a cohesive global brand strategy. It is indeed the launchpad of brand monetization!"
– **Moustapha Sarhank**, Chairman Emeritus, Sarhank Group for Investment (Egypt)

"*Global Brand Strategy* is a reference on the power of brands, old and new, and a joy to read. It is an enthralling journey that makes a reader value branding as a competitive tool. This is particularly true in a fast-changing global economy, where competitors have instant access to markets through the Internet and ever-evolving digital technologies."
– **Raja Habre**, Executive Director Lebanese Franchise Association

"Anyone involved in the development of brand strategies will treasure this book because it provides an organized framework that makes sense in current market conditions of intensive competition. Companies and brand managers will gain a strategic perspective on the Brand Value Chain that helps to understand processes, structures and strategies required to build a brand on the global context."
– **Maria Elena Vázquez**, Dean School of Business and Humanities, Tecnologico de Monterrey (ITESM), Mexico

"*Global Brand Strategy* represents the best combination of theory and practice. The book clearly indicates how a well-defined brand strategy can allow firms to leverage their resources in an increasing competitive global business context."
– **Dheeraj Sharma**, Chairman of the Marketing Department, Indian Institute of Management Ahmedabad

"Steenkamp presents useful insights and a thoughtful framework that outlines the ways that global brands can create value. *Global Brand Strategy* should prove to be a very useful read for any executive aspiring to build a great and lasting global brand."
– **Richard Allison**, President of Domino's Pizza International

"Each day more companies are becoming global; as a result the global community is becoming smaller. Nevertheless, it is important to understand the differences of each culture and how global brands need to adapt to them. This is exactly what Jan-Benedict Steenkamp does in his book transmitting novel concepts that can apply to any organization."
– **Alejandro Romero**, Latin America Marketing Manager, Alltech

Jan-Benedict Steenkamp

Global Brand Strategy

World-wise Marketing in the Age of Branding

palgrave
macmillan

Jan-Benedict Steenkamp
Kenan-Flagler Business School
University of North Carolina at Chapell Hill
North Carolina, USA

ISBN 978-1-349-94993-9   ISBN 978-1-349-94994-6   (eBook)
DOI 10.1057/978-1-349-94994-6

Library of Congress Control Number: 2016955973

Cover illustration: mattjeacock/Getty

Printed on acid-free paper

This Palgrave Macmillan imprint is published by Springer Nature
The registered company is Macmillan Publishers Ltd.
The registered company address is: The Campus, 4 Crinan Street, London, N1 9XW, United Kingdom

To the loving memory of my parents: to my father, Prof. dr. Piet Steenkamp, Founder of the Christian Democratic Party, Chairman of the Senate, Commander in the Order of the Netherlands Lion, Holder of the Grand Cross of Merit of France and of Germany, and Commander in the Pontifical Order of St. Gregory the Great; and to my brilliant and iron-willed mother, Constance Steenkamp. I am deeply grateful for their support, wise counsel, and inspiration during my entire life.

Also by the Author

Product Quality (Assen: Van Gorcum, 1989).
Private Label Strategy: How to Meet the Store Brand Challenge (with Nirmalya Kumar; Cambridge: MA: Harvard Business School Press, 2007).
Brand Breakout: How Emerging Market Brands Will Go Global (with Nirmalya Kumar; New York: Palgrave Macmillan, 2013).

Contents

List of Figures

List of Tables

List of Tools

Preface

Not since our species emerged from Africa have we seen such integration of human commerce as we do today. When I was born in Amsterdam, the Netherlands had no free flow of goods and people across the German border. The Dutch government restricted the convertibility of the guilder, few people had journeyed to other countries, and even fewer had traveled by air, while entering China was all but impossible. The Iron Curtain divided Europe, and the wind of change had yet to sweep through colonial Africa. Making a telephone call from Amsterdam to New York City cost several US dollars per minute and knowledge of far-away events was sketchy.

We ate the typically stern Dutch meal: potatoes, meat, and cabbage. If your family ate zucchini, pasta, and olive oil, whatever those were, we eyed you with mild suspicion. People drove DAF Variomatics, owned Philips televisions, spread Blue Band margarine on their bread, drank Raak soda and Heineken beer, ate Royco soup, De Hoorn smoked sausage, and Campina ice cream, rode Gazelle bikes, dreamed of flying on KLM Royal Dutch Airlines, rooted for Amsterdamsche Football Club Ajax, and banked with the Boerenleenbank. Koninklijke Hoogovens delivered its steel to Stork machinery on DAF heavy trucks and shipped steel overseas through Verolme dock and shipyard. Many filled their gas tanks at a Royal Dutch Shell station, unaware of its global stature.

In my youth, my brand awareness was local because the products I could buy were local, even though I lived in one of the world's most open economies at the time, an economy that even in 1960 depended on global trade for over half its national wealth.

How different is the brandscape of today's youth. Not even Dutch children would recognize half these brands. Many have disappeared from the marketplace (e.g., Fokker, Raak, Royco, DAF cars) and others are but a pale image of their former glory (Philips, Ajax). Still others sold themselves off to foreign firms (Hoogovens to Tata Steel, DAF trucks to Paccar) or merged with them (KLM with Air France). At the same time, several (largely) local Dutch brands became powerful global brands, not just Shell and Heineken but ING bank, Grolsch beer, KPMG professional services, and Omo laundry detergents.

Of course, Dutch brands are not unique in this respect. You can probably think of several retail or consumer brands, maybe even your childhood favorites, that did not survive the arrival of the global economy. Britain's storied car brand Rover went bankrupt, while once proud British Steel—now part of India's Tata Steel—is fighting for survival. Germany's renowned consumer electronics brands Schneider and Dual were sold to China's TCL and all but disappeared from the marketplace. France's Simca was acquired by Chrysler and afterwards taken from the market and Belgium's SBR went bankrupt. Chrysler bought American Motors Corporation only to be eliminated later. General Motors' car brands Oldsmobile, Pontiac, Hummer, and Saturn ceased operations, the victims of the onslaught brought on by foreign car brands and the global financial crisis of 2008–2009.

Brands would not have emerged from their country of origin without the dramatic drop in the costs of international connectivity. A turning point was 1989: people everywhere watched the Berlin Wall come down. Goods, services, capital, and ideas move freely about the cabin of planet Earth. Via the Internet, people follow local weather and global news. Before I graduated from college, I had the privilege of traveling widely across the world because my father served as an independent (nonexecutive) director of KLM. But my travels were nothing compared with my daughter's. Before her 25th birthday, she had traveled from Argentina to Zimbabwe: that is, not just the countries of the European Union but also Botswana, Brazil, Burma, Chile, Ethiopia, India, Namibia, Nepal, South Africa, Thailand, the United States, Uruguay, and Vietnam.

It's a small world after all. People around the world covet the prestige of Gucci, the reliability of Toyota, the taste of French Haut-Médoc wine or Coca-Cola, the soccer played by Real Madrid, the café experience of Starbucks, Hollywood blockbusters, McDonald's French fries, the latest iPhone, and Zara's fashion.

In corporate headquarters around the world, many purchase managers prefer the technological prowess of Caterpillar machinery, Honeywell process controls, John Deere tractors, General Electric medical equipment, and Airbus aircraft over any local manufacturer; the expertise of McKinsey consulting services, Deloitte accounting services, Sodexo hospitality services, and FedEx logistics services. Along with their market success, global brands have become immensely valuable assets. While the total value of the world's 100 most valuable global brands was $1.4 trillion in 2006, the global top-100 was worth a staggering $3.4 trillion in 2016, according to brand consultancy Millward Brown. Few, if any, firm assets exhibit a compound annual growth rate of 8.8 % year after year.

Yet, more than a few firms stumble in taking their brands global while others misjudge market developments or cut corners with scandalous results. Chrysler's efforts to go global have failed, Walmart flopped in Germany and South Korea, Sony rose and faded in global consumer electronics, BlackBerry misread the consumer market, and Volkswagen's emission testing fraud has scandalized the brand.

Why do some brands succeed in all the big markets of the world and others never make it beyond their own borders? What can executives learn from their successes and failures in building and managing their global brand? These questions inspired me to write this book.

Drawing on my own research in branding and global marketing over the last 25 years, the work of my academic peers, interviews with senior executives, trade publications, and my consulting work, I analyze brand strategies in a global economy where the forces of globalization are strong but not friction free: national and cultural differences cause turbulence, even resistance. I lay out actionable strategies for executives to launch and fly strong global brands, no matter the headwinds. My book contains many examples, visuals, and tools for you to use in analyzing your situation and discussing your aspirations with fellow executives, board members, and direct reports. My goal is to enable heads of business units and managers to navigate effectively and profitably in today's global marketscape.

Acknowledgments

Many colleagues, companies, and marketing practitioners have made an invaluable contribution in making this book a reality. I am deeply grateful to all executives who shared their unique experiences during my long odyssey. I owe special thanks to Ramzi Abou-Ezzeddine (Bank Audi), Vindi Banga (Unilever), Giuseppe Caiazza (Saatchi & Saatchi), Peter Dart (WPP), Arvind Desikan (Google), Annick Desmecht (Samsonite, Wedgwood), Mark Durcan (Micron Technology), John Edwards (Jaguar Land Rover), Rebecca Enonchong (AppsTech), Vaughan Ensley (P&G), Brian Feng (SUMEC), Juliet Guo (Sand River), Raja Habre (Lebanese Franchise Association), Peter Hubbell (P&G), Rob Malcolm (Diageo), Anna Malmhake (Pernod Ricard), Kathrine Mo (Telinor), Franck Moison (Colgate), Sunil Nayak (Sodexo), Paul Polman (Unilever), Raji Ramaswamy (JWT), Yannig Roth (eYeka), Riad Salame (Banque du Liban), Moustapha Sarhank (Sarhank Group for Investment), Eric Solovy (Sidley Austin LLP), Paulus Steenkamp (Royal Dutch Shell), Pierpaolo Susani (Barilla), Luca Uva (Barilla), C.K. Venkataraman (Titan), Zhang Jianhua (SAIC Motor Corp.), and Peter Zhang (Volvo).

I have had the privilege to test and refine my ideas in lectures to participants at conferences on all continents and in various MBA and executive programs. I learned as much from them as they learned from me. I also owe much gratitude to a number of colleagues whose insights have sharpened my thinking over the years. The contributions of David Aaker

(Berkeley & Prophet), Kusum Ailawadi (Dartmouth College), Dana Alden (University of Hawaii), Rajeev Batra (University of Michigan), Steven Burgess (University of the Witwatersrand), Yubo Chen (Tsinghua University), Martijn de Jong (Erasmus University), Marnik Dekimpe (Tilburg University), Pankaj Ghemawat (IESE & NYU), Justin He (East China Normal University), Kevin Keller (Dartmouth College), Miguel Angel López Lomelí (ITESM), and Dheeraj Sharma (Indian Institute of Management Ahmedabad) were especially helpful. I am grateful for the help and suggestions I received from my colleagues at UNC-Kenan-Flagler Business School, especially Barry Bayus, Isaac Dinner and Katrijn Gielens. I thank Erin Mitchell for preparing the art work—tables, figures, and tools.

A very special word of thanks to my friend and colleague of 25 years, Nirmalya Kumar, who left academia in 2013 to join Tata & Sons. Academia's loss is India's gain. His insights over the years have significantly influenced my thinking. I sorely miss the countless hours we spent discussing ideas in his London apartment, fueled by excellent French wine from his personal cellar.

I am grateful for the support of my wife, Valarie Steenkamp. She is my sounding board, not only for many of the ideas in this book, but for all my life's decisions.

Finally, I want to acknowledge all those executives who work hard every day of their lives to enrich our lives with high quality global brands. If they find this book useful, it will be worth all of my efforts.

1

The Cambrian Explosion of Brands

Imagine a world without brands. Perhaps it is the world before language, before mankind could distinguish earth from sky, flora from fauna, or dreams from reality. Or it is the world before money, at the dawn of specialization, where people were called by what they did best—fisher, farmer, baker, barber, sailor, smith—and bartered for what they needed. Or it is the world before industry, where the rich coveted Florentine wool, Venetian glass, and Toledo steel, all from artisanal communities. Their products were relatively unsophisticated, rivals were few, and most sales were local. If consumers weren't satisfied with their purchases, word got out quickly, and a craftsman's reputation took a hit.

Then came movable type, electricity, the steam engine, railroads, the light bulb, the telegraph, mass production, and unprecedented choice. Technological progress in the late nineteenth century outstripped the average consumer's ability to understand the products, let alone know their producers personally. Copycats sprung up to exploit the popularity of certain goods. Which product was the genuine article? Which producer was trustworthy? In response to this customer uncertainty, firms started to introduce brands in various industries, ranging from steel and armaments (Krupp, Vickers), automobiles (Mercedes, Ford), and

© The Author(s) 2017
J.-B. Steenkamp, *Global Brand Strategy*,
DOI 10.1057/978-1-349-94994-6_1

banks (Barings, Rothschild) to toothpaste (Colgate), soap (Ivory), and soft drinks (Coca-Cola). In what we might call the "Precambrian" era of branding, a diversity of brand-savvy entrepreneurs emerged.

Take the Lever brothers, William and James. In 1884, they launched Sunlight, a soap for washing clothes and cleaning house. The chemist who invented the Sunlight formula, William Watson, used glycerin and vegetable oils instead of animal fat (tallow). The resulting soap was a free-lathering product of uniform high quality. Where most soap makers were selling big blocks of soap, the Lever brothers had the marketing insight to cut their product into small bars, wrap them in bright yellow paper, and brand them Sunlight to appeal to sun-starved housewives of Victorian England. Over time, the Lever brothers started to advertise their brand. In one World War I advertisement, they claimed that the British Tommy was the cleanest fighter in the world because he used Sunlight. The Lever brothers were also among the first to understand the brand as an assurance of quality. They offered a £1000 guarantee of purity on every bar. That's £71,570 in today's terms. Sunlight quickly became one of the world's first consumer brands.[1] In 1930, Lever Brothers merged with the Dutch company Margarine Unie (Margarine Union Ltd.), led by the brand-savvy Van den Bergh and Jurgens families, to become Unilever, still one of the largest consumer packaged goods firms in the world.

The Global Branding Phenomenon

With the advent of mass media in the 1960s, immortalized in the TV series Mad Men, the pace of brand introduction, sophistication, and importance accelerated dramatically. The world has witnessed a "Cambrian explosion" of brands.[2] The digital revolution of the twenty-first cen-

---

[1] https://en.wikipedia.org/wiki/Sunlight_(cleaning_product); accessed October 14, 2015.

[2] The term Cambrian explosion of brands was first used by Marc de SwaanArons; http://www.the-atlantic.com/business/archive/2011/10/how-brands-were-born-a-brief-history-of-modern-marketing/246012/. It is inspired by one of the greatest—if not the greatest—explosion of species in the history of the world, which took place in a relatively short time (geologically speaking) of about 20–25 million years in the Cambrian era, which started 542 million years ago; http://burgess-shale.rom.on.ca/en/science/origin/04-cambrian-explosion.php; both sites accessed January 21, 2016.

tury with cheap mobile, big data, social media, and global connectivity has further accelerated this process. Brands have become ubiquitous in today's marketplace. And when you look at annual rankings of the world's most powerful brands by consultancies Brand Finance, Interbrand, and Millward Brown, you will notice that the strongest brands in about any industry are almost invariably global brands.[3]

In this book, I define a global brand as a *brand that uses the same name and logo, is recognized, available, and accepted in multiple regions of the world, shares the same principles, values, strategic positioning, and marketing throughout the world, and its management is internationally coordinated, although the marketing mix can vary.*[4]

I do not include a market share criterion in my definition as that confounds strategy with its outcomes and restricts me to proven successes as opposed to emerging successes. In principle, a global brand has broadly the same positioning around the world. If the brand is a premium-priced brand, it is premium-priced around the world. If it is positioned vis-à-vis an income segment of the market (e.g., global elite), its positioning must be consistent in every market. Of course, this is an ideal that managers cannot always realize because the competitive environment of markets may vary and companies need to adapt positioning. For example, Heineken has a premium positioning in most of the world, but it is a middle-of-the-road brand in its home market. For most global brands, the marketing mix will vary (somewhat) to meet local needs and competitive requirements. For example, Coca-Cola is sweeter in the Middle East than in the USA. However, its brand name, logo, and packages are similar worldwide, and consumers can easily distinguish Coke from its competitors worldwide. The issue is not exact uniformity; rather, it is whether the company is offering essentially the same product.

---

[3] Millward Brown: http://www.millwardbrown.com/brandz; Brand Finance: http://brandirectory.com/; Interbrand: http://interbrand.com/best-brands/. A notable exception is banking, where the average value of a top ten regional bank (e.g., Wells Fargo, ICBC) is more than twice the average value of a top ten global bank (e.g., HSBC, Citi), according to Millward Brown. This is due to the great complexities in running global banks in a context of ever stricter, but country-specific legislation (think about compliance officers).

[4] My definition is based on De Mooij, Marieke (1998), *Global Marketing and Advertising: Understanding Cultural Paradoxes*, Thousand Oaks, CA: Sage.

The rise and dominance of global brands is a logical consequence of one of the axial principles of our time, the globalization of the marketplace, accelerated by rapidly falling transportation and communication costs. For example, a three-minute telephone call from New York City to London cost $1004.78 in 1927 and $0.06 in 2014 (both in 2014 US dollars). Transporting a single container via ship from Los Angeles to Hong Kong cost $14,365 in 1970 and less than $1500 in 2014 (in 2014 US dollars).[5]

Other factors contributing to global integration of markets include falling national boundaries, regional unification (EU, ASEAN, NAFTA), global standardization of manufacturing techniques, global investment and production strategies, rapid increase in education and literacy levels, growing urbanization in developing countries, free(er) flow of information, labor, money, and technology across borders and the World Wide Web, increased consumer sophistication and purchasing power, and the emergence of global media.

Brands help consumers everywhere in the world to determine which product or service to choose – which baby formula is safest for our newborn, which cars have airbags that will inflate properly, which consultancy has the experience we need without conflicts of interest, or which excavator is the most durable with the best warranty. Firms invest massive amounts of money to build, nurture, and defend their brands. In 2014, global advertising spending alone exceeded half a trillion dollars (see Table 1.1). And brand advertising is only part of brand investment; think about brand-related R&D, distribution channel cultivation, personal selling, and market research. Why do firms spend so much money on building their brands? Because brands perform several functions that make them valuable to companies. Read on.

---

[5] US Department of Commerce; https://cps.ipums.org/cps/cpi99.shtml.

Table 1.1 Worldwide media spending for selected MNCs

Global rank	Company	Home country	Industry	Media spending ($ millions)
1	Procter & Gamble	USA	Consumer packaged goods	10,125
2	Unilever	UK/ Netherlands	Consumer packaged goods	7394
3	L'Oréal	France	Personal care	5264
4	Coca-Cola	USA	Beverages	3279
5	Toyota Motor Corp.	Japan	Automotive	3185
6	Volkswagen	Germany	Automotive	3171
7	Nestlé	Switzerland	Food	2930
8	General Motors	USA	Automotive	2849
9	Mars Inc.	USA	Snacks/pet food	2569
10	McDonald's	USA	Restaurants	2494
13	Sony	Japan	Electronics	2346
18	Pfizer	USA	Pharmaceuticals	1984
21	Samsung	South Korea	Technology	1905
30	Apple	USA	Technology	1390
35	Disney	USA	Entertainment	1256
36	Walmart Stores	USA	Retail	1236
40	Bayer	Germany	Chemicals/ pharmaceuticals	1161
46	Vodafone Group	UK	Telecom	1020
48	LVMH	France	Luxury	994
61	Sanofi	France	Pharmaceuticals	688
63	Amazon	USA	Retail	672
66	IKEA	Sweden	Retail	647
74	Novartis	Switzerland	Pharmaceuticals	552
84	American Express	USA	Payments	451
86	Mattel	USA	Toys	447

Source: Adapted from *Advertising Age* (December 7, 2015); reported is worldwide measured media spending
Note: Throughout the book, unless noted otherwise, $ refers to US dollars

Why Consumers Value Brands

We live in a branded world. The average number of brand exposures per day per person exceeds 5000.[6] For comparison, the average male speaks about 7000 words a day.[7] Five thousand brand exposures per day seem rather overwhelming, although the average person only consciously notices a fraction of them. Nevertheless, the sheer ubiquity of brands has led so-called critical thinkers to suggest that brands are in some way not real, that they are mere ploys to mislead consumers, and that the world might be better off without them.[8] I have met executives with engineering, finance, or accounting backgrounds who are equally unsure about the importance of brands. When I was working with a major player in the infant formula market, the chief financial officer asked me openly: "The marketing department tells me all the time that brands are important. Can you explain that to me? I don't really get it." Why do brands matter? Brands perform three important functions for consumers.

Brands Make Decision Making Easier

First, brands *ease consumer decision making*. The human brain stores product knowledge in associate networks largely organized around the brand. If you recognize a brand and have some knowledge about it, then you can easily access and use related product knowledge in your decision making. You need not engage in additional thought or data processing to make a purchase decision. Absent brands, you need to study each offering, and analyze product detail for multiple offerings before you can choose among them. Most people do not want to expend this time and effort on their everyday purchases. For example, on average, consumers take

---

[6] http://sjinsights.net/2014/09/29/new-research-sheds-light-on-daily-ad-exposures/; accessed October 15, 2015.

[7] http://www.dailymail.co.uk/sciencetech/article-2281891/Women-really-talk-men-13-000-words-day-precise.html; accessed January 21, 2016.

[8] Boorman, Neil (2007), *Bonfire of Brands: How I Learned to Live Without Labels*, Edinburgh, UK: Canongate; Klein, Naomi (2000), *No Logo: Taking Aim at the Brand Bullies*, New York: Knopf; Ritzer, George (2004), *The McDonaldization of Society*, Thousand Oaks, CA: Pine Forge Press; Ritzer, George (2007), *The Globalization of Nothing 2*, Thousand Oaks, CA: Pine Forge Press.

four to five seconds to make a purchase decision in a local supermarket.[9] Compare that with, say, the amount of time you'd need to shop for groceries while vacationing in another country, where you'd recognize few of the brands on the shelves. From personal experience, I know that it easily takes three times as much time to reach a decision. And grocery shopping is not cognitively very demanding. Imagine selecting a car—new or used—in a world without brands!

Brands Reduce Risk

A second function of brands is to reduce consumer *risk*. Brands signify the source or maker of the product. As the former chief marketing officer (CMO) of Unilever, Simon Clift said, "a brand is the contract between a company and consumers. And the consumer is the judge and jury. If (s) he believes a company is in breach of that contract either by underperforming or reducing quality service rendering, the consumer will simply choose to enter a contract with another brand."[10] Executives who invest in brands know these investments would yield poor returns if the brands failed to fulfill their promises. Therefore, *companies have a strong incentive to deliver on quality*. Consumers intuitively understand this connection and use brand name as an indicator of product quality. Consider how a Chinese consumer, Wang Weixin, searched for a new smartphone. Although he contemplated buying the Xiaomi brand, he went with a Huawei Honor 7 because of the company's reputation. He explained, "To be honest, regular folk don't know that much about specs [mobile phone specifications]. But Huawei phones have a good name among my friends, and I know it's an international brand."[11]

The link between a strong brand name and perceived quality is such that it can affect consumer judgments even if consumers are verifiably

---

[9] Hoyer, Wayne D. (1984), "An Examination of Consumer Decision Making for a Common Repeat Purchase Product," *Journal of Consumer Research*, 10 (December), pp. 822–829.

[10] https://www.linkedin.com/pulse/power-brand-building-your-own-personal-corporate-world-onyebuchi?forceNoSplash=true; accessed January 21, 2016.

[11] Osawa, Juro and Eva Dou (2015), "Huawei Catches Up To Xiaomi in China," *Wall Street Journal*, October 23, p. B1.

wrong. In one study of customer perception, consumers could not distinguish the taste of ten beer brands when the bottles were unlabeled. However, when they could see the labels, they could differentiate the flavors of the beers.[12] Consumers use a well-known brand name to infer product quality; that is their most important mechanism to reduce purchase risk.

If the brand does not fulfill its promises, if the company reneges on its implied contract with consumers, then consumers will feel betrayed, even violated; so violated that they may sue the company for false advertising, misleading brand statements, and other transgressions. Consider what then-CEO Martin Winterkorn said, after the September 2015 revelation that Volkswagen had been cheating on emission tests of its diesel cars: "I personally am deeply sorry we have broken the trust of our consumers and the public."[13] Apologies may not be enough—according to branding consultancy Brand Finance, its brand stature declined significantly and lawsuits are in the making.[14]

Brands Provide Emotional Benefits

A third important function of brands is to fulfill consumers' emotional needs. Marketers have long known that consumers can attach emotional meaning to brands. People value Tide laundry detergent not only because it removes stains effectively but also because it makes them feel better caretakers of their family. Jaguar does not give consumers the best functional quality per dollar paid—Lexus would be a more rational choice on that deliverable—but it does convey British heritage and royalty. Harley-Davidson stands unequivocally for rebellion, machismo, freedom, and

---

[12] Allison, Ralph I. and Kenneth P. Uhl (1964), "Influence of Beer Brand Identification on Taste Perception," *Journal of Marketing Research*, 1 (August), pp. 36–39. Steenkamp, Jan-Benedict E.M. (1989), *Product Quality*, Assen: Van Gorcum.

[13] Rieger, Bernhard (2015), "The End of the People's Car: How Volkswagen Lost Its Corporate Soul," *Foreign Affairs*, October 4 https://www.foreignaffairs.com/articles/germany/2015-10-04/end-peoples-car; accessed October 10, 2015.

[14] http://brandfinance.com/news/press-releases/vw-risks-its-31-billion-brand-and-germanys-national-reputation/; http://www.hgdlawfirm.com/vwemissionslawsuit/#top; both accessed January 21, 2016.

America. Riding a Harley is an escape from the drudgery of rules and routines. The Harley Owners Group is "the granddaddy of all community-building efforts," serving to promote not just a consumer product, but a lifestyle. It has over one million members. Starbucks is a popular place for business meetings in China as it makes the host seem international and sophisticated.[15]

Emotional benefits are becoming ever more important. As prices fall for virtually all commodities and mass-manufactured goods, the real competition takes place not on the shelves or on website pages but in the hearts of consumers.

In sum, brands provide value to consumers by:

- Decreasing the time, money, and cognitive load of making purchase decisions;
- Reducing consumer uncertainty by signaling quality and identifying the source or maker of the product; and
- Providing emotional satisfaction.

The Role of Business Brands

While business-to-business (B2B) executives readily recognize the importance of brands for their business-to-consumers (B2C) customers, what about B2B markets? Many B2B executives are uncertain about the role of business branding in their industry. After all, their customers are usually well-informed about the product alternatives and their specifications. Moreover, compared with households, industrial buyers have far fewer purchase decisions to make per week; and they do not expect the decision process to be emotional.

Yet we ought not underestimate the importance of brands in B2B markets. Why? First, many industrial buyers are employed in small business enterprises. They do not always have the time or the specialized know-how to evaluate each purchase in detail. Second, many of the decisions

---

[15] Beattie, Anita Chang (2012), "Can Starbucks Make China Love Joe?" *Advertising Age*, November 5, pp. 20–21.

that large and small companies make are routine purchases of limited significance. These decisions simply do not warrant extensive problem solving. Third, purchase managers are still human beings! They experience cognitive limitations, time pressure, distractions, and social influences, whether they head the procurement department, a small business, or a household.

Suppose you are the CMO who needs advice on your firm's strategy. There are countless consultancies, and you can hardly evaluate them all before making a choice. You may prefer to deal with a prestigious consultancy as it will make you feel more important. So you hire McKinsey, the strongest brand in consultancy according to brand consulting firm Brand Finance. McKinsey is not an exception. Most B2B industries have strong brand names: investment banking (Goldman Sachs, Morgan Stanley), accounting (Deloitte, PwC, KPMG), business software (Oracle, SAP), telecom infrastructure (Cisco, Ericsson, Huawei), engineering (Siemens, General Electric), heavy equipment (Caterpillar, Komatsu), and IT services (Accenture, IBM).

But, while B2B brands do expedite decision making and provide emotional benefits, their most important function is to reduce risk. For B2B buyers, the product or service purchased is an input in their firm's own value-creating process. If the quality of this input falls short, senior management will be looking for somebody to blame. If the purchase manager bought a brand of high reputation, he or she can hardly be blamed for choosing the best, the most trusted, or the most used brand. If you were a purchase manager in mining industry, you could consider the US firm Caterpillar as well as the Chinese company Sany. Even if the Sany equipment were superior in features, price, service, and warranty, you would still hesitate to buy it because if the Sany equipment broke down, it would be *your* fault and put *your* job at risk After all, why did you risk the project by buying this second-tier brand? If the Cat excavator broke down, it would be *Caterpillar's* fault, and your job would be secure. To paraphrase an earlier saying, "No one ever got fired for buying a Cat."

The Global Competition for Consumers and Business Customers

In the twenty-first century global integration means truly the entire world, not just the West. The last four decades have witnessed the most profound change in the global economy since the dawn of the Industrial Revolution in eighteenth-century Britain. While the West accounted for 80% of global GDP in 1980, in 2016, emerging markets generate more than half the world's GDP. Thirty years ago, Eastern Europe was still chafing under Soviet domination, China had only just started to reform its economy, high tariffs sheltered the markets of India, Brazil, and Mexico, and South Africa was an international pariah. All these countries have become key competitive arenas for today's multinational companies (MNCs).

Recognizing the increased globalization of the marketplace, firms have increasingly turned to overseas markets to meet their growth targets. Nowadays, nearly 50% of revenues of S&P 500 companies are from overseas business, up from 30% in 2000.[16]And globalization is not restricted to large MNCs; foreign sales account for 50% or more of the sales of many smaller enterprises, especially in B2B where they can dominate global niches. Thus, global brands are increasingly the name of the game. The goal today is to create consistency and have impact, both of which are a lot easier to manage with a single worldwide identity. That approach is also more efficient, since MNCs can apply the same strategy everywhere.

However, a strategy that relies on global brands is not without risks. Global brands bring organizational and managerial complexity, a source of frustration and countless hours lost in meetings, time that people could have spent more productively on other activities. Even worse, if the global brand strategy is ill-conceived and poorly executed, it destroys rather than creates firm value. After all, we may conceive the world as flat, but most world citizens beg to differ. Many customers either do not know or do not care whether the brand is global. Moreover, the opportunities and threats to creating global brand for Chinese smart-

---

[16] http://www.prnewswire.com/news-releases/sp-500-foreign-sales-report-sales-to-asia-rise-uk-moves-lower-taxes-paid-to-us-climbs-dramatically-300112741.html; accessed January 6, 2016.

phone brand Xiaomi are different from those of Apple, let alone Vertu. Toyota's are as different from Ferrari's as Uniqlo's are from Zara's. The successful executive needs to understand what these differences are and why they matter in order to tackle the global branding challenge head-on. Otherwise, the global brand may turn out to be a basket case rather than a bread winner. This is what this book is about: securing the good and avoiding the ugly.

The Plan of the Book

I've structured this book around the Global Brand Value Chain (Fig. 1.1). It consists of three parts. Part I examines the key activities in building successful global brands. Chapter 2, "The COMET Framework: How Global Brands Create Value," maps out the most traveled paths that multinational corporations take to create global brand value. Chapter 3, "Customer Propositions for Global Brands," outlines five of the most viable customer propositions for global brands. Chapter 4, "Global Marketing Mix Decisions: Global Integration, Not Standardization,"

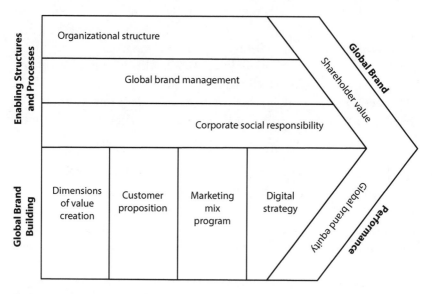

Fig. 1.1   Global brand value chain

walks through the key decisions that managers must make about the marketing mix for the global brand. The key challenge is to decide on the degree of global integration versus local adaptation for the various elements of the marketing mix. Finally, Chapter 5, "Global Brand Building in the Digital Age," explores the implications of the rise of the Internet and digital media for global brand building.

In Part II, I examine the structures and processes needed for building and maintaining the global brand. Chapter 6, "Organizational Structures for Global Brands," lays out four organizational solutions to manage the inherent tensions between global standardization, local adaptation, worldwide learning, and the need for speed and agility. Chapter 7, "Global Brand Management," delves into effective global brand management. Chapter 8, "Corporate Social Responsibility," highlights the importance of firm-wide corporate social responsibility in managing global brands. Communities hold global brands to a higher standard because of their great visibility and impact on societies around the world.

In Part III, I examine the performance of global brands. Financial markets demand ever greater accountability for the huge investments the firm makes in global brand building. Chapter 9, "Global Brand Equity," focuses on global brand equity, the goodwill adhering to the global brand. Chapter 10, "Global Brands and Shareholder Value," covers what the C-suite cares most about, the creation of shareholder value. By showing CEOs how global brands create shareholder value, marketing executives retain their seat at the top table.

Finally, in Chapter 11, "The Future of Global Brands," I draw together various themes and lessons of the book and will look into the future.

Before starting Part I of the book, two comments about terminology. I use the word *product* in a general sense, referring to both goods and services. I use the term *customer* broadly, referring to all organizations and persons who might potentially be interested in your brand, including (potential) consumers, purchase managers, and other companies. I prefer to use *customer* over *consumer* as many executives strongly associate the word consumer with one particular type of market entity that is, the buyer of consumer goods and services.

Part I

Global Brand Building

When Apple launches a new product, people wait for hours in cities around the world to be among the first to buy it. If ZTE of China introduced the same product, would anyone line up anywhere? When Coca-Cola changed its formula in 1985, consumers revolted from Atlanta to Havana even though they actually preferred it to traditional Coke in blind taste tests. The "Ultimate Driving Machine" stands not only for great automobiles but also for great speed. Car lovers link the machines of Bayerische Motoren Werke with the German Autobahn, which has no speed limit. By driving a BMW, they enjoy this unique experience, no matter how fast their highway allows them to go.

To build strong global brands, multinational corporations (MNC) such as Apple, Coca Cola, and BMW manage a portfolio of interlocking activities and processes, which need to achieve four goals. The first goal is to create value for the MNC (Chapter, "The COMET Framework: How Global Brands Create Value"). There are five types of value:

- **C**ustomer preference for global brands – the very fact that the brand is global adds luster to the brand through associations of higher quality (e.g., Nivea), global culture (Starbucks), or country of origin (Wedgwood).

- **O**rganizational benefits such as rapid rollout of new products (Magnum ice cream), ability to make global competitive moves (Daimler-Benz trucks), or the creation of a corporate identity (Zurich insurance).
- **M**arketing benefits associated with superior branding programs such as media spillover (HSBC), pooling marketing resources across countries (Nike), or leveraging the best marketing ideas globally (MasterCard).
- **E**conomic benefits of cost reduction in production and procurement (Caterpillar, IKEA).
- **T**ransnational innovation pooling of R&D globally to make better products (Olay), bottom-up innovation (Nissan), or frugal innovation (Aldi).

You can remember those five types through the acronym COMET. Building a strong global brand generally involves maximizing all five dimensions. If your brand falls short on certain aspects, assess whether this is a conscious choice or that action is required. Yet, even in the best of cases, your brand will do better on some aspects than on other aspects. Managers should design subsequent brand-building strategies to leverage rather than interfere with the brand's main source of value. For example, if a brand's primary source of value is economic (cost reduction), then the strategy calls for a high degree of global integration in the production process. If it leverages transnational innovation, then the strategy must involve procedures for rapid introduction of new products around the world. If its source of value is being symbolic of the global consumer culture, then its strategy should restrict localized advertising.

The second goal of the global brand is to offer a compelling customer proposition (Chapter, "Customer Propositions for Global Brands"). Most individual global brands can be classified as one of five types of brands, each with their own customer proposition:

- Value brands like Kirkland (Costco), Norwegian, or Sany offer the best possible value in the marketplace by offering acceptable quality for a very low price.
- Mass brands such as Samsung, Olay, and Lufthansa offer good quality for a price that is (slightly) above market average.

- Premium brands such as Apple, Mercedes, or Bose offer top quality for a high price. These brands excel in combining logic (functional performance) with magic (emotional benefits).
- Prestige brands like Ferrari, Hermès, Breitling, or McKinsey are sold at an extremely high price. Their primary raison d'être is exclusivity, buying something that few others can afford.
- Fun brands such as Zara, Swatch, and Disney provide stimulation, change, and excitement for a low price.

Each type of brand caters to a different global target segment defined by unique universal needs, has a distinct value proposition in terms of price and benefits offered, and faces unique challenges. Of course, within these five types, there is diversity as each global brand seeks to differentiate itself from others.

The third goal is to deliver the brand's promise to the target segment with a balanced marketing strategy (Chapter, "Global Marketing Mix Decisions: Global Integration, Not Standardization"). The global executive is a twenty-first-century Odysseus. He or she must sail between Scylla of global uniformity and Charybdis of excessive localization. How to navigate the choppy waters between the global and the local is the most hotly contested issue in global marketing. To what extent should we locally adapt the global brand's marketing mix? Should we rename the brand, alter the product, or localize pricing? Today, executives have both considerable company experience and a large body of research to make better decisions than ever before. I make recommendations that you can use as benchmarks for your own brand.

The fourth goal is to seize the opportunities and respond to the demands of the digital environment (Chapter, "Global Brand Building in the Digital Age"). More than three billion people use the Internet, and this number increases daily. While digital technologies change every day, what will not change quickly are the underlying trends that have a profound effect global brand building:

- The rise of the digital sales channel allows any brand to go global at a keystroke, especially start-up brands like Dollar Shave Club that intend to compete against yours.

- The move toward co-creation with customers of your brand program, which is practiced successfully by brands like Lego and Dell.
- The unrivaled transparency of your global brand's activities, which you ignore at your own peril, as IKEA and Starbucks learned the hard way.
- The connected customer and the sharing economy give rise to new global brands such as Airbnb and Uber that might disrupt your industry unless you move fast.
- The Internet of Things, which offers tremendous potential for new entrants like Tesla and for manufacturers like General Electric transitioning into services.

Collectively, these chapters will help you to develop or modify the customer proposition and marketing mix strategy for your global brand, taking into account the type of global brand you have and its specific sources of value.

2

The COMET Framework: How Global Brands Create Value

In the daily grind of global brand management, many marketing executives get hung up on customer preference for global over local brands. Yet customers may not even know or may not care that a brand is globally available. And many global brands, such as Aldi, Pampers, Gillette, Dove, and Heinz do not tout their globalness, perhaps because some customers reject global brands as signs of cultural homogenization or foreign hegemony.[1] A singular focus on customer preference for global brands is far too narrow. In my research, I have observed five different ways by which global brands create value for their firms, namely *C*ustomer, *O*rganizational, *M*arketing, *E*conomic, and *T*ransnational innovation (Fig. 2.1). The COMET framework helps executives to map out ways for their companies to create global brand value. This chapter describes all five ways and then provides a scorecard for management teams to step back and see their global brands anew.

---

[1] Steenkamp, Jan-Benedict E.M. and Martijn G. de Jong (2010), "A Global Investigation into the Constellation of Consumer Attitudes toward Global and Local Products," *Journal of Marketing*, 74 (November), pp. 18–40.

© The Author(s) 2017
J.-B. Steenkamp, *Global Brand Strategy*,
DOI 10.1057/978-1-349-94994-6_2

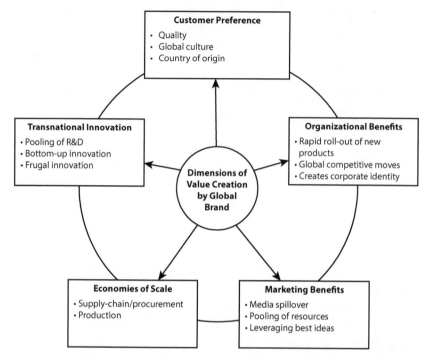

Fig. 2.1 Dimensions of value creation by global brands—the COMET framework

Customer Preference

Many customers have a strong preference for global over local brands for various reasons, three of which stand out—perceived quality, global culture, and country of origin.[2]

---

[2] Steenkamp and de Jong (2010); Steenkamp, Jan-Benedict E.M., Rajeev Batra, and Dana Alden (2003), "How Perceived Brand Globalness Creates Brand Value," *Journal of International Business Studies*, 34 (1), 53–65; Holt, Douglas B., John A. Quelch, and Earl L. Taylor (2004), "How Global Brands Compete," *Harvard Business Review*, 82 (September), pp. 68–75; Verlegh, Peeter, W.J. and Jan-Benedict E.M. Steenkamp (1999), "A Review and Meta-Analysis of Country-of-Origin Research," *Journal of Economic Psychology*, 20 (5), pp. 521–546.

Perceived Quality

Many people take global availability and sales as evidence that the brand is of high quality. They infer that a bad product could not be successful around the globe. Consider what 20–35 years old urban consumers said in qualitative research about global brands:

- "The more people who buy [a] brand...the better quality it is." (Russia)
- "I like [global] brands because they usually offer more quality and better guarantees than other products." (Spain)
- "[Global brands] are expensive, but the price is reasonable when you think of the quality." (Thailand)
- "[Global brands] are very dynamic, always upgrading themselves." (India)
- "[Global brands] are more exciting because they come up with new products all the time, whereas you know what you'll get with local ones." (Australia)[3]

German MNC Beiersdorf AG uses the worldwide acceptance and success of its personal care brand, Nivea, as an asset. In one print ad, Nivea Visage Q10 cream had a picture of four women of different ethnicities (Asian, African, Latin, and Germanic) with the headline: "64 countries, 1 face care line, 0 wrinkles." In supporting text, Beiersdorf claimed that Nivea is "the world's #1 selling anti-age face care line." In TV ads for Nivea for Men, Beiersdorf claimed that Nivea is the world's best-selling brand among men, and in a TV ad for sunscreen that it is the world's best-selling sunscreen brand.[4] Not surprisingly, in my seminars, executives scored Nivea high on perceived quality item in the COMET scorecard that I'll introduce at the end of this chapter.

---

[3] Holt et al. (2004).

[4] See for an example of an ad for Nivea Men: https://www.youtube.com/watch?v=bzjNdwI5cp4; and for an ad for sunscreen: https://www.youtube.com/watch?v=zsYlCA6ClIo. Notice also the stark difference in the 'tone' of the ads; accessed September 26, 2016.

Global Culture

Some consumers look to global brands as symbols of cultural ideals. They use these brands to form a global identity that they share with like-minded people. For them, consumption of global brands is a passport to global citizenship, a vehicle for participation in a global world and a pathway to belonging to the global world. To these consumers, global brands signify modernity, progress, and a promise of abundance. They appreciate the convergence of consumer culture around a common set of traits and practices and are attracted to the shared consciousness and the cultural meanings of global brands. Coca-Cola is a prime example of a brand that rates high on being an icon of global culture. A famous early example is Coca-Cola's 1971 multi-racial advertising campaign, "I'd Like to Buy the World a Coke." The *Financial Times* is well known for its print ads that show a cityscape composed of famous buildings from metropolises from around the world, together with the tag line "World business. In one place."[5]

The aforementioned global qualitative study uncovered many associations supporting the relevance of the association of global brands with global culture among young urban consumers:

- "Global brands make us feel citizens of the world, and we fear their leaving because they somehow give us an identity." (Argentina)
- "Global brands make you feel part of something bigger, and give a sense of belonging." (New Zealand)
- "Global brands speak a universal language that can be shared by all." (Italy)
- "Local brands show what we are, global brands show what we want to be." (Costa Rica)[6]

---

[5] The Coca-Cola ad can be found on https://www.youtube.com/watch?v=2msbfN81Gm0; accessed January 6, 2016; see for the FT ad http://adsoftheworld.com/media/print/financial_times_cityscape; accessed January 6, 2016.

[6] Holt et al. (2004).

In many countries, consumers perceive Starbucks as an aspirational global brand offering an international café experience. For example, a trip to Starbucks is a see-and-be-seen occasion for China's brand conscious middle class, especially for millennials who are less wedded to tea. Starbucks is also a popular place for business meetings as it makes "the host seem international and sophisticated."[7] In 2016, Starbucks had about 2,000 across 100 Chinese cities, making China Starbucks' second largest market after the United States. That is pretty impressive for a global brand in a country given that tea has been at the core of the Chinese culture for the last 2,500 years. That's what global brands do: they influence culture. On the other hand, it is exactly such influences on local culture that rile the anti-globalists.

Country of Origin

Customers around the world prefer global brands that have associated themselves (or have become associated) with a particular country of origin. Certain countries have particular qualities – real or imagined – which are globally recognized and appreciated. Wedgwood (now owned by Finnish Fiskars Group, known for its high end scissors, knives, and other hand tools) is a premium brand in tableware and home decoration, and Fiskars skillfully uses Wedgwood's British origin to build customer preference around the world. According to its chief of strategy and marketing Annick Desmecht, "Wedgwood is treasured by aristocracy and stylish consumers on four continents for more than two centuries, making it one of the first global luxury brands." Yet the brand is also seen as a bit old-fashioned. To address this, its brand management team has turned to young upper-crust English aristocrats such as Lady Tatiana Mountbatten as spokespersons in advertisement in countries like China, Japan, and South Korea where its English heritage is an important source of the brand's appeal. On the other hand, Fiskars's Waterford crystal does not

---

[7] Beattie, Anita Chang (2012), "Can Starbucks Make China Love Joe?" *Advertising Age*, November 5, pp. 20–21.

play up its Irish origins. Beyond the target market of the Irish diaspora, Irishness is not seen as an advantage for luxury crystal products, according to Desmecht.

Entire German industries, from cars to machinery benefit from the universal association of Germany with engineering prowess. No wonder that US ads for Bosch appliances emphasize that they are "German engineered."

Japan, Germany, Switzerland, and the United States have a positive country-of-origin image across a broad range of B2C industries. The contribution of the country image to brand preference of other countries is specific to the product category. For example, Barilla ("Italy's No. 1 Pasta") and L'Oréal ("L'Oréal Paris") benefit from their country image in food and personal care, respectively, but this is not the case for Pirelli (tires) or Peugeot (cars).

Purchase managers are not immune to country-of-origin connotations either. Research on the effect of country of origin on the product evaluations of industrial buyers has yielded the following:

- Country of origin influences purchase managers' assessment of the quality of industrial products. Japan, Germany, Switzerland, and the United States have the most positive country-of-origin image among industrial buyers around the world. Newly industrializing countries (e.g., India, Brazil, Mexico) have the least positive image. China's image is in between and improving.
- Country of origin plays a bigger role in purchase managers' assessment of complex products with high performance risk (e.g., complex machinery, heavy equipment) than in their assessment of relatively simple, less risky products (office supplies, small power relay unit).
- Country of development (where the product is conceptualized, designed, and engineered; this is often an advanced country such as Japan, the USA, Sweden, or Germany) has a larger effect on purchase managers' assessment of product quality than country of assembly (e.g., China, Mexico) because manufacturing know-how has spread much more widely around the world than research and development capabilities.

- Purchase managers consider the country of sourcing for industrial parts that go into the final product. The B2B firm can mitigate an unfavorable country-of-development or country-of-assembly image (e.g., China, India) by sourcing components from a highly regarded country (e.g., Japan, the USA, Germany).[8]

Limits to Country-of-Origin Benefits

As the legendary Dutch soccer player Johan Cruyff said, "Every advantage has its disadvantage." No single brand owns a country-of-origin image. If a brand draws customer strength from its country of origin, then events beyond its control can adversely affect its equity. Two types of events especially concern global brands—rogue actions by other brands and customer animosity.

Rogue Actions

The rogue actions of bad actors can severely damage the positive image of the country, and hence of the brands originating from that country. The 1985 diethylene glycol wine scandal nearly killed the Austrian wine industry. Several Austrian wineries illegally adulterated their wines with this toxic substance to make the wines appear sweeter and more full-bodied. The scandal made headlines around the world. The short-term effect of the scandal was a complete collapse of Austrian wine exports and a total loss of reputation of the entire Austrian wine industry, which took over a decade to recover. Of more recent date is the Volkswagen emission scandal that broke in September 2015. When the public learned that Volkswagen had installed software in diesel vehicles that enabled them to cheat emission tests, there was widespread concern among CEOs and politicians

---

[8] Albarq, Abbas N. (2014), "Industrial Purchase among Saudi Managers: Does Country of Origin Matter?" *International Journal of Marketing Studies*, 6 (1), pp. 116–126; Tamijani, Seyedeh et al. (2012), "The Importance of Country of Origin in Purchasing Industrial Products: The Case of the Valves Industry in Iran," Proceedings, University of Bamberg, pp. 1–25 and the literature referenced in these publications.

alike that VW's illegal behavior would lower the world's opinion of "Made in Germany," and hence the equity of other German brands too.[9]

Customer Animosity

Customer animosity—the anger deriving from historical or ongoing political, military, economic, or diplomatic actions—profoundly influences customer behavior toward brands from that particular country.[10] Even though customers who loathe a country's activities may very well acknowledge that the reviled country can produce high-quality products, they will still reject them. French nuclear testing in the South Pacific in the mid-1990s prompted Australians to boycott French products from wine and cosmetics to jewelry and cars. A year after France announced it would cease all further nuclear testing, Australian sales still had not recovered to previous levels.[11]

As the world's dominant power, the United States generates disproportionate emotions, both positive and negative. In the aftermath of the 2003 Iraq invasion, Coca-Cola sales in Germany declined by 16% in 2004, while Marlboro sales in France and Germany declined by 25% and 19%, respectively. The animosity toward the US policy in the Middle East offered an opportunity for a new entrant, Mecca Cola. Launched in November 2002 in France by Tawfik Mathlouthi, the brand was launched as an alternative to American brands and to take advantage of anti-American feelings. It is now available in over 60 countries around the world.[12]

Anti-Americanism continues to haunt US companies. In November 2015, the global investment management business of US insurance group Prudential Financial changed its name from Pramerica to PGIM, and announced it in full sized advertisements in the *Financial Times* and the

---

[9] https://en.wikipedia.org/wiki/1985_diethylene_glycol_wine_scandal; accessed October 21, 2015; Wagstyl, Stefan and James Shotter (2015), "Blow to 'Made in Germany' Label Leaves Nation's Pride Bruised," *Financial Times*, September 25, p. 19.

[10] Klein, Jill G., Richard Ettenson, and Marlene D. Morris (1998), "The Animosity Model of Foreign Product Purchase: An Empirical Test in the People's Republic of China," *Journal of Marketing*, (January), pp. 89–100.

[11] Ettenson, Richard and Jill G. Klein (2005), "The Fallout from French Nuclear Testing in the South Pacific," *International Marketing Review*, 22 (2), pp. 199–224.

[12] http://fizzyzist.com/entries/mecca-cola/; accessed February 16, 2016.

Wall Street Journal. CEO David Hunt explained, "We have been building out more in Southeast Asia, in India, Malaysia and other places where the America part of that wasn't necessarily something that people wanted to meet with."[13]

One of the most pertinent cases of customer animosity is the Chinese view of Japan's role in World War II and the ownership of a group of uninhabited islands known as the Diaoyus in China and the Senkakus in Japan. I know from personal experience that highly educated and otherwise composed Chinese people become visibly agitated when Japan comes up in conversations. A flare-up over the island group in September 2012 led to a large drop in the sales for various Japanese companies such as Nissan (−35% from a year earlier), Honda (−41%), and Toyota (−49%). Anti-Japanese sentiment has cooled somewhat, but the two countries have not resolved either dispute. Their global brand equity remains at risk. Mitsubishi Materials did not want to wait for another political incident. In July 2015, it apologized to China and committed to paying compensation of CNY100,000 to each Chinese victim of forced labor during World War II, even though Japan's Supreme Court had rejected such claims.[14] Imagine that: a corporation valued its global brand equity so much that it stepped up to apologize and compensate the victims of political actions. It was a bold and unprecedented brand play.

Organizational Benefits

Rapid Rollout of New Products

Today's new products are tomorrow's old news. With product lifecycles shortening and rival companies hastening to copy one's new products, companies need to launch new products quickly everywhere in the world.

---

[13] Foley, Stephen (2015), "Investment Group Takes 'America' Out of Its Name," *Financial Times,* November 11, p. 16.

[14] Burkitt, Laurie, (2012) "Dispute Tests Japanese Brands," *Wall Street Journal,* September 27, p. A11.; http://www.japantimes.co.jp/news/2015/07/24/national/history/mitsubishi-materials-apologize-settle-3765-chinese-wwii-forced-labor-redress-claims/#.Vikn0X6rRhE; accessed October 22, 2015.

A global brand expedites rapid rollout of innovations. If it fails to do so, local brand managers will lose much time finding the "right" brand name for each country. Moreover, since the brand name is the linchpin of any marketing strategy, a brand policy that accommodates different brand names almost invariably opens the door to other adaptations in the marketing strategy, causing further delays.

In the past, Unilever struggled to bring innovations quickly to the marketplace because of the time spent on local adaptation. Nowadays, by focusing its innovations on fewer, bigger projects with global appeal, it can speed new products to market. Under such global brand names as TRESemmé and Magnum ice cream, Unilever gets its innovations into stores in São Paulo, Mumbai, Jakarta, London, and New York faster than ever before. These are examples of brands that rate high on facilitating rapid rollout of new products in the COMET scorecard. In 2005, Unilever had 5000 new-product projects in its pipeline and could bring only eight (0.16%) of them to hundred or more countries within a year of their debut. In 2012, it had cut the pipeline to 600 with 90 of those (15%) rolled out globally within 12 months.[15] That represents a hundred fold improvement in speed-to-global-market!

Strength in Global Competitive Moves

If you organize the strategy around the global brand, you can make global competitive moves. You could use cash flows from one country or region to pay for competitive offense in another part of the world where the return may be higher ("cross-subsidization"). For a long time, global powerhouses like Toyota and Samsung subsidized global offense using cash generated in their home market. Or you could defend against a competitive attack in one country by countering in another country ("counter-parry"). Take Philip Morris, which rates high on aspect. In 1993, it reduced the US price of its Marlboro brand by 20% while substantially increasing the brand's domestic advertising budget. In response, Reynolds dropped the price of its own premium brands such as Camel

---

[15] Wuestner, Christian (2013), "Unilever: Taking the World, One Stall at a Time," *Bloomberg Businessweek*, January 7, pp. 18–20.

and Winston and increased their advertising. This play depleted Reynolds' cash resources just when the Eastern European market was opening up. Philip Morris then expanded aggressively into Eastern Europe where it invested $800 million. Reynolds had no cash to do the same, and so Philip Morris won the battle for Eastern European market share, with enduring results. In 2016, the brand value of Marlboro was nearly three times that of Winston and Camel combined.[16]

Truck maker Daimler-Benz faced growing competition from Chinese manufacturers in the medium-duty truck segment, which were using their leading position in the world's biggest commercial-vehicle market to expand in other emerging economies. What if these Chinese rivals reached the critical scale that would allow them to become formidable global competitors? Wolfgang Bernhard, the head of Daimler's global truck business, recognized the threat: "The Chinese are gaining a foothold in these markets. We need to do some fore-checking." (In ice hockey, fore-checking refers to playing an aggressive style of defense, checking opponents in their own defensive zone, before they can organize an attack.) Daimler relied on its growing BharatBenz operation in India to execute its global competitive move. Opened in 2012, BharatBenz had become India's fourth-largest truck maker by 2015. Daimler plans to use India as the company's development and manufacturing hub to counter the Chinese expansion in Southeast Asia and Africa.[17]

Corporate Identity to Rally All Employees

The global brand gives the firm an identity which serves as an organizational rallying cry. Swiss insurance company Zurich replaced its worldwide portfolio of local brands with the Zurich brand. This simplification not only created synergies for its branding investments, but also gave local companies and their employees a sense of belonging to one and the

---

[16] MacMillan, Ian C., Alexander B. van Putten, and Rita Gunther McGrath (2003), "Global Gamesmanship," *Harvard Business Review*, 81 (May), pp. 62–71; brand value taken from Brand Finance.

[17] Boston, William (2014), "Daimler Looks to India as Truck Hub," *Wall Street Journal*, September 22, p. B3.

same company. Ultimately, the change opened up parochial cultures and disrupted the associated not-invented-here syndrome. The Zurich brand name's role in creating a corporate identity around the world was instrumental in it entering the top ten list of most valuable insurance brands for the first time in 2015, according to brand consultancy Millward Brown.[18]

At Unilever, employees in local subsidiaries (often with a local company name) did not feel a part of the global conglomerate. The distance fostered a culture of localism, hindering global initiatives. To cultivate a corporate identity that included every employee in the world, Unilever started adding its corporate brand logo to packaging and advertisements.

A strong(er) corporate identity derived from its brands can also attract the best and the brightest of each cohort of new managers. People identify with brands and want to work for those companies whose brands their social circle know and love. Anybody who teaches MBA students knows this. While beloved brands can be local brands, global brands have disproportionate appeal among newly minted MBAs in today's global world.

Superior Marketing Programs

Media Spillover Across Countries

Global marketing efforts benefit from customers' exposure to media from other countries. Over one billion people cross borders each year, and that figure does not include visits to foreign websites. HSBC leveraged this fact by placing "point-of-view" billboards in airports. Hundreds of millions of travelers have been exposed to the HSBC brand. Unknown in the late 1990s, its high score on media spillover contributed to making HSBC the world's most valuable global banking brand in 2010, a position it retained since then.

Let's look at the marketing spillover of global brands in the pharmaceutical industry. Most countries prohibit direct-to-consumer adver-

---

[18] In the remainder of the book, unless otherwise indicated, brand value is taken from Millward Brown Brand Z; http://www.millwardbrown.com/brandz.

tising of prescription drugs. So the large pharma firms promote the corporate brand. According to George Mitchinson, GlaxoSmithKline's vice-president strategy, "Leveraging the company name to define quality, value, and alignment to customer needs is a powerful way to position the company as a brand. As products become more complex [and cannot be advertised] … there is an interesting question as to how to leverage the corporate brand advantage."[19] No wonder GSK has begun to put its logo on its products and consolidated the bulk of its $600 million global media buying and planning account with WPP. Like Bayer, GSK has the advantage that it also sells over-the-counter drugs which it can advertise with potential spillover benefits for prescription drugs.

Pooling Marketing Resources Across Countries

Global brands can offset the disadvantage of low local market shares by pooling marketing resources across countries, allowing them to associate with globally recognized celebrities (e.g., Pantene with Gisele Bündchen; H&M with Beyoncé; Nike with Cristiano Ronaldo; Cover Girl with Katy Perry; Breitling with John Travolta) and globally watched events such as the FIFA World Cup, the Olympic Games, FIA Formula One racing, and Wimbledon.

Coca-Cola, Visa, Adidas, and Hyundai are among the FIFA partners. Coca-Cola and Visa are also Worldwide Olympic Partners, along with other well-known B2C brands like Omega, Panasonic, McDonald's, and Samsung. Association with worldwide events is not the prerogative of B2C brands only. Dow, General Electric, and IT services provider Atos are also Worldwide Olympic Partners, costing each more than $25 million per year in rights fees alone.[20]

---

[19] *Campaign Asia* (2015), "What's Really Next for Pharma?" July/August 2015, pp. 48–49.
[20] http://m.sportsbusinessdaily.com/Journal/Issues/2013/09/23/Olympics/IOC-TOP.aspx; accessed October 21, 2015.

Leveraging the Best Marketing Ideas

Even cursory exposure to TV ads reveals that creative ideas are scarce. 54% of US executives rate improving creative excellence as a key challenge facing marketing and advertising, second only to making marketing more efficient.[21] Global brands allow the best creative positioning ideas and advertising campaigns that brand managers can leverage across countries. One company that rates very high on the ability to leverage the best creative ideas globally is Red Bull. How to sell an energy drink that, according to many customers, does not taste good? Red Bull solved this quandary by developing a global campaign around the slogan, "It Gives You Wings." Its campaign targets young men with extreme sports, ranging from snowboarding and skateboarding to cliff-diving, freestyle motocross, and Formula One racing. The company went from 35 million cans sold in 1993 to 5.4 billion cans across 166 countries in 2013. In 2016, its brand value stood at $11.7 billion.[22]

Few products are as functional as credit cards. How can you distinguish yourself? MasterCard came up with an answer, the "Priceless" advertising theme. In the very first commercial, a dad takes his son to a baseball game and pays for a hot dog and a drink with his MasterCard, and the conversation between the two is priceless. The ad ends with, "There are some things money can't buy. For everything else, there's MasterCard."[23] "Priceless" became MasterCard's unifying brand platform in over 200 countries, albeit its execution varies across countries.[24] According to MasterCard's former CMO Alfredo Gangotena, the "Priceless" theme "has unified the brand to make it meaningful whether you are Chinese, Brazilian, American, or Russian."[25] This campaign has fueled the brand's increase in value, which exceeded $46 billion in 2016.

---

[21] *Advertising Age* (2016), "Creativity, Efficiency, Exploration," January 11, p. 18.

[22] For an example of a Red Bull ad: https://www.youtube.com/watch?v=hoSVI7ovEIw; accessed September 23, 2016.

[23] https://www.youtube.com/watch?v=71KAO_bmc2o; accessed October 16, 2015.

[24] For example, a "Priceless" commercial in the Netherlands featured soccer legend Johan Cruyff playing for the team that made him great, Ajax Amsterdam. This ad can be found on https://www.youtube.com/watch?v=XAf37y4Wjh4; accessed October 16, 2015.

[25] Learmonth, Michael et al. (2010), "CMOs Discuss Their Brands; Keith Weed," *Advertising Age*, June 14, pp. 18–20.

In 2014, Starbucks launched its first global campaign ever, organized around the "Meet me at Starbucks" theme. The campaign chronicled a day in the life of Starbucks through a mini-documentary shot in 59 different stores in 28 countries.[26] The idea originated from Starbucks monitoring its customers on social media. Starbucks spokeswoman Linda Mills said that the company noticed Starbucks fan videos on YouTube: "There were stories that were taking place inside our stores." Individual markets could use the mini-documentary to develop TV spots. For example, the US team developed a 60-second spot, a distilled version of the documentary.[27]

MNCs increasingly realize that great brand campaigns can emerge from local subsidiaries. If the company uses the same brand everywhere, then it can more easily leverage locally developed creative ideas in other countries. McDonald's successful "I'm lovin' it" campaign originated in Germany in 2003, and McDonald's subsequently rolled it out in other countries. It was the company's first global advertising campaign.

Executives in Australia came up with the "Share a Coke" campaign, first launched in 2011. The campaign tapped into self-expression and individual storytelling, and deepened the connection between the famous brand and millennials. By placing popular first names and colloquial nicknames on its cans and bottles, "Share a Coke" sought to get on a first-name basis with younger consumers. The campaign has since spread to about 80 countries.[28]

Economies of Scale

Global brands can generate significant economies of scale in production and procurement. In principle, MNCs can sell global products under local brand names, but doing so profitably is the exception, not the rule. Global brands typically go hand in hand with global products—that is, products

---

[26] https://www.youtube.com/user/Starbucks; accessed February 17, 2016.

[27] http://www.ispot.tv/ad/7Nly/starbucks-meet-me-at-starbucks; accessed February 17, 2016.

[28] Esterl, Mike (2014), "'Share a Coke' Credited with a Pop in Sales," *Wall Street Journal*, September 25; http://www.wsj.com/articles/share-a-coke-credited-with-a-pop-in-sales-1411661519; accessed February 17, 2016.

that are largely standardized around a common core. Standardized production means rationalizing the number of different products, manufacturing a few global ones rather than many local ones, thereby cutting the costs of setup, production runs, downtime, and inventory and securing bigger discounts in raw materials purchases. For example, in the highly competitive household cleaning market, a US consumer packaged goods (CPG) company saved 15% in manufacturing and inventory handling costs by unifying product ingredients across countries. Another leading CPG company found that it could reduce the cost of goods sold by 17% if it replaced all its local brands by a single pan-European brand.

Lack of economies of scale is a key vulnerability of Japan's industrial conglomerate Hitachi. While its overall sales stood at an impressive $89 billion in 2014, this was spread over machinery, trains, electronics, telecommunications equipment, information system, and power plants. It lacks the overall scale of rivals such as General Electric and the industry-level scale of more focused competitors like Caterpillar in machinery or Huawei in telecommunication equipment. Its relatively weak position showed up in its operating margin, just 5.5% versus 16.2% for GE, 9.6% for Caterpillar, and 11.7% for Huawei.[29]

Transnational Innovation

Pooling of R&D to Make Higher Quality Products

By pooling financial and human resources across countries, overall research and development will generally perform better than local R&D alone. For example, P&G recognized a worldwide desire to achieve a soft, moisturized, clean-feeling skin. Its leadership pooled local resources to assemble the best technologists from P&G's laboratories around the world at an R&D facility in Cincinnati. The team found that a 10-micron fiber, when woven into a mesh, was effective in trapping and absorbing dirt and impurities. By impregnating this substrate with a dry-sprayed formula of cleansers and moisturizers activated at different moments in

---

[29] Data refer to 2014 and are obtained from the companies' annual reports.

Table 2.1 Innovativeness of selected countries

Country	Global rank 2015	Global rank 2008	Change in rank
Switzerland	1	7	▲
UK	2	4	▲
Sweden	3	3	–
Netherlands	4	10	▲
USA	5	1	▼
Singapore	7	5	▼
Hong Kong SAR	11	12	▼
Germany	12	2	▼ ▼
South Korea	14	6	▼
Japan	19	9	▼ ▼
China	29	37	▲
Russia	48	68	▲ ▲
South Africa	50	43	▼
Vietnam	52	64	▲ ▲
Mexico	57	61	▲
Turkey	58	51	▼
Brazil	70	50	▼ ▼
India	81	41	▼ ▼

Source: Dutta, Lavin, and Wunsch-Vicent (2015)
Notes: ▲ / ▼ = change in rank <10
▲ ▲ / ▼ ▼ = change in rank ≥10

the cleansing process, the technologists were able to develop a disposable cleansing cloth. P&G introduced this innovation globally as Olay Daily Facial Cloth.[30]

Pooling R&D resources does not mean concentrating R&D activities in one location, especially not in the country of corporate headquarters. The evidence suggests that global R&D networks can generate better R&D performance.[31] Why?

1. There are systematic differences in innovativeness between countries, because of institutional differences, human capital and research infra-

---

[30] These and other innovations were instrumental in the global success of Olay, with sales exceeding $3 billion in 2016.

[31] Eppinger, Steven D. and Anil R. Chitkara (2006), "The New Practice of Global Product Development," *MIT Sloan Management Review*, 47 (4), pp. 22–30; Lahiri, Nandini (2010), "Geographical Distribution of R&D Activity: How Does It Affect Innovation Quality?" *Academy of Management Review*, 53 (5), pp. 1194–1209. Innovation performance is measured as the number of granted patents weighted by the number of citations each patent received.

structure (e.g., universities), market sophistication, knowledge and creative outputs. Table 2.1 gives the innovation rank of nations. By establishing R&D facilities in an innovative country, your firm can tap into these skills.[32]

2. Over and above the innovativeness of a country, within industries there exist asymmetries in technical knowledge at different locations. Each location contributes unique knowledge that comes from the interaction among firms in that location. If you place R&D facilities in a particular location, your firm benefits from knowledge spillovers from industry peers, research institutes, and firms in related industries.

3. Using input from different R&D labs can facilitate globally inclusive product development as opposed to ethnocentric product development.

4. R&D internationalization takes advantage of differences in labor costs. For example, the median salary of a US mechanical engineer is more than four times that of his Czech counterpart.

Many Western MNCs are setting up R&D centers in China, despite concerns about intellectual property protection to tap into local market knowledge and to create goodwill with the Chinese authorities. At the same time, Chinese companies are increasingly taking advantage of highly experienced engineers in the West to develop new technologies and connect with international markets. Consumer appliances' giant Haier has set up R&D facilities in Germany, Japan, and the United States, paying wages of an order of magnitude greater than in China. It has established a global R&D platform, drawing on strengths from specific countries to seize opportunities in local markets as varied as Pakistan and America.[33]

Yet R&D globalization has its limit. A firm can spread its resources too thinly, and geographical dispersion poses coordination, monitoring, and communication challenges that the Internet alone cannot mitigate. Here are three guidelines:

---

[32] Dutta, Soumitra, Bruno Lavin, and Sacha Wunsch-Vicent (2015), *The Global Innovation Index 2015*, Cornell University.

[33] Steenkamp, Jan-Benedict E.M. (2013), "Haier – The Quest to Become the First Chinese Global Consumer Brand," The Case Centre Case #514-042-1.

- Assign a primary area of investigation to each R&D subsidiary to avoid overlap and duplication of R&D efforts. Hyundai Motors has established R&D centers in India, primarily tasked to focus on manufacturing and engineering of small cars, in Japan for cutting-edge electronics and hybrid technology, in America for vehicle styling and high-temperature testing (Californian desert), and in Germany for engines that meet environment regulations.
- Compare the geographical spread in your R&D activities with that of your peers. If you are in the upper one-third of R&D internationalization, you can likely reduce R&D costs while increasing quality of the output by consolidating R&D in fewer locations.
- Cultivate extensive connections among your R&D locations. The greater the intraorganizational linkages across R&D locations, the greater the likelihood that knowledge created at one location can benefit a different location.[34]

Bottom-Up Innovation to Overcome Scarcity of Great Ideas

MNCs increasingly realize that overseas markets are a source of new product ideas, not only for the local but also for overseas markets. Global brands leverage bottom-up innovation on a worldwide scale. L'Oréal traditionally developed new products in France by pooling market requirements from the major continents. But it is turning more to local markets for new product concepts. Its Elsève Total Repair 5, which fights five signs of damaged hair, was conceived in Brazil. Garnier Mineral Deodorant, which contains mineralite (a natural mineral ingredient that locks in four times its volume in water) was conceived in Russia. In 2015, L'Oréal's Lancôme brand launched Miracle Cushion in Europe and North America, a sponge infused with liquid foundation.

---

[34] A straightforward way to measure the extent of intraorganizational R&D linkages is the fraction of a firm's patents that are coauthored by scientists from different locations of the firm in a given time period. Co-authorship of a patent requires frequent interaction between individuals, which results in the formation of an ongoing relationship. These relationships are more likely to enable transfer and sharing of knowledge across locations in the future.

The idea came from South Korea where consumers preferred these so-called cushion compacts to even out skin tones. Industry insiders believe this new product concept is just the beginning. Asian women's skin-care regimens may include as many as ten steps—each a potential lucrative opportunity—compared with three or four steps in the West. "We are in the early days, but we are completely convinced that the best of innovation will travel from the East to the West," said Fabrice Weber, president of Asia Pacific for Estée Lauder. "The most discerning skin-care consumers are Asian women and men."[35] In all these examples, taking local innovations global was greatly facilitated by them being introduced under a global brand.

Bottom-up innovation is not limited to the CPG industry. Nissan's Chinese development center unveiled its Friend-Me concept car—a four-passenger sedan-with-a-hatchback. It was developed for the 240 million Chinese born in the 1980s, bereft of siblings due to China's one-child policy. The exterior is meant to be most imposing at night, when Nissan figures these single children will be getting together with their friends. For a generation that grew up without siblings, leisure time—usually at night—shared with peers is treasured. With an assertive, imposing exterior featuring boldly flowing sculpted lines, Friend-Me is meant to be seen in bright city lights. Inside is a carefully considered space designed to give four friends a sense of shared adventure without hierarchy in which the "oracle stone" plays a central role. Instead of a driver and three passengers, everyone gets access to the same information and the ability to alter the ambiance of the car—dash readouts are provided for all of the occupants, and anyone can move content from their phones to the in-car screens to be shared throughout. While the Friend-Me car is tailored for Chinese drivers, Nissan believes the concept is applicable globally.[36]

---

[35] Chu, Kathy (2015), "Cosmetics Industry Applies Asian Trends to West," *Wall Street Journal*, May 5, p. A1.

[36] http://www.autoblog.com/2013/04/20/nissan-friend-me-concept-shanghai-2013/;   accessed February 8, 2016.

Frugal Innovation to Redefine the Value Proposition

Frugal innovation is the process of eliminating nonessential features of a product without compromising on its basic reliability or desirability, thereby reducing the complexity and cost of manufacturing. By confronting each element of cost in the product line by line against the objective value added to the consumer, you can create a good quality product at remarkably low prices. Among the champions of frugal innovation are global hard discounts chains Aldi (owner of Trader Joe's) and Lidl (Schwarz Gruppe), both headquartered in Germany.[37] Aldi and Lidl sold over $70 billion each in 2016. The Aldi brand ($12.1 billion in 2016) is worth more than those of storied global full-service retailers Tesco ($8.9 billion) and Carrefour ($7.7 billion).

Emerging markets are a natural laboratory for frugal innovation. Their lean economic environment makes customers very cost conscious. Yet they demand high reliability because they have no money to pay for frequent maintenance and repair. So they are an ideal test market for entirely new products that redefine the price-value. Renault developed its frugal innovation, the Dacia car brand, in Romania. Launched in 2004, the Dacia combined low-cost engineering and no-frills specifications; Renault could sell it for about 30% less than mass brands like Ford or Toyota. Renault targeted Eastern Europe first, and then North Africa, the Middle East, and Latin America. Dacia models proved popular with western European car buyers as well. In short, the Dacia brand greatly facilitates Renault's ability to take frugal innovation to the global marketplace. By 2016, the brand accounted for nearly 20% of total sales of the Renault group.[38]

GE Healthcare was selling basically the same medical-diagnostic equipment in India as it was in the United States. However, it found that only 10% of Indian medical practices were rich enough to afford those US-designed products. That insight led GE to develop a portable,

---

[37] Steenkamp, Jan-Benedict E.M. and Nirmalya Kumar (2009), "Don't Be Undersold!," *Harvard Business Review*, 87 (December), 90–95.

[38] Foy, Henry (2013), "Dacia Leads Charge of Emerging Market Cars in Europe," *Financial Times*, August 23, p. 14; Foy, Henry (2014), "GM in European No-Frills Push," *Financial Times*, July 21, p. 15.

battery-operated electrocardiogram machine that sold for $800. Intended as a solution for rural Indian markets where bulky, $20,000 machines made little sense, the product is now making inroads as a solution for US first responders.

The COMET Scorecard

Which pathways are you using in your global branding strategy? Not every manager is able to step back and assess their global brand's particular strengths and weaknesses objectively. Most have a good sense of one or two areas in which their brand may excel or may need help. But if pressed, many (understandably) would find it difficult even to identify all of the factors they should be considering. When you're immersed in the day-to-day management of a brand, it's not easy to keep in perspective all the parts that affect the whole.

To help your strategic assessment, Tool 2.1 poses a series of statements about your brand's actual performance on each facet of the COMET dimensions. Give the scorecard to a group of managers from different functions and different locales (headquarters, major-country subsidiaries) and aggregate the results. Use the snake diagram to generate discussion among all those individuals who participate in the management of your brand. You will learn a lot about how your managers view the brand, its potential, and quality of current plans. Looking at the results in that manner should help you identify areas that need improvement, recognize areas in which you excel, and learn more about how your particular brand is configured.

Building a strong global brand involves maximizing all five dimensions. A strong global brand generates benefits from enhanced customer preference, brings organizational benefits, leverages superior marketing programs, yields economies of scale, and uses its global footprint to come up with innovations its customers desire. Take Nike. It commands strong customer preference due to the credibility it derives from its global availability (resulting in a high score on statement C1). Its slogan "Just do it" resonates globally, especially with more risk-taking, individualistic young people (C2). Its global brand allows for rapid rollout of new products

This tool is designed to assess your global brand's particular strengths and weaknesses. For this, take the following steps:

Step 1: Administer the Scorecard
Administer the scorecard to a group of managers from different functions and different locales (headquarters, major subsidiaries).

Instructions: Rate Brand X on a scale from 1 (strongly disagree) to 7 (strongly agree) on each statement below. These statements deal with your assessment of the extent to which Brand X *actually* achieves what is described in the statement, not what you wish it to be! If you are uncertain about a particular response, skip the statement.

Customer Preference   Score (1-7)

C1. Brand X is seen by our target segment as being of high quality *because* of its global availability, acceptance, and success. ☐

C2. Brand X is seen by our target segment as an icon of the global culture. ☐

C3. Brand X is seen by our target segment as being associated with a favorable country of origin. ☐

Organizational Benefits

O1. We rapidly roll out new products around the world under Brand X. ☐

O2. We make global competitive moves with Brand X. ☐

O3. Brand X creates a corporate identity for our firm. ☐

Marketing Program Superiority

M1. Brand X benefits from significant cross-national media spillover and/or exposure to international travelers. ☐

M2. We pool marketing resources across countries for Brand X. ☐

M3. We leverage the best marketing ideas from around the world to promote Brand X. ☐

Economies of Scale

E1. We generate significant economies of scale in supply-chain/procurement for Brand X. ☐

E2. We generate significant economies of scale in production of Brand X. ☐

Transnational Innovation

T1. We pool R&D resources across countries to develop new products for Brand X. ☐

T2. We take local innovations to the global marketplace under Brand X. ☐

T3. We take frugal innovations to the global marketplace under Brand X. ☐

Step 2: Construct Snake Diagram
Average the scores per statement and create a snake diagram.

Step 3: Develop an Action Plan
Use the following interpretation of the scores:

Score	Interpretation	Action
< 4	Not used to create brand value	Missed opportunity or conscious choice?
4-5	Some use	Intensify use of this factor
> 5	High use	Maintain, possible further increase

Tool 2.1   The COMET diagnostic test

such as the green incandescent shoes introduced at the 2012 London Olympics (O1). Its brand name and the swoosh symbol define the company and are a magnet in attracting the best and the brightest MBAs (O3). Pooling of resources has led to superior marketing campaigns such as well-executed ads like "Secret Tournament," "The Mission," "Winner Stays," and "Risk Everything" (M2).[39] Production of such ads exceeded the advertising budgets of local Nike brand managers. At the same time, Nike's global scale allows it to generate significant economies of scale by outsourcing large orders of its products, from soccer balls to running shoes to low-cost countries like Vietnam and Indonesia (E1). And finally, Nike is consistently ranked among the world's most innovative companies according to *Forbes, Fast Company*, and the Boston Consulting Group (T1). No wonder the Nike brand name is worth $37.5 billion in 2016, making it the world's most valuable apparel brand, up from $12.6 billion in 2010.

But while maximizing all five dimensions is a worthy goal, this is not always feasible because when the brand focuses on improving one, another may suffer. Consider a luxury brand like Louis Vuitton that has to trade off country-of-origin mystique (France) with economies of scale (outsourcing production to China). Outsourcing to China is possible if customers associate the brand with country of design (France) and not with the country of manufacturing (China), and if there is little that is unique in French craftsmanship. Obviously, this is a risky proposition. If your brand scores low on a COMET facet, carefully think about whether this is intentional or a lost opportunity that calls for action. In this analysis, it can also be helpful to create a snake diagram for competitors' brands simply by rating those brands based on your own informed judgment. What are they doing differently? Are our competitors more or less effective in using particular COMET dimensions?

---

[39] These ads can be found at https://www.youtube.com/watch?v=7zlX0Sm65zA, https://www.youtube.com/watch?v=kNhrE0z4-qs, https://www.youtube.com/watch?v=3XviR7esUvo; https://www.youtube.com/watch?v=gwxdEECNpZY; accessed October 10, 2015.

Managerial Takeaways

Customer preference for global brands can be a major source of brand value in B2C and B2B markets. But even when customers neither know nor care whether the brand is global, global brands provide organizational, marketing, economic, and innovation advantages. Managers need to assess their global brands systematically across the various value-creating functions. Here is a summary of the four-step process for global brand evaluation:

1. Administer the COMET scorecard to a group of managers, both at headquarters and in major-country subsidiaries, who are associated with a particular global brand. Gather scores from different functions including marketing, sales, and R&D.
2. Plot the mean scores in a snake diagram. Assess whether you are missing opportunities. A strong global brand ideally receives high scores on items pertaining to each COMET dimension. If a brand scores low on many facets it is not leveraging its globalness effectively.
3. Calculate the variation in scores per item across the group of managers. If there are significant differences of opinion, ask for explanation in follow-up communications. If different parts of the company have divergent views, probe to find out what you are missing.
4. Benchmark against competing global brands. On which facets do you rate better than your competitors? On which items lower? Is your lower score due to a conscious decision and a fundamentally different view of the market? If so, what evidence can you bring to the table to support this? Alternatively, are you overlooking particular possibilities to create value to the firm that put you at a competitive disadvantage? If so, what should you do differently?

3

Customer Propositions for Global Brands

Vertu and Xiaomi are both global brands, yet they could have come from different planets. Xiaomi handsets are sold in the millions over the Internet, to value-conscious shoppers. They offer good quality for a price that is easily 50% below that of a comparable iPhone. The Vertu Signature Touch collection is handmade in England and comes with a dedicated 'concierge' offering 24-hour worldwide assistance, recommendations, and priority bookings. Undoubtedly, the Vertu is a great phone but, given the rate of technological change in this industry, it will be obsolete in a few years' time. However, with an entry level price of $10,800, the Vertu sets its (few) owners apart from three billion other smartphone users. Clearly, global brands come in very different guises.

In the previous chapter, we looked at the five potential benefits—customer preference, organizational competitiveness, marketing strength, economies of scale, and transnational innovation (COMET)—that a global brand can deliver to a multinational corporation (MNC). The snag is in the word *potential*: if your brand's marketing strategy is ineffective or incomplete, or if you drift in implementation and are slow to course-correct, you may never realize these benefits. The marketing strategy of any global brand requires (1) the development of a compelling

© The Author(s) 2017
J.-B. Steenkamp, *Global Brand Strategy*,
DOI 10.1057/978-1-349-94994-6_3

customer proposition, specifying the target segment and connecting the core features with the benefits of the brand, and (2) a marketing strategy to deliver that proposition to the target segment. This chapter focuses on the customer proposition, and the next two chapters delve into the marketing mix.

In my research and analysis of diverse global brands, I have observed a surprisingly simple handful of customer propositions. In general, the most successful fall into one of five categories, which I refer to as *value, mass, premium, prestige,* and *fun* brands. Each of these targets a different global segment defined by the segment's universal needs, ranging from the biggest value per dollar to the most fun per dollar. Table 3.1 highlights the differences among the five types of global brands, their distinct positioning, and their unique challenges. Of course, within these five types, brand managers seek to differentiate their offerings from others in the MNC's portfolio and from competitors in the space. For example, PepsiCo's mass brand 7 Up is differentiated from Pepsi Cola on taste ("The Uncola") and on caffeine content ("Never Had It, Never Will"). Pepsi Cola is differentiated from Coca-Cola by being positioned as the soft drink for the new generation, aiming to "capture the excitement of now" by linking the brand to entertainment and pop culture. On the other hand, in its new global campaign "Taste the Feeling," launched in January 2016, Coca-Cola is positioned on refreshing taste, linking this to stories about special moments in life.[1]

Sometimes managers draw from the characteristics of the other four categories, and so the five types blur at the edges. In fine-tuning and repositioning your global brand proposition, you can increase your strategic options by understanding each of these categories, the customers they serve, the needs they fulfill, the challenges they face, and the value they deliver to the corporation.

---

[1] Examples of the new campaign can be found at: and https://www.youtube.com/watch?v=-AmKP9VE2Ms and https://www.youtube.com/watch?v=F411acOyIzw; accessed September 23, 2016.

Table 3.1 Customer proposition for five types of global brands

	Value brand	Mass brand	Premium brand	Prestige brand	Fun brand
Example brand names	IKEA, Xiaomi, Aldi, Kia, Norwegian, Haier, Dacia, Uniqlo, Sany	Samsung, Olay, L'Oréal Paris, Toyota, Lufthansa, Komatsu	Apple, Jaguar, Emirates, Scania, *Financial Times*, Caterpillar	Loro Piana, McKinsey, Ferrari, Bang & Olufsen, Breitling, WEF	Zara, Swatch, Cosmopolitan, Nintendo, H&M, Disney, SEAT
Universal need	Best possible value for money	Desire for quality Risk aversion	Desire for best product Risk aversion	Social distinction	Stimulation, change, excitement
Value positioning	Acceptable quality Lowest price	High quality Priced above average	Best quality Emotional benefits High price	Aspirational, selective, scarcity Very high price	Lifestyle, enjoyment, change Low price
Global target segments	Cash-strapped customers Smart shoppers Customers for whom category is unimportant Routine purchases of low risk	Middle class Mainstream firms	Affluent customers Firms for which product is crucial to operations Customers who are highly involved with the category	Global elite Imitators of the global elite	Global youth
COMET factor: customer	Perceived quality Country of origin	Perceived quality Country of origin	Perceived quality Country of origin	Global culture Country of origin	Global culture

(continued)

Table 3.1 (continued)

	Value brand	Mass brand	Premium brand	Prestige brand	Fun brand
COMET factor: other	Economies of scale Frugal innovation	All factors except frugal innovation	Rapid rollout new products Pooling of R&D resources	Media spillover Pooling of market resources	Rapid rollout new products Pooling of market resources Economies of scale
Challenges	Segment of price-oriented buyers is limited Low customer loyalty Low price position may not travel well globally	Need for continuous product improvements Vulnerable to attacks from below and above Success varies with state of economy	Continuous stream of breakthrough R&D Recoup R&D costs Temptation to go down market	Maintain scarcity Global backlash against elitism Retain relevance among millennials	Remain relevant to a fickle segment Segment is declining in many countries Conflict with corporate social responsibility

Note: The use of country of origin as pathway to creating brand value depends on the favorability of the country for the category in question. In principle, almost any COMET factor can serve as pathway to generate value for almost any brand. I specify the most pertinent factors

Value Brands

Value brands cater to a universal need for getting the best functional value for the least available money. Successful value brands deliver adequate quality for a low price, with little if any emotional benefit, also known as *badge value*. This is what a car analyst writes about Kia, "You want … the theoretical maximum amount of SUV you can get for your dollar. You don't care about brand. You are one dead-eyed materialist. That's why we've come to Kia."[2] Japanese fast-fashion retailer Uniqlo operates over 600 stores around the world (and over 800 in its home market). It differentiates itself from fun brands like H&M and Zara with a focus on basic designs and functional fashion, relying on large volumes of high-quality cheap items that last all season. And with success: it rates highest among global apparel retailers on value for money, with a score of 137 versus 112 for H&M (an average brand rates 100).[3]

Among the best examples of value brands are the store brands (i.e., *private label brands*) carried by international grocery retailers like Costco, Walmart, Tesco, and Aldi. For example, Costco's Kirkland Signature store brand is sold in the United States, Canada, Mexico, United Kingdom, Spain, Australia, South Korea, Taiwan, and Japan, and approximates 25% of its global sales.

When it comes to launching value brands, emerging market companies have an edge over Western firms. They have developed their core competencies in lean economies. Take China's Huawei. In a span of two decades it has become the world's second largest mobile network equipment provider with its fast follower strategy, undercutting Western companies like Ericsson and Nokia by 5 to 15%.[4] Huawei is now transitioning into a mass brand. Peru's AJE Group brand, Big Cola, has shown strong growth internationally in a category dominated by Coca-Cola and Pepsi Cola.

---

[2] Neil, Dan (2015), "Kia Sorento: The SUV for the Dispassionate Investor," *Wall Street Journal*, September 5, p. D12.

[3] Millward Brown (2015), *BrandZ Report of Top 100 Most Valuable Brands*.

[4] Steenkamp, Jan-Benedict E.M. (2014), "Huawei: Taking a Chinese Brand from B2B to B2C amidst Political Resistance," The Case Centre Case #514-043-1.

Although most consumers agree that Coke and Pepsi taste better, Big Cola's price advantage of around 25% proves irresistible to consumers at the bottom of the pyramid. For example, in just four years, the AJE Group, captured more than a third of the one billion dollar carbonated drinks market in Indonesia.[5]

Value brands appeal to three target segments. The largest market is lower income customers who lack the resources to purchase a better quality product. A second group consists of so-called smart shoppers, people who do not *need to* buy value brands but do so anyway because they consider it "smart" not to be "ripped off" by higher priced brands. A third target segment is comprised of customers of all economic strata for whom the product category is not important in their lives (B2C) or for their business processes (B2B). For example, US consumers care more about the paper towel category than do European consumers. Consequently, leading mass brands like Bounty had a hard time justifying their price premium in Europe. In 2007, P&G exited this business in Europe to focus on prospects in North America.

IKEA: Democratizing Furniture

According to its founder Ingvar Kamprad, IKEA's mission is to democratize an industry characterized by high prices by offering simple, durable, well-designed furniture, at a low price to value-conscious buyers. From its humble beginnings in Sweden in the 1950s, IKEA has grown into one of the world's strongest value brands, which in 2016 stood at $18.1 billion, the fifth most valuable retail brand globally. It positions itself as a "smart brand." One of its longest running and most successful campaigns was, "Not for the rich but for the wise."

How is IKEA able to offer great value? CEO Peter Agnefjäll explained, "We are engineering costs out of our value chain that don't contribute anything." Kamprad explained the challenge, "To design a desk which

[5] Bland, Ben and Andres Schipani (2014), "A Peruvian Upstart Takes on Asia," *Financial Times*, July 22, p. 10; Bland, Ben (2014), "Soft Drinks Battle Rages in Indonesia," *Financial Times*, November 6, p. 18.

may cost $1000 is easy for a furniture designer, but to design a functional and good desk which shall cost $50 can only be done by the very best. Expensive solutions to all kinds of problems are often signs of mediocrity." For example, it cut the price of its Bjursta dining table to €199 from €279 after choosing to make the legs hollow, reducing weight and raw-material costs.

Next comes the supply chain. It has over 1800 suppliers located in over 50 different nations. IKEA's suppliers are mostly located in low-cost nations with close proximity to raw materials and distribution channels. Efficient packing—and the concomitant benefit of lower transport costs—is key to IKEA's ability to stay affordable. IKEA reduced the number of components in its Textur lamp down from 33 to nine. That cut packaging weight by 28% and allowed IKEA to fit 128 lamps on a pallet that previously took just 80. In 2010, IKEA changed its Ektorp sofa from one solid piece into several, with detachable arm rests and a hinged back. The move translated into a package size that is 50% smaller, removing 7477 truck trips from the roads annually, and a price tag that is 14% lower.

IKEA also saves costs by transferring costly activities to its customers, many of whom have more time than money. Its self-service model in which catalogues and in-store labels provide most of the information, allows it to reduce expensive sales staff. Selling products as flat packs reduces transportation costs and shifts assembly to the customer (sometimes to their despair). Out-of-town locations are cheaper and more easily accessible by car, allowing for cash-and-carry.[6]

Value Brand Challenges

Although there are many successful global value brands, they face several challenges. The size of the segment of value buyers is limited. Many consumers and purchase managers buy a value brand for a negative reason, because they cannot afford a better quality mass brand. Quite some value

---

[6] Sources include Milne, Richard (2015), "IKEA Store Planners Think Outside the Big Box," *Financial Times*, December 5, p. 14; Chaudhuri, Saabira (2015), "IKEA's Favorite Design Idea: Shrink the Box," *Wall Street Journal*, June 18, p. B10; http://cmuscm.blogspot.com/2013/02/ikeas-low-price-strategy.html; accessed February 10, 2016.

brands are, for all practical purposes, what economists call an *inferior good*. A good for which demand declines with rising incomes, as it does in emerging markets each year, where millions of people enter the middle class. IKEA tries to counter this by expanding its assortment with higher-priced items and by opening city-center stores. Of course, if pushed too far, the value brand risks losing its value position to even lower-cost entrants. This leads to the second challenge, namely that customer loyalty to value brands is often skin deep, something Xiaomi experienced when Oppo and Letv smartphones were launched and its growth slowed substantially in 2015. In 2016, Xiaomi's sales were in decline and the future of the company which in 2014 was the world's most valuable technology startup, with a private valuation of 46 billion dollars was in doubt.

To remain successful in their target segment, value brand managers need to relentlessly focus on keeping costs down. As the brand becomes more successful, containing costs becomes increasingly difficult as bureaucracy takes hold, moves to fancier offices, and extinguishes the pioneering spirit that was willing to make sacrifices. When you work for the fastest growing car brand in Europe chances you'll want a raise are high. And this happened at Dacia. The unions betted successfully on the fact that Dacia will have to heed their demands because strikes mean lower sales, which in turn results in money lost. Executives who start rewarding themselves cannot credibly turn around and deny their employees on the grounds of keeping a brand's costs low.

Finally, a low price position may not always travel well globally. In many markets, low-cost local incumbents already occupy the space and are difficult to dislodge. When Walmart entered Germany, it found Aldi and Lidl in its customary position, and it could not budge them. Low prices in the West may not translate into low prices in emerging markets because of lower incomes. Chinese consumers perceive IKEA's Billy bookcase as a luxury item. In response, IKEA China is positioning itself as a company with unique competences in interior design.

Mass Brands

Mass brands offer good quality at prices that are (slightly) above market average. These brands cater to the universal appeal of quality products, even if they cost a bit more. For many customers, quality weighs more heavily than price in their purchase decisions, and purchasing a well-known, good quality mass brand is the most common way to reduce purchase risk. For these two reasons, mass brands constitute the majority of sales in most industries. They occupy the sweet spot on the value map between low quality (value brands) and expensive (premium brands) (Fig. 3.1). In emerging markets, mass brands target the middle class, whereas in developed markets, these brands are generally accessible to all but the lowest income households.

Mass brands are the backbone of companies. They provide the revenue that supports growth in firms ranging from General Motors, Komatsu, Tata Steel, Alcatel-Lucent, Lufthansa, Hyundai, and Toyota to Levi's, L'Oréal, Unilever, P&G, and Nestlé. While lucrative, this position is pre-

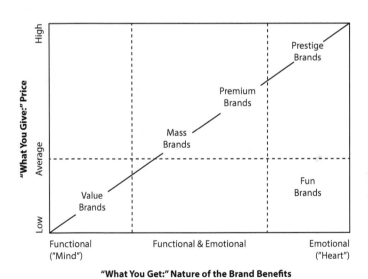

Fig. 3.1 Value map for global brands

carious: value brands can attack them from below, and premium brands can attack them from above.

Samsung: Rising from the Ashes

Samsung Electronics began as a domestic producer. Through joint ventures, alliances, and technology licensing agreements over the years, it developed the capabilities to start exporting electronic products. Initially, it sold its commoditized products as value brand to price-sensitive buyers in overseas markets. Then came the Asian financial crisis, which nearly brought Samsung down. Radical change was needed. It decided to focus on innovation, design, and brand building. To develop innovative new products, Samsung invested in upgrading its market research and product development capabilities, increased the R&D budget, conducted extensive consumer research, and set up manufacturing and distribution operations in major export markets.

It opened an in-house design school where Samsung designers, marketers, and engineers began taking six-day-a-week classes in cutting-edge design techniques. To convey its commitment to product quality, it ordered factory workers wearing headbands with the slogan "Quality First" to smash the entire product inventory of wireless phones after customer complaints about its phones began to multiply. It committed one billion dollars to make Samsung a global brand, and deleted other brands from its brand portfolio.[7]

These investments paid off handsomely. Samsung Electronics' 2015 worldwide sales were $166 billion, with profits of $16 billion and a brand value of $21.6 billion. It is a global leader in consumer electronics, including appliances, TVs, and computers, and the largest seller of smartphones in the world. Its products sell at an above-average price rather than at a discount and it received the largest number of design awards at the International Design Excellence Awards (IDEA) 2015, one of the world's most prestigious design competitions, including for a mirrorless camera with exchangeable lenses, a dishwasher that features an effective

---

[7] Slywotzky, Adrian J. (2007), *The Upside*, New York: Crown.

spray bar that achieves corner to corner coverage of dishes inside in a way that rotary bars cannot, and the world's first smartphone cover that displays information and messages from a smartphone with its LED display.[8] Samsung now regularly shows up on global lists of most innovative companies, and ranks high in *Consumer Reports* tests. Its strategy is the blueprint for Chinese brands like Huawei and Haier in their efforts to move from value to mass brand.

Value Brands Closing the Quality Gap

The greatest threat for mass brands comes from value brands that narrow the performance gap so that the difference in quality is no longer worth the difference in price. We can see this threat clearly in the consumer packaged goods industry, where store brands have largely closed the quality gap with national (mass) brands. Consumers have become less willing to pay a price premium for mass brands, and that unwillingness is a key factor in the shrinkage in their market share.[9] This danger also looms in the smartphone industry. Declining sales of Samsung's smartphones in 2015–2016 came at the gain of Chinese value brands Huawei and Xiaomi, which retail at significantly lower prices than Samsung's handsets. Thus, mass brands must continually race to improve product performance. If R&D fails to deliver meaningful technological improvements, or if innovations fail to catch on, a mass brand can quickly lose its luster. Do you or any of your friends own a smartphone by Nokia, Sony, Blackberry, or Motorola?

Mass brands can counterattack value brands by taking the fight to the latter's mattress. Brand managers stretch the mass brand downward. For example, P&G introduced Bounty Basic paper towels and Tide Simply Clean & Fresh laundry detergent. In *Consumer Reports* tests, the quality of Tide Simply Clean & Fresh was 37% lower than that of Tide Ultra

---

[8] http://www.samsungvillage.com/blog/2015/08/24/samsung-design-awards-idea-2015/; accessed February 11, 2016.
[9] Steenkamp, Jan-Benedict E.M. and Inge Geyskens (2014), "Manufacturer and Retailer Strategies to Impact Store Brand Share: Global Integration, Local Adaptation, and Worldwide Learning," *Marketing Science*, 33 (January-February), pp. 6–26.

and its price was 56% lower. Savvy firms realize that the segment of value conscious consumers varies over time, and grows in size during recessions, when companies are most desperate to keep their factories running.[10]

Stretching downward can potentially stabilize the mass brand's sales, but it can easily go awry. At the time when Kodak Gold dominated the global market, Kodak launched the discount Kodak Funtime brand to compete with lower-priced Fuji film. Cannibalization of the Kodak brand soon followed and its flagship brand's market share declined significantly. Here are three questions you need to consider in deciding whether downward stretching is for you:

- Do we attract new shoppers or are we mainly cannibalizing sales of the mass brand ('parent brand')? A rule of thumb is that there is a problem if substitution with the parent significantly exceeds fair share.[11]
- Do we earn money on the downward extension if proper accounting rules are followed? This means that the downward extension should not only recoup variable costs but also its commensurate share of fixed costs. Otherwise, you 'tax' the parent brand to subsidize the extension.
- Can we be confident we can contain negative spillover in brand image from the downward extension to the parent brand? In my work with companies, it is especially this concern that held executives back from introducing downward extensions. Negative image spillovers can be contained by using a sub-brand (e.g., Courtyard by Marriott).

---

[10] Lamey, Lien, Barbara Deleersnyder, Jan-Benedict E.M. Steenkamp, and Marnik G. Dekimpe (2012), "The Effect of Business-Cycle Fluctuations on Private-Label Share: What Has Marketing Conduct Got to Do with It?" *Journal of Marketing*, 76 (January), pp. 1–19

[11] Fair share loss means that the parent brand loses sales volume proportional to its share of the market. For example, if the parent brand has 40 % market share by volume, fair share loss means that 40 % of the downward-stretch version comes from the parent brand. Cannibalization exceeding fair share is the norm rather than the exception due to brand spillover.

Premium Brands Stretching Downward

When premium brands stretch down market to achieve economies of scale, they threaten mass brands. A counterstrategy for the mass brand is to stretch up market into the premium segment, where profit margins are higher and premium extensions can strengthen brand equity. Think of the presence and visibility of your higher-end products as a signal of the quality of your total product line. Hyundai executives told me that they decided to launch their premium Genesis line in 2008 to improve customer perception of the Hyundai brand. P&G stretched its best-selling Pantene brand upward with its "Pantene Expert Collection."

So why are not all mass brand managers rushing to extend their brands upward? Because extending a mass brand upward poses significant challenges, which executives ignore at their own peril. Priced north of $70,000, the Phaeton was Volkswagen's attempt to extend the brand into the premium segment. Although the car has excellent technology and features, its success has been minimal and production ended in 2016. Why? Because you are still driving a Volkswagen. If you really want to make your mark as a lover of premium German cars, you purchase Audi (incidentally, part of the Volkswagen Group), BMW, or Mercedes-Benz. Here are three critical questions to help you decide whether upward extension is suitable for your brand:

- Is the upward extension credible? Or will customers question whether your mass brand has the know-how to deliver the superior functional benefits expected of a premium brand in which case you should not do it.
- Is there among the premium-brand buyers in your industry a viable sub-segment that primarily buys on functional attributes (e.g., latest technology) rather than on badge value?
- Can we use a sub-brand that may be imbued with the badge value that is expected by the typical premium-brand buyer? American Express successfully extended upward by introducing a Platinum card. On the other hand, Hyundai realized that the strategy fell short of expectations, and in 2015 announced that it was launching Genesis as standalone premium brand.

Premium Brands

Premium brands promise the best functional performance in the marketplace at a premium price. Think of BMW, "The Ultimate Driving Machine," or Bose, "Better Sound Through Research." As such, premium brands cater to the universal appeal of the best product one can buy. Premium brands also appeal to risk averse B2B purchasing managers who buy the best quality brand as the ultimate safeguard against the unexpected. Most premium brands (especially in B2C) overlay functional logic with emotion in their appeals. SK-II is proven effective in fighting wrinkles (logical appeal) but it needs the myth of a monk finding pitera and the celebrity status of Cate Blanchett to persuade consumers to fork over $125 for a 14.5 ml pot of eye cream.

Some companies operate almost exclusively in the premium space, such as car makers BMW and Mercedes-Benz, consumer electronics manufacturer Apple, audio equipment maker Bose, and camera maker Hasselblad. Singapore Airlines, Emirates, and Etihad have become premium brands, especially in the lucrative business and first-class segments that European and US carriers envy. Other MNCs have a portfolio of mass and premium brands in the same category. So has Toyota Motor Co. Toyota and Lexus, and P&G has Olay and SK-II.

Premium brand buyers are of two types: First and foremost are consumers and companies that have the financial resources. Premium brand managers find them in the high income group of emerging markets and the upper-middle to high income groups of developed countries, and among financially strong firms. Second are customers who depend on the product category to achieve their own goals. Purchase managers will be more inclined to buy a premium brand when the product is a key input in their own value-adding process. Consumers will be more inclined to purchase a premium brand if they are intrinsically interested in the category (e.g., photography as a hobby) or if the brand itself is important for the person's identity. For example, for many young people, their smartphone is their most cherished possession. Consumer psychology research has found that people who are willing to make this financial sacrifice are generally highly involved with the category. They often possess some of technical knowledge about the category as well: and so they truly appreciate the superior quality they buy.

Sand River: Magic in Cashmere

Around the world, cashmere conjures up images of sophistication, but cashmere products tend to emphasize quality rather than design. The Chinese company Sand River saw an opportunity for cashmere products that combined authenticity, superior tactile quality, and modern, fashionable aesthetic designs. Sand River's CEO Juliet Guo explained, "Cashmere is very classical fabric, which is utilized in a traditional way. My dream is to reinterpret cashmere in a more contemporary and fashionable style." China's best cashmere can be found in the Alashan Plateau. But high-quality raw cashmere from purebred Alashan goats has become rarer and rarer. Therefore, Sand River built its own sourcing base by establishing long-term supply relations with herdsman families. It only uses cashmere with length of 36-plus mm and fineness around 14–15 microns.

Sand River works with avant-garde fashion designers like Japan's Junko Koshino to create contemporary apparel for its target segment of sophisticated, high-income urban, independent women in the age bracket of 35–50 years. While advanced technology is perhaps not associated with cashmere, Koshino's designs are so complex that transforming them into actual products poses significant technical challenges. Sand River's R&D team, led by Guo herself, accomplishes just that. And with success—Sand River apparel is showcased at various fashion shows such as the Tokyo Roppongi Hills Mori Tower fashion show. Prices for its women's cashmere apparel ranges from approximately $160 to $2,100, and for scarves up to $350, which is broadly similar to those of foreign premium brands in China. Although the primary market is still China, sales to overseas consumers through a Hong Kong website and websites in France, Germany, the United Kingdom, and the Netherlands made up 10% in 2015, and is expected to double in the next few years. My (American) wife, for one, is an enthusiastic customer. In 2016, Sand River started efforts to sell through upscale European retailers like Galeries Lafayette.[12]

---

[12] For more information on Sand River, see Steenkamp, Jan-Benedict E.M. (2014), "Sand River: Branding a Chinese Natural Resource," The Case Centre Case #514-065-1.

Premium Brand Challenges

Premium brands operate at the frontier of technology. They pioneer new technologies and are the first to implement them. However, product lifecycles are becoming ever shorter, even as R&D costs are increasing rapidly. This profit squeeze creates two challenges. First, even more than mass brands, premium brands need to excel on R&D capabilities and on their ability to commercialize basic discoveries. Second, premium brands need to increase prices or expand sales. Since pricing power in a competitive environment has its limits and the market for premium-priced products is by definition limited, premium brand managers are under constant pressure to increase sales and economies of scale. Moving downward into the mass segment is a tempting strategy.

And a hazardous one. Remember the lower-priced iPhone 5C, with its multicolored plastic casing, aimed to reach the mass market in emerging markets? Probably not and for good reason because it flopped largely due to image issues. In China and other countries, it received "cheap iPhone status," and its owners were ridiculed by their peers.[13] Or look at the auto industry. The Cadillac Cimarron and the Jaguar X-Type nearly killed their respective premium brands. *Time* magazine rightfully included both in its list of the 50 worst cars of all time.[14] Is history repeating itself, with entry-level models like the CLA (Mercedes), A1 (Audi) and the BMW 1? These firms hope to attract young, upwardly mobile consumers who might become loyalists and upgrade to more expensive models later. Said Steve Cannon, the head of Mercedes-Benz US, "If you make your brand accessible ... you're feeding your ecosystem." However, this assumes that the CLA meets the driving experience associated with a Mercedes, which is not borne out by the facts. *Consumer Reports* is damning in its verdict: "the driving experience [of the CLA] falls well short of a typical Mercedes... and lacks refinement." It goes on noting that the car rides very stiffly, power delivery is uneven, and the cabin is noisy. With

---

[13] Dou, Eva and Yang Jie (2016), "An iPhone Built for China?" *Wall Street Journal*, March 23, p. B5.

[14] "The 50 Worst Cars of All Time", *Time*. September 7, 2007; http://content.time.com/time/specials/packages/completelist/0,29569,1658545,00.html; accessed October 16, 2015.

a road-test score of 64 and an overall score of 53 (on a 100-point scale), the CLA rates lower than the Hyundai entry-level Accent, not the place Mercedes wants to be.[15] I myself heard people complain that the entry-level BMWs were anything but an ultimate driving machine. Such tests and sentiments undermine rather than strengthen brand equity.

Prestige Brands

Premium and prestige brands together constitute luxury brands. The purveyors of prestige brands price them very high and design them to deliver unique, exclusionary emotional benefits. The quality of prestige brands may not necessarily surpass that of premium brands. For example, a Bentley salesman in London acknowledged to me that Lexus offered higher reliability. Rather, Bentley's raison d'être is its emotional pay-off. Prestige brands are aspirational and selective—their purpose is to exclude the many to appeal to the few. Prestige brands thrive on—and critically require – scarcity. We can find prestige brands in many B2C categories, either as standalones or sub-brands. They are disproportionately strong in display categories with high aspirational value, such as wine (Château Mouton Rothschild), cognac (Rémy Martin XO Excellence), cigars (King of Denmark), watches (Patek Philippe), apparel (Canali, Loro Piana), consumer electronics (Bang & Olufsen), smartphones (Vertu), credit cards (American Express Centurion), and cars (Aston Martin, Rolls-Royce). Prestige brands can also be found in B2B, albeit they are less ubiquitous. Nevertheless, more than a few companies hire McKinsey because they want to brag about they hired McKinsey, or they send their executive team to a Harvard Business School seminar, hold their national sales conference in Davos, or participate in the World Economic Forum.

Prestige brands cater to the human desire to differentiate oneself from others, to divide the world between haves and have-nots. These brands are often unashamedly elitist. For example, Sergio Loro Piana described the market for his company's products (e.g., a knitted jacket priced $28,995 or a St. Petersburg coat for $46,500) this way: "These are not

---

[15] *Consumer Reports* (2016), "Best & Worst New Cars," April.

the needs of a Boston fireman, who wouldn't wear a cashmere coat if you gave it to him, but needs that I have, that my customers have."[16] Prestige brands benefit from origin associations, whether the origin be a country (Wedgwood) or a larger-than-life, "mythical" founder (e.g., Coco Chanel). They are also part and parcel of the global consumer culture of sophistication and good taste.

The primary target group for prestige brands is the global elite consisting of people with very high income, wealth, and social status, as well as those who aspire to belong to this group. They typically are well-educated and well-traveled. Although this segment is small in numbers, it is economically disproportionally influential. In the United States alone, the top 0.1% of families owns 21.5% of total wealth.[17] The global elite also have outsized aspirational influence over other segments of customers because of their high exposure in the media. This exposure benefits the brands they use.

Ferrari: Selling Less than You Can

Ferrari is one of the most hallowed car brands—despite the fact that there are so few of them on the road. Its brand value in 2016 stood at $4.4 billion according to Brand Finance. This places Ferrari above Peugeot ($2.6 billion) or Citroën ($1.9 billion), which sell many more cars. Ferrari understands that a prestige brand thrives on scarcity, that there should be unfulfilled demand in the marketplace. Under chairman Luca di Montezemolo, Ferrari therefore safeguarded its exclusivity by limiting production to 7000 units annually, considerably fewer than the 10,000+ he could sell. He reasoned that scarcity increased consumer demand and pricing power. On average, new customers spend a year on its waiting list before they take possession of their car. If you wait so long, you are not going to haggle about the price – starting at $190,000. The company has an operating profit margin of 14% that is the envy of other car brands.

[16] http://dealbook.nytimes.com/2013/07/08/lvmh-to-buy-control-of-loro-piana-for-2-6-billion/?_r=0; accessed June 24, 2016.
[17] http://www.businessweek.com/articles/2014-04-03/top-tenth-of-1-percenters-reaps-all-the-riches; accessed November 17, 2014.

An integral part of Ferrari's brand mystique is its involvement with Formula One racing. Who has not seen the red bolides racing to one of more than 200 victories in Grand Prix motor races? Formula One success is what makes the brand tick – it is not an optional extra. The *Financial Times* described the symbiosis, "Toys for the rich generate money for the [Ferrari] racing team, which in turn gives luster to the toys."

In 2014, Sergio Marchionne succeeded Montezemolo as chairman. He will increase production from 7000 to 10,000 units per year to keep up with the growing number of wealthy customers around the world. Only time will tell whether this strengthens or hurts the brand. But there are limits to what Marchionne wants to do. Some pundits are recommending that Ferrari enter the sport-utility vehicle or cross-over categories. His response: "You'd have to shoot me first."[18]

Prestige Brand Challenges

Prestige brands, particularly publicly owned ones, struggle to thrive under the pressure of quarterly reports. The greatest threat for prestige brands is internal, a brand team's short-term incentive to increase production in order to achieve or exceed investor expectations and to earn bonuses. Prestige brands thrive on scarcity, which makes for unfulfilled demand in the marketplace. This requires iron self-discipline as the firm leaves money on the table. If the prestige brand increases production, profits will soar in the short term but will hurt its ability to charge premium prices in the long run.

A second challenge is the looming backlash against the global elite and income inequality, as evidenced by the success of Thomas Piketty's *Capital in the Twenty-First Century*, the anti-extravagance campaign in China, and the American public's revulsion of the ultra-rich's behaviors captured by such movies as *The Wolf of Wall Street* and *The Big Short*. If this criticism continues to grow, global elites may be less willing to flaunt

[18] Sylvers, Eric and Jeff Bennett (2015), "Ferrari Tunes Up for IPO," *Wall Street Journal*, October 19, p. B3; Driebusch, Corrie and Eric Sylvers (2015), "Ferrari Gets Fast IPO Start," *Wall Street Journal*, October 21, p. B3; *Financial Times* (2015), "Ferrari: Bourse Power," October 24, p. 16; Sylvers, Eric (2016), "Ferrari Outlook Tramples Shares," *Wall Street Journal*, February 3, p. B4.

their wealth through prestige brands. Some brands such as Louis Vuitton are already responding to this outcry by showing a gentler, more discreet face, reducing logos and other brand identifiers. This is an ironic strategy, to remove a key reason for purchasing these brands in the first place, signaling to others that you are different from, and perhaps richer than, other people.

Finally, the new generation of consumers has a harder time aligning luxury purchases with their views about consuming responsibly and expecting brands to serve a higher societal purpose. Many millennials view luxury products as expensive indulgences that are inconsistent with a modest and sustainable lifestyle. To reach this new generation of affluent consumers who value authenticity very highly, prestige brands may want to focus on how they make things, how they preserve skills, crafts, jobs, and the environment, and how their products are heirlooms to preserve and pass down from generation to generation, not to dispose of and contribute to the world's landfills.

Fun Brands

Value brands and fun brands have in common a low price positioning. While value brands connote the best functional performance per dollar spent, fun brands are about lifestyle, enjoyment, and change. Fun brands cater to the universal need for stimulation and new experiences. Brand strategy calls for planned obsolescence, that is, the rapid roll-over of products because thrill seekers do not stick with the same item for a long time. They want to vary their product assortment with the occasion. The quality of fun brand products may not be the best, but it does not have to be when the consumer's interest in it is so short.

One of the pioneers of the concept of fun brands is Swiss watchmaker Swatch. In the past, young people (including me) got a watch on a special occasion (e.g., confirmation or graduation) and they would wear this watch for many years. I received mine (an austere Dutch Prisma watch) when I was ten years old and wore it for 12 years until it stopped working.

Swatch's research determined that such behavior was becoming increasingly atypical. People wanted funky rather than staid watches, preferring to own multiple watches to go with multiple occasions rather than being stuck with the same watch for a long time. So, the quality did not have to be very high. Swatch (a contraction of "Second Watch") used cheap plastic casing instead of metal, fully automated assembly of the watches, and reduced the number of parts from the usual 91 or more to only 51 components. The Swatch watch was 80% cheaper to produce than conventional watches at the time. Conceived at the beginning as a standard, cheap value brand to fight off the threat of Asian value brands that had entered Western markets, Franz Sprecher, a marketing consultant hired by Swatch's CEO Ernst Thomke to give the project an outsider's consideration, soon led the brand into what it has become: a trendy line of watches with a full brand identity and marketing concept—instead of developing just another watch collection, which could have soon been matched by the competition. Introduced in 1983, Swatch watches were a runaway success and a new category was born—the fun watch.[19]

In print media, fun brands need to keep up with the latest developments in fads and fashion. For example, through its 64 editions, printed in 35 languages, *Cosmopolitan* has spread its 3F ethos of "Fun, Fearless, Female!" around the world. Fun brands almost by definition also are ubiquitous in the entertainment industry – Disney's brand value stands at a whopping $49 billion in 2016) – and the gaming sector (online, video, casinos).

Fun brands have also been introduced in car industry but success has proved elusive. Toyota's funky brand Scion was introduced in 2002 to appeal to finicky younger buyers but never quite made its mark with them as millennials regarded it a lesser Toyota rather than its own brand. In August 2016, the line was discontinued. Volkswagen A.G.'s car brand SEAT is positioned on "Enjoyneering," described as, "[Enjoyneering] makes you feel young. It makes you feel nervous and excited at the same time." With sales of 544,000 in 2015, it did considerably better than

---

[19] https://en.wikipedia.org/wiki/Swatch; http://www.swatchgroup.com/en/group_profile/history; both accessed February 14, 2016.

Scion but with an operating loss of €10 million the brand added little to the overall value of the Volkswagen Group.

The primary target segment for fun brands is the global youth segment (as well as the young at heart), accounting for more than half of the world's population. This segment tends to share values of growth, change, optimism, future, learning, and play. Its members seek trendy images and want to make fashion statements. They are looking for novelty, modernity, and affordability, exactly the benefits that fun brands deliver. In the past, brand managers reached this segment through traditional unidirectional media like TV and magazines. Nowadays, fun brands need a strong presence on social media and the ability to engage their customers through omnidirectional channels.

Social media are not only important to reach the target segment; they also fuel the growth of fun brands, especially among fashion-conscious members who do not want to be seen wearing the same thing over and over again in their online photos. The rise of the selfie is driving the fashion conscious to buy something new to wear more often. But, since they have no more disposable income to spend on clothes, they are gravitating toward the lower end of the fun brand range, benefiting retailers such as Primark and Forever 21.[20]

Zara: Refreshing the Assortment Twice a Week

There is no industry that has been reshaped more by fun brands than apparel, where global chains like H&M, Forever 21, Victoria's Secret, and Primark have popularized the concept of disposable clothing, aka *fast fashion*. You wear the item for a short time; and when you get bored, you purchase something else, something that is new and thus more exciting. But none has been as successful as Spain's Zara.

Zara is by far the most valuable fun brand in apparel with a brand value of $25.2 billion in 2016. Zara has over 2000 stores in 2016 (up from 723 stores a decade ago) in 88 countries and sales exceeding $15 billion. How is Zara able to remain relevant to its fickle customer base

---

[20] Felsted, Andrea and Hannah Kuchler (2015), "Instagram: Retail's Holy Grail," *Financial Times*, June 19, p. 7.

each purchase cycle? And how is it able to earn an impressive EBIT margin of 18% on sales? Pablo Isla, CEO of Inditex (Zara's parent company) explained, "Our business model is the opposite of the traditional model. Instead of designing a collection long before the season, and then working out whether clients like it or not, we try to understand what our customers like, and then we design it and produce it." Only 15–20% of Zara's total production is pre-made; the other 80–85% is produced according to the market reaction. By comparison, H&M produces 80% of its clothes in advance and introduces remaining 20% based on the most current market trends.

Zara gathers its intelligence in its own stores. Shop assistants meet every day to pool customer feedback and requests. Zara combines this information with the design team's own ideas to design new items. Variations on basic designs can be sketched ready for production in only a few hours. Zara's 350 designers are located together with other functions including marketing and a manufacturing facility at Inditex sprawling headquarters in Arteixo, Galicia (Spain). Designers work in tandem with the commercial staff to assess market viability of new ideas.

Where Zara truly excels in its ability to turn design sketches into products ready to be shipped to its stores. Many of the items you see in Zara stores today will have been designed back in Arteixo as little as two weeks before. It can do that because more than 60% of production takes place close to home—in Spain, Portugal, Morocco, and Turkey. While this is more expensive, speed is of the essence in fast fashion. Every Zara store receives new products twice a week, which encourages customers to return to the store again and again. Indeed, Zara customers typically visit the shop four or five times more often than clients of a more traditional fashion store, to check out the 18,000 new items it introduces each year.

Zara typically produces small batches of any new design. This means, crucially, that it has much lower inventories than its rivals. Moreover, it leaves the decision what to stock to individual store managers. Twice a week, they 'bid' for the items they think will sell well with their clientele. Small batches and empowering store managers result in less need to discount unsold goods. Only 15–20% of Zara's stock is marked down versus 45% for a competitor like H&M.

Zara also saves money by not advertising. This in contrast to H&M, which is famous for using celebrities. The lack of mass advertising is compensated, up to a point, by the group's flagship stores, which are often located in fancy shopping streets, side-by-side with the luxury brands whose styles Zara designers and shoppers hope to emulate. The aim is to convince not just the locals but shoppers everywhere that Zara is hip. Why have its competitors not copied Zara's business model? An executive at the Gap gave the answer, "I would love to organize our business like Inditex, but I would have to knock the company down and rebuild it from scratch."[21]

Fun Brand Challenges

The global youth segment is always looking for new experiences and, like value brand buyers, is more fickle in its preferences and loyalties than older consumers or customers of premium and prestige brands. Therefore, fun brands need to continuously monitor the environment, especially through social media, for new trends. The brand team requires an exceptionally high degree of market sensing skills. What are the new trends? Which trends will catch on, and which will not? Missteps can quickly turn today's fun brand into yesterday's bad news. For example, in 2011, formerly hip clothing retail chain Gap announced that it would close 200 stores in North America to focus on its international expansion. Then, in June 2015, it announced it will close another 175 North American stores. It said it would also close a number of Gap stores in Europe over the next few years. One of its few bright spots is China, where its sales have reached $500 million in just four years.

Another challenge in many parts of the world, including Western countries, China, and Russia is that the youth segment is shrinking because

---

[21] Based on Buck, Tobias (2014), "A Better Business Model," *Financial Times*, July 27, p. 6; *The Economist* (2012), "Fashion Forward," March 24, pp. 63–64.

of rapidly falling birthrates. Some brands like Swatch try to counter this trend by introducing more expensive product lines, a strategy for holding on to their existing customer base before they age out. By 2015, Swatch had expanded its assortment beyond its $50 plastic model to sophisticated timepieces like the YVS403G selling for over $500. At that price, Swatch may lose its original fun brand essence, a viable option for neither the older nor the younger segment.

Finally, fun brands may not sit well with the increased emphasis society places on corporate social responsibility, an issue we explore further in chapter "Corporate Social Responsibility." A business model that depends on the rapid disposal of products means a lot of waste, waste that is especially visible in fast fashion. Americans, for example, discard over 11 million tons of clothes and shoes *each year*, amounting to more than 4% of the country's waste. Moreover, ultra-cheap prices require ultra-low costs in the supply chain. Primark sells dresses for as little as eight dollars, pointed men's brogues for $17, and faux-reptile cross-body bags for $12. At such prices, human rights advocates are bound to question the wages and labor conditions of those making these products.

Developing a Customer Proposition for Your Brand

Usually, your brand falls into one of the five customer propositions outlined in Table 3.1. You will typically need to tailor it to the specific strengths and competitive context of your brand. Specify a compelling customer proposition within the contours of one of the five customer propositions unless you see an opportunity to cross boundaries in order to:

- Serve the needs and characteristics of your global target segment;
- Drive purchase decisions;
- Fit with firm capabilities;

- Turn a profit in the short and long run; and
- Distinguish your brand from competitors.

Lexus, BMW, and Jaguar are all premium brands. Yet they have a clearly differentiated customer proposition. Lexus excels on reliability. There is little mystery about the Lexus brand. BMW excels on driving performance and technology, and it associates these functional benefits with the German Autobahn. Jaguar excels on prestige and heritage. Consider what a US owner of a Jaguar XJ wrote: "My wife was pleasantly surprised and proud she is riding the same car as the British royalty members. I told her how lucky we are to own such a car and enjoy it on an everyday basis."[22]

I cannot overstate the importance of a meaningful and compelling customer value proposition. A global brand needs a big idea at heart, a meaning that resonates globally with customers. It needs to stake out a unique position, which is different from anything else that exists out there and grounded in what the brand can credibly deliver. Nirmalya Kumar, Chief Corporate Strategist and member of the Group Executive Board of the Indian conglomerate Tata & Sons, even goes so far as stating that the test of a great customer proposition is: "does anybody hate you?" Brands often wish to be universally liked. However, *liked* by everyone usually means *loved* by no one in particular. Great brands are loved by some and hated by others because they actually stand for something. Of course, if everyone hates you then the brand will not be able to generate enough sales. So the challenge is to strike the right balance. As your brand becomes larger, the need to reach greater numbers of customers makes it less edgy and dilutes its unique positioning as it tries to please a broader spectrum of customers. It is therefore not surprising to find such brands go into decline before they are (hopefully) able to reinvent themselves. Think of Burberry's about being more than checked trench coats or Starbucks about being more than coffee. Thus, as your brand's success increases, you will need to update its customer proposition to ensure that it continues to stake out a unique position that is loved by many customers but still being hated by some ….

---

[22] http://www.jaguarforums.com/forum/xj-x351-53/our-car-being-used-british-royalty-86050/; accessed October 17, 2015.

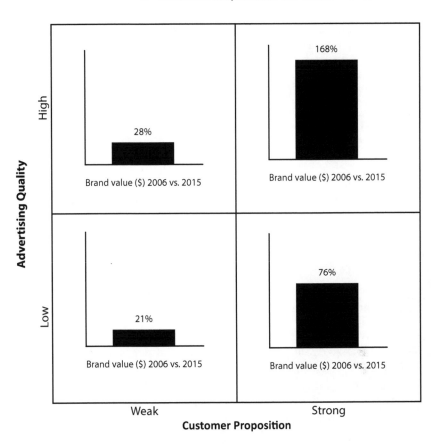

Fig. 3.2 The value of a strong customer proposition. *Source:* Adapted from Millward Brown (2015).

Research has shown that a strong customer proposition is associated with an increase in the value of the global brand, especially when a firm uses compelling advertising to communicate its proposition to the market (Fig. 3.2). Brands, which consumers say have a strong proposition and excellent advertising, grew 168% in brand value in the period 2006–2015. Brands with a strong proposition but no excellent advertising grew 76% over 10 years. However, if the brand failed to develop a strong proposition, then good or bad advertising is largely wasted. Brand value increased less than 30% over a 10-year period.

Blueprint for a One-Sentence Customer Proposition

The result of all your efforts is the customer proposition for your brand. While you can make it as many words as you wish, the more words, the fuzzier the message, both internally and externally. As part of your brand strategizing, develop a succinct one-sentence statement of your brand's raison-d'être. In my experience, many brand managers have difficulty succinctly formulating what is unique and different about their brand. If company managers have difficulty articulating it, then imagine how difficult it is for customers to grasp. When working with companies and executive MBAs, I have found the following blueprint useful for developing customer proposition statements. I also give this blueprint as an 'assignment' to executives to 'force' them to focus on the essentials:[23]

> *For* .... (definition of the global target segment), *Brand X is* .... (definition of the category) *which gives the most* .... (definition of differentiating functional/emotional benefits), *because of* .... (reason to believe).

To illustrate, this is the statement for Sand River: "For urban, sophisticated, cosmopolitan women, Sand River is a premium apparel brand which provides unparalleled elegance and comfort because of its unique combination of authentic Alashan cashmere, cutting-edge manufacturing, and Junko Koshino's innovative designs."

---

[23] Based on Kapferer, Jean-Noel (2012), *The New Strategic Brand Management*, Sterling, VA: Kogan Page, 5th edition.

Managerial Takeaways

Successful global brands align the target segment with their value positioning. Usually, individual global brands have one of five customer propositions with which to compete. You can use these labels – value, mass, premium, prestige, and fun—as a framework to refine the customer proposition and strategy for your own brand. I recommend that executives work through the following checklist:

- Determine the customer proposition that fits your brand. Are you a value brand? Mass? Premium? Prestige? Or fun?
- Customize this proposition. Does it address the needs and characteristics of your global target segment? Will it drive purchase decisions? Does it fit with your firm's capabilities? Does it make for both short- and long-term profitability? Will it distinguish your brand from competitors in the minds of your customers?
- Summarize the results in a one-sentence statement. Discuss it with colleagues. Do they understand it without much difficulty or explanation? If not, you may have to rethink it. If your colleagues do not get it or do not find it compelling, you can be confident the market will not like it either. Rethink it and give special attention to the component "reason to believe." It is the ultimate test of the credibility in a world filled with skeptical buyers.
- Evaluate the size of the target segment and geographical spread around the world for your customized proposition. Is the segment economically viable? Can you reach it?
- Contrast your brand's customer proposition with that of global competitors. Is your brand superior on one or more aspects that are important to the target segment? If not, what can you do to change that?
- Contrast your customer proposition with that of local competitors in key markets. Is your brand superior on one or more aspects that are important to the target segment? If not, what can you do to change that?
- Be aware of the challenges your particular type of brand faces (Table 3.1). Will they seriously harm global brand success in the near future? If so, start working on counterstrategies.

4

Global Marketing Mix Decisions: Global Integration, Not Standardization

In Chapter, "The COMET Framework: How Global Brands Create Value," we saw that the global brand can perform important value-creating functions for the firm. *In theory*, the brand performs these functions most effectively if the firm markets it around the world with a uniform, standardized marketing strategy. In Chapter, "Customer Propositions for Global Brands," we looked at different value propositions and why managers have to develop statements that demonstrate the superiority of their brand over competitors in satisfying the needs of their global target segment. Again, *in theory*, a globally standardized strategy is the best approach to consistently delivering the global value proposition to the target segment. *In practice* though, standardization of the brand marketing strategy is often unrealistic. Despite increasing globalization, significant differences between countries remain. You are dealing not only with a foreign language that no one on your team may speak fluently, but also with local competition, regulations, and numerous subtle nuances of local tastes and culture. Failure to accommodate these differences in global branding strategy has resulted in many brand failures.

In 2004, Home Depot entered the Chinese market by acquiring Home Way, only to exit China six years later with $160 million of losses.

© The Author(s) 2017
J.-B. Steenkamp, *Global Brand Strategy*,
DOI 10.1057/978-1-349-94994-6_4

Home Depot failed because its US executives approached China with a mindset of "If it's good enough for us, it will be good enough for them." Big mistake. Chinese consumers tend to rely on designers and contractors to plan, build, and repair their homes. They value social status and reputation, and buying do-it-yourself products signals poverty or low social standing.

Home Depot is not alone. Kraft's famous Oreos cookies struggled for years outside the US market. Kraft even considered pulling Oreos from huge markets like China. Why? It offered overseas consumers the same type of Oreos that it sold in its home market. Only after Kraft developed new flavors to suit local tastes, such as green tea Oreos in China, and a chocolate and peanut flavor in Indonesia, did sales really take off. In 2016, approximately 50% of total sales of Oreos (now owned by Mondelez) was from overseas markets Oreos was now be found in more than 100 countries. And while the United States is still the biggest market, China and Indonesia are number 2 and 3.

eBay executives ignored the advice of local Chinese employees to run servers out of China and switched hosting to the United States. "The day they switched to the U.S. servers despite our protests, traffic dropped 50 percent because access speeds were too slow. We never recovered. We lost because headquarters tried to implement what worked in the U.S., from interface design to customer service help," a China-based eBay executive said.[1]

Gillette is the dominant shaving brand in most markets around the world, but it struggled to make inroads in India. Its products were too expensive, and many consumers did not care about Gillette's promise of a clean, smooth shave. On the contrary, from Bollywood to high tech, men were adopting the designer-stubble look. To unlock the demand of the huge Indian market, Gillette developed a more affordable razor, the Gillette Guard, and came up with an innovative marketing campaign, the "Shave India Movement." It began in 2009 when Gillette publicized a study commissioned by Gillette and conducted by Nielsen, showing that 77% of women in India preferred clean-shaven men. In 2010 Gillette

[1] Rein, Shaun (2012), "Why Global Brands Fail in China," http://www.cnbc.com/id/46009614; accessed February 27, 2015.

sponsored "Women Against Lazy Stubble," to encourage women to ask their men to shave. By 2013, Gillette's share in the Indian razor blade category exceeded 50%.[2]

Global Integration Options

The dichotomy that one often encounters in executive seminars and the literature between global standardization and local adaptation is a false one. These are endpoints on a continuum ranging from complete global uniformity to complete local diversity (Fig. 4.1). Abandon the idea that global marketing means standardization. You should focus on global integration—i.e., on the degree of coordination of marketing mix activities across countries. This requires a mindset that is oriented toward looking for cross-national similarities, not differences. Cross-national differences in actual behavior may disguise potential for a globally integrated approach. Ask your team, "Is our target segment happy with the outcome? Are there globally unfulfilled needs?"

Thus, as long as elements of the marketing mix strategy are set within the context of the overarching global branding framework, we are talking about a globally integrated marketing strategy. We can consider this at the level of the overall marketing strategy—but that is too abstract. My research has identified various global integration options per mix element as they can be found in companies around the world (see Table 4.1). The global brand executive along with national marketing managers should check carefully what degree of global integration is feasible for each element of the marketing mix. This chapter brings together pertinent insights and recommendations.[3]

---

[2] Reddy, Srinivas and Christopher Dula (2013), "New Tactics to Revitalise a Brand – Gillette's 'Shave India Movement,'" *Financial Times*, November 5, p. 10; https://www.pg.com/en_IN/invest/gillette/company_updates/pdf/Gillette_India_Company_Presentation_vF.PDF; accessed February 16, 2016.

[3] In various places in this chapter, I also draw on an extensive academic literature which covers thousands of managers, working for thousands of international companies that. Key references are: Leonidou, Leonidas C., Constantine S. Katsikeas, and Saeed Samiee (2002), "Marketing Strategy Determinants of Export Performance: A Meta-Analysis," *Journal of Business Research*, 55 (1), pp. 51–67; Tan, Qun and Carlos M.P. Sousa (2013), "International Marketing Standardization: A

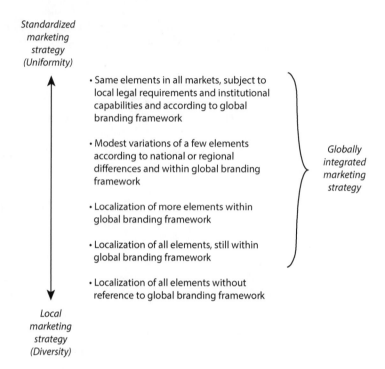

Standardized marketing strategy (Uniformity)

- Same elements in all markets, subject to local legal requirements and institutional capabilities and according to global branding framework

- Modest variations of a few elements according to national or regional differences and within global branding framework

- Localization of more elements within global branding framework

- Localization of all elements, still within global branding framework

- Localization of all elements without reference to global branding framework

Globally integrated marketing strategy

Local marketing strategy (Diversity)

Fig. 4.1 Global marketing mix strategy options

Brand Name

Many global brand managers default to using the same brand name around the world (i.e., uniformity). For example, the Chinese technology firm Huawei and South Korea's Hyundai use the same brand name everywhere, despite the difficulty overseas consumers have in pronouncing the name correctly. Yet this can create serious challenges if the original brand name is hard to pronounce and meaningless (e.g., France's Groupe Bel soft cheese brand, La Vache qui rit), or when you have to deal with

Meta-Analytical Estimation of its Antecedents and Consequences," *Management International Review*, 53, pp. 711–739; Theodosiou, Marios and Leonidas C. Leonidou (2003), "Standardization Versus Adaptation of International Marketing Strategy: An Integrative Assessment of the Empirical Research," *International Business Review*, 12 (2), pp. 141–171.

Table 4.1 Major marketing mix options for the global brand

Brand name	Product	Pricing	Advertising	Sales promotion	Sales	Distribution
Global integrated strategy						
Same brand name everywhere	Standardized product	Same price around the world	Same advertising everywhere	Sales promotion mix the same everywhere	Standardized personal selling strategies and systems	Own channel
Dual branding	Standardized product core	Transaction price band	Select advertising message from a global list	Global sales promotion coordinator	GAM	Use same existing channels everywhere
Transliteration/translation with common logo, color, etc.	Modular product	Value-optimized pricing	Glocal advertising—globally conceived, locally executed		Sales management program varies by culture type	GAM
Local strategy						
Local brand name	Product locally conceived and sold locally	Local pricing for local markets	Locally conceived and executed advertising	Sales promotion mix set locally	Personal selling strategies and systems set by local manager	Local distribution decisions

Note: Options ranked from most tightly globally integrated (uniformity) to local. The uniformity option is subject to legal restrictions and basic adaptions necessary for product functioning (e.g., voltage or left- vs. right-hand steering wheel)

radically different language systems, especially Chinese, Korean, and Japanese, all of which are based on *ideographs*, characters that represent a whole idea but not its pronunciation.

If you opt not to use the global brand name as is in a country, you can decide to retain the sound of the global brand name (transliteration). For example, the Chinese name for Samsung is 三星 (Sān Xīng) and La Vache qui rit is called ラッフィング カウ (Raffingu Kau) in Japan. Another option is to retain the brand essence (translation). La Vache qui rit is "The Laughing Cow" in English-speaking countries, "La Vaca Que Ríe" in Spanish, "Die lachende Kuh" in German, and "Vessiolaia Bourionka" in Russia. Nestlé uses 雀巢 (Què Cháo) in China, meaning "bird's nest" (after its brand logo).

Coca-Cola uses both transliteration and translation —its Chinese brand name being 可口可乐 (Kě -Kǒu- Kě- Lè) which sounds like the English brand name (transliteration) and means "delicious happiness" (translation). In Coca-Cola's case, the font of Chinese characters is cleverly adapted to closely resemble its famous wavy Roman font. Table 4.2 provides some other examples of branding practices of global brand names in China.

A final option is to use a local brand name, without any connection to the global brand name. Unilever's worldwide fabric softener, developed in Germany under the brand name Kuschelweich, was subsequently introduced in Belgium and the Netherlands as Robijn, in France as Cajoline, Yumos in Turkey, Snuggle in the United States, Fofo in Brazil, and Pomi in South Korea. Costco is called 好市多 (Hǎo Shì Duō) in China, and Oishi is called 上好佳 (Shàng Hǎo Jiā), neither of which bears any relation to the global brand name.

Transliteration and translation qualify as retention of the global brand name if they use the same logo and other branding elements. For example, despite its heavy use of translation and transliteration, all local versions of La Vache qui rit use the logo and other branding elements; and the brand is instantly recognizable everywhere. The importance of using the same logo everywhere should not be underestimated. After analyzing the world's most famous brands, advertising agency Bartle Bogle Hegarty

Table 4.2 Global brand names in China

Global name	Chinese name	Pinyin	Meaning of Chinese name	Translation/ transliteration
BMW	宝马	*Bǎomǎ*	Precious horse	Translation + transliteration
Mercedes-Benz	梅赛德斯-奔驰	*Méisàidésī-Bēnchí*	Running fast	Translation + transliteration
Jaguar	捷豹	*Jiébào*	Fast leopard	Translation
Pepsi	百事可乐	*Bǎishì kělè*	Everything is enjoyable	Translation
Johnson & Johnson	强生	*Qiángshēng*	Make life stronger	Translation
IKEA	宜家	*Yíjiā*	Good for the home	Translation
Samsung	三星	*Sānxīng*	Three stars	Transliteration
Budweiser	百威	*Bǎiwēi*	–	Transliteration
Gillette	吉列	*Jíliè*	–	Transliteration
P&G	宝洁	*Bǎojié*	Preciously clean	Translation
Disney	迪士尼	*Díshìní*	–	Transliteration
Marlboro	万宝路	*Wànbǎolù*	Roads with many treasures	Transliteration
Toyota	丰田	*Fēngtián*	Fertile fields	Translation
Caterpillar	卡特彼勒	*Kǎtèblè*	–	Transliteration
McDonald's	麦当劳	*Màidāngláo*	–	Transliteration
Oracle	甲骨文	*Jiǎgǔwén*	Inscriptions on bones	Translation
Microsoft	微软	*Wēiruǎn*	Micro + soft	Translation
Apple	苹果	*Píngguǒ*	Apple	Translation
Volkswagen	大众	*Dàzhòng*	People	Translation
Rolls-Royce	劳斯莱斯	*Láosī láisī*	–	Transliteration

concluded that each transcended geography, culture, and language via a universally recognized logo symbolizing what the brand represents.[4]

A company can further strengthen the link between its global brand name and the translated/transliterated brand name by *dua branding*, that is, showing both brand names, and that's what most Western brands do in China.

Regardless of the brand-name strategy chosen, it is crucial that the phonetic sound (standardized brand name, transliteration) or the translation work out locally. While that seems obvious, there are many examples

---

[4] De Swaan Arons, Marc and Frank van den Diest (2010), *The Global Brand CEO*, New York: Airstream.

where it went wrong. Goodyear's Servitekar tire stores ran into problems in Japan where its phonetic sound means "rusty car," P&G's Vicks introduced its cough drops into the German market without realizing that the German pronunciation of "v" is "f" making "Vicks" slang for sexual intercourse. General Mills' Jolly Green Giant was originally translated as "intimidating green ogre" in Saudi Arabia. Mercedes-Benz entered the Chinese market under the brand name 奔死 (Bēn Sǐ), which means "rush to die."[5]

Yet it is easy to avoid these mistakes. Just ask some people on the street in the country in question what comes to mind when they hear the phonetic sound of the brand name you have in mind. Thirty minutes of your time saves millions of dollars lost in using a unfortunate brand name.

Product

Managerial practice indicates that product-related elements such as quality, design, and features are among the most standardized elements of the marketing program. But despite the widespread corporate use of product standardization, its effect on firm performance in overseas markets is negative on average. That is, firms that standardize their product strategy tend to do worse than firms that localize some product elements. Uniform products do not satisfy diverse and demanding local customers, since usage conditions, income levels, and needs vary in different parts of the world. Yet the economic, organizational, and innovation drawbacks of locally developed products are formidable. In response, MNCs have turned to standardized core products and product modularity (Fig. 4.2). Both are effective solutions, which, according to research covering thousands of companies (footnote 3), lead to higher market share and profitability compared with local products.

---

[5] http://www.inc.com/geoffrey-james/the-20-worst-brand-translations-of-all-time.html; accessed February 22, 2016.

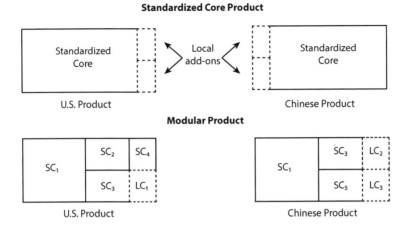

Fig. 4.2 Product adaptations within a global framework (*Note:* Rectangle size reflects the share of cost of goods sold; *SC* = standardized component, *LC* = localized component)

Standardized Core Product

You can give your core product a local look and feel with *add-ons*. This is based on the fact that the standardized core easily accounts for 75–90% of the total product configuration. Sometimes, the changes are minor, such as varying ingredients. For example, Starbucks has added an extra shot of coffee shot to its standard formulations in the Netherlands to accommodate local preference for stronger coffee, and McDonald's has added beer to its menu in its Belgian restaurants and wine in its French restaurants. Varying the packaging size also unlocks demand of poor consumers in emerging markets. For example, low-income Mexicans prefer small portions of soap, laundry detergent, and single diapers because they cannot afford full-size goods.

In other cases, the technology is more sophisticated. Honda is the pioneer of adjustable-width platforms, which allowed it to inexpensively customize and design different versions of its best-selling Accord for different regions around the world. In Europe, it gave the Accord a shorter, narrow body to handle narrow streets; in North America, it stretched the body for a roomier interior. Industry analysts attribute the success of General Motor and Volkswagen in China to aggressive localization of their cars.[6]

Product Modularity

Pioneered in 1950s by Swedish truck manufacturer Scania, product modularity as a strategy has appealed to brand managers beyond the automotive sector to markets as diverse as capital goods, energy, consumer electronics and appliances, as manufacturers seek to come to grips with the complexity of producing for global markets. By assembling a product largely from standardized components or subsystems, modularity allows manufacturers to preserve quality, creative flexibility, and mass customize products while achieving economies of scale and higher functional reliability. Scania executives believed that its modular design system has enabled the company to achieve higher margins on revenue than any other truck marker in the world.[7]

This modular approach to global production is especially effective when the standardized components are (1) not easily observable by the customer ("out of sight"), (2) a considerable part of the total cost of goods sold, and (3) R&D intensive, that is, development costs are high but give the product a technological edge over local offerings. To satisfy the needs of regional drivers, fleet operators, and standards and emission regulators, Daimler-Benz embarked on a modular strategy starting with its power train, which accounts for more than half of the value of a truck. Sweden's appliance maker Electrolux started with a modular approach in 2009. Its purpose was to increase the number of components common to its various brands and products without homogenizing or enforcing rigid product dimensions. In the white goods industry, Electrolux uses common cabinets, technology, and electronics such as fluid flow, heat exchange, electric motors and compressors across a range of products,

---

[6] Yip, George S. and G. Tomas Hult (2012), *Total Global Strategy*, Boston, MA: Pearson, 3rd ed.; Mitchell, Tom (2013), "Ownership Surges in Beijing, Shanghai, Guangzhou and Shenzhen," *Financial Times*, December 16, p. 19.

[7] Egan, Michael (2004), "Implementing a Successful Modular Design – PTC's Approach," paper presented at the 7th Workshop on Product Structuring, Göteborg, March 24–25.

from ovens to refrigerators. "Our strength is being able to deliver differentiated products for various regions and brands that are geared towards consumer preferences," said Jan Brockmann, chief technology officer at Electrolux.[8]

Pricing

Pricing decisions are usually more localized than product or advertising decisions. From an economic point of view, that makes sense: maximizing profit in a country depends on the price sensitivity of local customers and the prices of competing products and services. Companies tend to more closely align pricing policies across countries similar in customer characteristics, economic conditions, and stage of the product lifecycle.[9]

However, firms that pursue a greater integration in their pricing strategy perform on average better than MNCs that cede pricing decisions to local hands. Why? Because of arbitrage pricing. Consider the Dutch company that charged its French dealers higher prices for its copying machines than it did its Belgian dealers, as the Belgian market was more price sensitive. It found that French dealers simply bought their machines in Wallonia (French-speaking Belgium) and pocketed the price difference.

In today's interconnected world, purchase managers and consumers alike arbitrage price. Luxury goods are especially prone to price arbitrage: they are small in volume, high in value, and priced quite differently across countries. No wonder that in 2015 tourists accounted for 55% of global luxury sales versus 40% in 2010, with China leading the way. Nearly half of the Chinese luxury buyers shop for luxury goods on overseas trips, where prices are much lower.[10] I noticed this first hand when I visited the flagship store of Dutch luxury retailer De Bijenkorf in Amsterdam.

---

[8] Bryant, Chris (2013), "Building Blocks to Cut Output Costs," *Financial Times*, May 20, p. 17.

[9] Theodosiou, Marios and Constantine S. Katsikeas (2001), "Factors Influencing the Degree of International Pricing Strategy of Multinational Corporations," *Journal of International Marketing*, 9 (3), pp. 1–18.

[10] Chu, Kathy and Megumi Fujikawa (2015), "Burberry Gets Grip on Brand in Japan," *Wall Street Journal*, August 15, p. B4. http://www.bloomberg.com/bw/articles/2014-01-14/more-chinese-luxury-shoppers-prefer-to-buy-overseas; accessed March 11, 2016.

It had two counters for value-added tax-refund for foreign tourists—one for Chinese nationals with a Mandarin-speaking clerk, and one for all other nationalities combined! In response to consumer arbitrage, luxury brands like Chanel are reducing their prices in China and increasing their prices in Europe and North America. It cut the price of popular items like the Chanel Boy handbags in China by 25% and increased the price of its bags in Europe by 20%. As a consequence, the price premium charged in China over Europe declined from 74% to 6%. "This decision will enable us to offer our products to all our clients at a harmonized price wherever they are in the world," Chanel reported.[11]

Large price differences can generate unwanted attention from local authorities. Several automotive, pharmaceutical, and dairy MNCs reduced their prices in China after Chinese customers learned that these MNCs were charging them significantly more than customers elsewhere. Moreover, since 2014, the Chinese government has pushed a parallel-import program whereby independent auto dealers can directly import vehicles "in a bid to help reduce the high prices that Chinese customers must pay for imported cars," according to *China Daily*.[12]

In sum, because of price arbitrage, MNCs that implement globally integrated pricing strategies perform better financially. Global brand executives would do themselves and their national managers a favor by developing an acceptable price band (i.e., price range or price schedule) in which local prices have to fall. They should anchor the price band in the main markets of the region (or globally; dependent on the geographical reach of price arbitrageurs) as the potential for lost sales and profits is greatest there. For example, due to its economic importance and central location, Germany would be an anchor for the European Union, the United States for NAFTA, and Brazil for South America. The MNC has to accept that it may lose sales and profits in smaller markets.

---

[11] Chaudhuri, Saabira (2015), "Burberry Feels a Chill From China," *Wall Street Journal*, July 16, p. B3; Thomson, Adam and Patti Waldmeir (2015), "Bag a Bargain – Chanel Cuts Price of Luxury," *Financial Times*, March 21, p. 8.

[12] Du, Xiaoying (2015), "China 'Accelerates' Plan to Boost Market for Parallel-Import Autos," *China Daily*, July 27, p. 19.

Value: Optimized Pricing

An innovative and flexible global pricing technique is value-optimized pricing, where the company charges prices that differ not among countries but among customers and that depend on the value of the good or service in the customer's own production process. This strategy works best for technology leaders, especially patent holders whose competitors offer no comparable alternatives.

For example, General Electric (GE), a global market leader in certain classes of stationary gas turbines, applies value-optimized pricing in its gas turbine business, where prices charged for spare parts may depend on the usage and on the specific customer. It should be realized that over the long lifecycle of such equipment, costs for spare parts far exceed those of the initial capital investment. Notably for Liquefied Natural Gas (LNG) plants, where GE holds a near monopoly, costs charged are often clearly higher for machines and certainly for spare parts in comparison to gas turbines used in e.g. the power generation industry.

List Price Versus Transaction Price

Setting a price band is a good start. But global brand managers need to do more as parties negotiate the actual price paid ("transaction price"). The sales representative or account manager starts with the list price and decides which discounts, allowances, payment terms, bonuses, and other incentives to apply. These on- and off-invoice reductions lead to profit leakage. Price discounts exceeding 50% are common. Consider what happened at a global lighting equipment supplier. Negotiations became a series of discounts and incentives that pushed the average transaction price to between 30% and 90% of the standard list price of every SKU (stock keeping unit). The chief marketing officer (CMO) was surprised to learn that the largest discounts and incentives were going not to the largest or most profitable accounts but to customers with close connections to overgenerous salespeople. The firm developed a schedule of new and explicit transaction price targets based on the size, type, and segment of each account. Whenever an account manager renegotiated an existing customer's prices or signed up a new customer, those targets guided the negotiation process. As a result of the new schedule, the average transaction price rose by 3.6% and operating profits increased by 51%.[13]

A global capital goods company implemented a similar approach with equally remarkable results. Its customers were global, but pricing was local, and so customers learned to source goods for their whole company from the cheapest local rep, typically based in an emerging market. Account managers negotiated price structure and discounts deal by deal, customer by customer; and these deals were supposed to be confidential—the terms prohibited disclosure of details—but price information still flowed rapidly across borders. The company harmonized prices around the world and then gave local managers limited pricing autonomy. As a result, prices stopped eroding and profitability increased.[14]

Advertising

Market research agency Nielsen conducted a survey in 60 countries to gauge consumer trust in seven traditional and digital advertising media.[15] Table 4.3 summarizes the responses of the 30,000 participants by region. Across all media, trust in advertising is highest in emerging markets and worrisomely low only in Europe.

The Nielsen study indicates that, while the media landscape has undergone—and is still undergoing—dramatic changes, trust in advertising remains strong. This news is good for global brands and their ad agencies: advertising remains a key instrument for building global brand awareness and imbuing the brand with imagery. Some travelers can still remember that, in the early 1980s, BA stood for Bloody Awful, not British Airways. BA worked hard to improve the quality of its service. To convince travelers around the world to give it another chance, it launched its famous

---

[13] Marn, Michael V., Eric Roegner, and Craig Zawada (2003), "The Power of Pricing," *McKinsey Quarterly*, February.

[14] Cressman, George (2006), "Profitable Pricing," presentation given at the MSI Trustees Meeting, Boston, MA.

[15] Nielsen (2015), *Global Trust in Advertising*, September.

Table 4.3 Trust in advertising around the world[a]

Advertising medium	Asia-Pacific (%)	Europe (%)	Africa/Middle East (%)	Latin America (%)	North America (%)
Branded websites	78	54	76	75	61
TV	68	45	70	72	63
Print	63	44	67	71	62
Radio	54	41	62	68	60
Online video	53	33	55	52	47
Social networks	50	32	47	54	42
Mobile	46	24	45	44	38
Average across all media[b]	59	40	61	62	55

Source: Adapted from Nielsen (2015)
[a]Notes: Reported is the percentage of respondents who completely or somewhat trust a particular advertising medium
[b]Reported is the unweighted percentage across all media included in the study (not all of which are included in the table)

advertising campaign, "The World's Favourite Airline."[16] Another example is Benetton's globally uniform "Colors of Benetton" campaign that featured interracial harmony as a central theme.

Originally, Dos Equis was a small beer brand from Mexico. To make a mark in a global market crowded by more than 20,000 beer brands, it introduced "The Most Interesting Man in the World" advertising campaign in 2007. Featuring actor Jonathan Goldsmith, the campaign was key to doubling Dos Equis' global sales volume from 198.5 million liters to 468.5 million liters in the period 2007–2014 and the brand's tagline, "Stay thirsty, my friends," is recognized around the world.[17]

One way the brand can retain the benefits of global advertising, while giving local managers a choice is by developing a series of global advertising messages from which local executives can choose the one(s) they like the most. This strategy has been used by brands like Mercedes-Benz and Absolut Vodka. For example, Absolut developed a series of ads in which the shape of the Absolut vodka bottle is blended with a famous

---

[16] Probably its most iconic commercial is the 1983 Manhattan commercial; https://www.youtube.com/watch?v=izkgAdISB4Q; accessed September 24, 2016.

[17] See for some commercials http://www.dosequis.com/videos/dos-equis-commercials; accessed October 8, 2015; data on Dos Equis sales volume are taken from Euromonitor.

city landmark, such as 10 Downing Street (London) or the entrance to a subway station (Paris). Some ads might only work locally but many had global appeal.

Glocal Advertising

But we should weigh these and many other successes against the countless international advertising blunders documented in the press. Producing ads with themes and stories that resonate with customers and reinforce the brand in every market is a challenge. Add the complexity of delivery channels, customer touchpoints, and competitive positioning, and we can appreciate the difficulty of teaching the world to sing. Advertising can benefit from local adaptation. Global brand advertising can rarely capture the idiosyncrasies of every market, but the alternative—locally designed advertising—sacrifices a consistent global message and misses out on economies of scope in pooling financial resources and creative talent across countries.

The solution is the adoption of a *glocal* advertising strategy, which combines a global creative strategy with locally conceived execution. The global creative team specifies the general nature and character of the advertising message. It must address a universal human motivation that will resonate with customers anywhere. The world's strongest brands are all founded on a fundamental human truth that can unite people around the world.[18] Each local creative team then figures out how to communicate the message to its segment of customers, that is, which words, sounds, people, images, and media to use.

The aforementioned Nielsen study looked at the appeal of various advertising themes around the world (Table 4.4). This study confirms that, while there are differences among regions—for example, humor resonates more with Western consumers than with people in Latin America or Asia-Pacific—the differences may be fewer than many global brand managers might think. The skill comes in identifying what to adapt

---

[18] Wind, Jerry, Stan Sthanunathan, and Rob Malcolm (2013), "Great Advertising Is Both Local and Global," HBR Blog Network; https://hbr.org/2013/03/great-advertising-is-both-local/; accessed February 27, 2016.

Table 4.4 Advertising theme appeal around the world

Advertising theme	Asia-Pacific (%)	Europe (%)	Africa/Middle East (%)	Latin America (%)	North America (%)
Slice of life	45	41	44	50	35
Humor	32	51	38	33	50
Sports	12	13	18	23	12
High energy/ action	30	16	22	20	17
Aspirational	26	17	20	23	13
Sentimental	18	14	19	23	15
Celebrity and/or athlete endorsement	22	13	24	18	13
Sexual	9	9	12	16	11

Source: adapted from Nielsen (2015)
Note: Reported is the percentage of respondents that indicated that the particular theme resonated with them.

locally. For example, a campaign anchored to an athlete's endorsement will more likely feature a baseball star in the United States and a football (soccer) star in Europe, Africa, and Latin America.

Diageo's Scotch brand Johnnie Walker uses the glocal model.[19] In the late 1990s, sales were in steep decline. Tactical, short-term promotion focused, and incoherent marketing sapped Johnnie Walker's brand appeal. Between 1997 and 1999, Diageo ran 27 different advertising campaigns for Red Label and Black Label across the world. To revitalize Johnnie Walker, Rob Malcolm, Diageo's President Global Marketing, Sales and Innovation embarked on a glocal strategy. The first step was to identify a fundamental human truth. Working with Bartle Bogle Hegarty, Malcolm and his team dug deep into the brand's history and identified success as defining brand property. But what does success mean? It is not just about the endpoint but also about getting there. Diageo and BBH realized that no matter the circumstances, every man (the target segment is males) has a hard-wired desire to move forward, to improve himself in some way. This innate universal need to advance and progress was identified as the fundamental human truth upon which to build the Johnnie Walker global brand.

---

[19] De Swaan Arons and van den Diest (2010).

The resulting campaign "Keep Walking" emphasized every man's determination to follow his dreams and pursue his agenda. But progress is defined differently in different countries. Diageo's global team tasked countries to work with BBH to bring to life the brand's fundamental human truth in a locally recognizable manner. For example, in post-war Lebanon with reconstruction in full swing, billboard advertising showed the Johnnie Walker logo—a cane-wielding man clad in boots and a hat—striding on a broken bridge, with the gap behind him.[20] Within three months of launch, brand recall increased from 22% to 50% and global revenue increased by 3.7%. The unified worldwide campaign gave Johnnie Walker high global brand consistency and it was the second world's most valuable spirits brand with a brand value of $4.6 billion in 2016, according to Brand Finance.

P&G's global "Thank You, Mom" campaign started with P&G's worldwide partnership with the Olympic Games. The campaign grew from fundamental human truth of the love and sacrifice of mothers for their children. Kirsten Suarez, Senior Brand Manager, Olympics at P&G, explained, "'Thank You, Mom' really touches hearts all over. Locally, of course, we have teams that adapt and amplify the message to ensure they're doing the best plans for their market. But, at an insight level, the message is extremely global."[21] To connect with consumers locally, P&G did two things. First, it featured (aspiring) sportspeople from different countries in its global ads. Second, it supplemented its global campaign with local ads that followed a common template but featured local sports stars and the brands deemed most relevant to the local audience. For example, around the 2014 Winter Games in Sochi, a print ad that ran in the US market featured three US heroes, Amy Purdy, Evan Lysacek, and Julie Chu.

---

[20] The print ad can be found at https://www.google.com/search?q=Johnnie+Walker+ad+Keep+on+Walking+in+Lebanon&rlz=1C1RNVG_enUS530&espv=2&biw=1920&bih=995&source=lnms&tbm=isch&sa=X&ved=0ahUKEwiciJewg5vMAhVEJR4KHZJjCEQQ_AUICCgD#imgrc=sHomphRwHmqdxM%3A; accessed April 19, 2016.

[21] Lopez, Ana et al. (2015), "Using the Olympics to Build a Global Brand," UNC Kenan-Flagler Business School report. Two examples of global ads featuring different slice-of-life stories from different countries can be found at https://www.youtube.com/watch?v=1SwFso7NeuA and https://www.youtube.com/watch?v=Y5lsZkJiUmM; accessed September 22, 2016.

Sales Promotion

Sales promotions refer to a collection of short-term customer incentives that lead to faster inventory turns and/or greater volume of sales of a particular product. For most MNCs, sales promotion policy is among the least integrated elements of their global marketing program. There are several reasons for this: economies of scope are few, and their effectiveness depends on the degree of economic development of the country, the product's stage in its lifecycle in each country, and the country's structure of the retail trade. Cultural perceptions of promotions tools also differ considerably between countries. For example, Taiwanese consumers have less favorable attitudes toward sweepstakes than Thais or Malaysians. Some 85% of Americans use coupons, with the overwhelming majority still preferring paper coupons, unthinkable in any form in Europe.[22]

Yet leaving sales promotion decisions completely in local hands has unintended consequences. During one of my trips to South Africa, I visited a store of a major retail chain and found Johnson & Johnson Baby Oil with labeling in Turkish. Someone had slapped an English sticker over the Turkish label. My colleague Steve Burgess, who once worked for J&J, explained that the South African retailer had noticed J&J Turkey's very deep price promotion and organized shipment of a container to South Africa, where he would sell it at the regular price. The retailer pocketed the profit, the Turkish subsidiary sold more, but J&J as a whole lost money.

To avoid such arbitrage, global brand executives need to harmonize the promotion policies of their global subsidiaries. The CMO should appoint a global sales promotion coordinator, with recognized experience in the promotion field, strong persuasion skills, and line marketing experience. This manager's set of responsibilities could include the following:

- Gathering performance data and develop monitoring systems to evaluate the effect of promotions of short- and long-term sales and profitability;
- Disseminating successful promotional ideas across countries;

---

[22] Huang, Jiayue (2015), "Americans Still Prefer Their Paper Coupons," *USA Today*, November 3, p. 5B.

- Training subsidiaries on how to limit their trade promotional expenditures;
- Setting limits to the intensity (frequency, percentage discount) of promotions to preserve global brand equity; and
- Creating incentives for local brand managers to maintain these promotion policies and practices.[23]

Global Sales Strategy

For most MNCs, sales strategy for global brands remains very much local. Salespeople typically get the majority of their sales within one country. Personal selling requires them to understand local aspirations, needs, and customs—which presumes a fluency in language and culture—well enough to forge an effective relationship with customers, be they households, entrepreneurs, or procurement managers. Consequently, MNCs have seldom standardized sales force techniques and management methods across markets. Standardization of sales in general tends to effect firm performance negatively.

Sales Management Control Systems

Sales managers oversee their sales representatives by monitoring output and behavior. In an outcome-based control system, managers provide relatively little guidance: they use straightforward objective measures of results (outcomes) to evaluate and compensate the salesforce. In other words, they hold salespeople accountable for their outcomes, not for how they achieve those outcomes. Firms using outcome-based control systems shift risk to the salespeople and share rewards with them in direct proportion to their measurable performance. Incentive-based (variable)

---

[23] Kashani, Kamran and John A. Quelch (1990), "Can Sales Promotions Go Global?" *Business Horizons*, 33 (3), pp. 37–43.

remuneration constitutes an important portion of a salesperson's total compensation.[24]

In contrast, in behavior-based control systems, managers actively monitor and direct their salespeople's activities and use their salesperson's inputs rather than sales outcomes to evaluate and compensate the salesforce. The advantage of behavior-based control is the sales managers' ability to reward certain behaviors as part of company strategy without having to sell that strategy to each salesperson. Salary-based (fixed) compensation constitutes the largest portion of salespeople's total remuneration. Thus, the firm assumes risk to gain cooperation.

Management's relative emphasis on, and effectiveness of, output-based and behavior-based control systems differ between countries. For example, British managers are more likely to use incentives in their salespersons' compensation plan than French, Italian, German, or Spanish managers.[25] Therefore, global brand strategy should accommodate local sales managers, allowing them to control sales programs and align them with local regulations. Yet there is room for global guidelines.

Cultural Variance of Sales Management Programs

A country's culture reflects the basic issues and problems that societies must confront to regulate human activity. The shared cultural priorities among members of a society help to shape the social and economic reward contingencies to which managers must adapt to function smoothly and effectively. MNCs benefit from using a framework for assessing how a country's *culture* could assist in designing and controlling local sales management programs. Two aspects of national culture are especially important: how people respond to uncertainty (tolerance/avoidance) and how they view individual achievement (competition/compassion).[26]

---

[24] Anderson, Erin and Richard L. Oliver (1987), "Perspectives on Behavior-Based Versus Outcome-Based Salesforce Control Systems," *Journal of Marketing*, 51 (October), pp. 76–88.

[25] Segalla, Michael et al. (2006), "A Cross-National Investigation of Incentive Sales Compensation," *International Journal of Research in Marketing*, 23 (4), pp. 419–433.

[26] Hofstede, Geert, Gert Jan Hofstede, and Michael Minkov (2010), *Cultures and Organizations: Software of the Mind,* New York: McGraw-Hill. Note that these authors use the terms masculinity/femininity rather than competition/compassion.

Uncertainty tolerance/avoidance refers to the degree to which a society tends to feel threatened by uncertain, risky, ambiguous, or undefined situations, and the extent to which they tend to avoid such situations by adopting strict and predictable codes of behavior. Since most sales jobs entail considerable uncertainty, salespeople who grew up in cultures where uncertainty avoidance is high are likely to prefer fixed-income compensation plans. To manage the salesforce in such countries, the firm will have to rely more heavily on behavior-based control systems. In societies that tend to tolerate risk and where laws and customs support entrepreneurial behavior, MNCs can deploy a variable-income compensation plan.

Competition/compassion refers to a society's orientation toward individual achievement, assertiveness, and material success at one end of the spectrum and toward equality, quality of life, and caring for and sharing with the weak. The country's orientation on this dimension will determine how the MNC should allocate incentives, according to individually differentiated performance (i.e., equity rule) or divided equally among all members of a sales team (i.e., equality rule).

Tool 4.1 shows the application of these cultural principles to the preferred sales management control system and assigns over 60 countries and regions—collectively comprising over 90% of the global economy—to a cell. A global sales coordinator can use this tool to evaluate proposed control systems in specific countries.[27]

Global Account Management

Many MNCs have major business customers with globalized supply chain management. These customers increasingly demand a single point of contact, contracts with uniform prices and terms of trade, standardized products and services, consistency in service quality and performance, and even after-sale support in countries where an MNC might lack presence. For example, Royal Dutch Shell has global accounts with three suppliers for its process control systems in its refineries and petro-

---

[27] Assignment is based on Hofstede et al. (2010). With the exception of Morocco, they only provide region scores for the Arab world, East Africa and West Africa.

		Competitive	Compassionate
Uncertainty Tolerance/Avoidance	*Avoidant*	• Emphasize behavior-based control systems • Low variable (incentive) component • Equity allocation of incentives	• Emphasize behavior-based control systems • Low variable (incentive) component • Equality allocation of incentives
	Tolerant	• Emphasize output-based control systems • High variable (incentive) component • Equity allocation of incentives	• Emphasize output-based control systems • High variable (incentive) component • Equality allocation of incentives

Competitive   *Compassionate*

Competition/Compassion

Uncertainty Avoidant/ Competitive	Uncertainty Avoidant/ Compassionate	Uncertainty Tolerant/ Competitive	Uncertainty Tolerant/ Compassionate
Arab countries	Brazil	Australia	Africa (East)
Argentina	Bulgaria	Bangladesh	Africa (West)
Austria	Chili	Canada	Denmark
Colombia	Costa Rica	China	Estonia
Czech Republic	Croatia	Great Britain	Finland
Ecuador	El Salvador	Hong Kong (SAR)	Indonesia
Germany	France	India	Iran
Greece	Guatemala	Ireland	Malaysia
Hungary	Peru	Jamaica	Netherlands
Italy	Portugal	New Zealand	Norway
Japan	Romania	Philippines	Singapore
Mexico	Russia	Slovakia	Sweden
Morocco	South Korea	South Africa	Vietnam
Poland	Spain	Trinidad	
Switzerland	Thailand	United States	
Venezuela	Turkey		
	Uruguay		

Tool 4.1 Sales management control systems in different cultures (*Source: Country allocation based on Hofstede et al. (2010)*)

chemical manufacturing installations. It consciously restricted its choice to suppliers with global presence, with which it negotiated so-called *global enterprise framework agreements*. These agreements are menus of offerings with set prices and conditions; they allow local managers to order process control equipment without having to pass through *tendering*, the often time-consuming process of responding to a *request for tender*, that is formally bidding on a customer's ongoing need for products and services.

In response, many global suppliers have begun to rely on global account management (GAM), where one person or team within the multinational supplier coordinates all activities to serve a particular multinational customer. For example, Xerox established relatively independent GAM units for global accounts such as Motorola and BP. These units are located near the customers' headquarters, and frontline employees in the units provide technical support and sales service. The fueling service of BP's Castrol division offers GAM to key multinational customers in the transportation industries for obvious reasons: Because international routes and their activity on those routes are constantly changing, global coordination is essential to ensure that their planes and ships don't run dry. Sodexo, a food services and facilities management MNC, has global account managers for various MNC clients such as Coca-Cola. Sodexo has a long-standing policy of rebranding acquired local companies to Sodexo. Its global customers want global account managers who represent the corporate brand, not the individual brand names in different countries. Sodexo's effective GAM contributed to its global success, with revenues of €20 billion in 2016, and its brand was valued at $2.6 billion according to Brand Finance.

Does Global Account Management Makes Sense for Your Company?

Global account management poses heavy challenges, least among them the cost of additional staff layered on top of existing national sales organizations, which easily adds between $100,000 to more than $1 million per customer (dependent on their size and global reach) to what the supplier had been spending in individual countries for sales and support.[28] Your sales management team will need to reconcile local salesforce incentives with global contracts. Your global account managers will need to deal with the pressure of uniform pricing, meaning the lowest price in the price band. And your sale service and after-sales support will need to deliver more or less standardized products and services of consistent quality everywhere in the world. Your firm might also have to enter countries that you had not planned to enter, so that you could serve the customer wherever that customer operates. Thus, global account management is not for every multinational supplier. To determine whether it is for your company, ask yourself the following questions:

- Do your goods or services need global coordination, where customers want a single point of contact? Prime candidates are complex products and services (e.g., process controls, global fueling contracts), commodities that add value to the customer's production process (e.g., specialty chemicals, food ingredients), and knowledge and expertise intensive services (e.g., high-end professional services such as corporate banking, advertising, marketing research).
- Do your products or services command a margin sufficiently high to justify the extra costs of a global account management layer in your organizational hierarchy, not to mention the potential internal turf wars and disruption of buyer–seller relationships?
- Are your multinational customers sufficiently important to merit GAM? Is at least one of the following criteria fulfilled: (1) one global customer accounts for 5% or more of your business; (2) more than 10% of your revenues come from multinational customers that coordinate their purchasing globally or regionally; (3) more than 25% of your revenues come from multinational customers, regardless of how they do their purchasing; (4) large multinational customers are your most profitable accounts?

[28]Yip, George and Audrey J. M. Bink (2007), "Managing Global Accounts," *Harvard Business Review*, 85 (September), pp. 103–111.

- Can you gain competitive advantage from GAM? That is, will it set you apart from your rivals?[29]

If you answered yes to at least three of the above four questions, you should seriously consider developing a GAM program to support your global brand. The next step would be to select multinational customers for the program. After all, not every multinational customer requires or merits the GAM effort and expense. Tool 4.2 presents a diagnostic tool for identifying the right customers for your GAM program.

Global Distribution Strategy

Developing One's Own Distribution Channel

You can most effectively ensure consistent brand policies around the world by setting up your own distribution system, either by directly operating distribution outlets or through contracts with independent distributors. If your firm is in the position to pursue an integrated global distribution strategy, then its performance should improve significantly. If you deploy the same channel structure in different countries, then you can leverage your experience in different markets. The efficiency of standardized channels improves sales and profits.

Not surprisingly, many global services companies, from hotels (e.g., Hilton, Holyday Inn) to restaurants (McDonald's, Starbucks) and retail (Aldi, IKEA) have set up their own distribution system, typically a mix of wholly owned outlets and agreements with independent distributors. However, brand-exclusive distribution channels also exist for selling such tangibles as cars, consumer electronics (Apple, Microsoft), or machinery. Caterpillar has over 150 independent licensed Caterpillar-only dealers around the world, many of which have been with Caterpillar for generations. It considers its dealer network as its primary route to market and a key advantage over competitors like Komatsu and Sany.

---

[29] Yip and Bink (2007).

Score each customer on a number of characteristics, tally the scores, and then use the key at the bottom to gauge their potential for global account management.

Customer Characteristics	Scoring Guidelines	Score (0-10)
Current account size	10 = our largest account 5 = half that size 1 = one-tenth that size	☐
Revenue potential	10 = our business with this customer can grow 100% or more in the next 5 years 5 = can grow 50% in the next 5 years 0 = no growth potential in the next 5 years	☐
Gross margin	10 = the highest margins among all our customers 5 = half that 0 = no profits	☐
Geography	10 = operates in countries that account for 100% of our market 5 = operates in countries that account for 50% 1 = operates in countries that account for 10%	☐
Integration capabilities	10 = all the capabilities required for global integration and coordination 5 = moderate capabilities 0 = no capabilities	☐
Strategic importance	10 = absolutely vital to our business 5 = moderately important 0 = of no strategic importance	☐
Strategic fit with our firm	10 = many joint strategies 5 = some joint strategies 0 = no joint strategies	☐
Cultural fit with our firm	10 = complete fit (might happen if customer is in the same industry, from the same country, and of similar size and age) 5 = partial fit 0 = no fit	☐
Geographic fit with our firm	10 = we operate in all the countries in which this customer operates 5 = we operate in half of them 0 = we operate in none of them	☐
Relationship	10 = we have a very close and trusting relationship in which vital information is shared 5 = moderate sharing 0 = no sharing	☐

Total score:	0-25	26-50	51-75	76-100	Total Score ☐
The customer:	Is not a good prospect for GAM	Is worth considering	Is a very promising prospect	Should be one of our key global accounts	

Tool 4.2   Scorecard for evaluating multinational customers as prospect for GAM (*Source:* Adapted from Yip and Bink (2007))

Expanding globally by working with independent distributors rather than developing your own distribution channel ties up less capital, is faster, and more fully capitalizes on local market knowledge. However, you relinquish considerable control over your brand strategy, the loss of which can hurt you in the longer run. For example, luxury brands like Burberry, Celine, and Yves Saint Laurent gave their licensees leeway to develop and sell their own products for the local market under those global brand names. But the global images were tarnished when licensees sold their locally conceived Yves Saint Laurent and Celine handkerchiefs and hand towels for about ten dollars in recent years in Japan or Burberry women's shirts for $70. By ending these licensing agreements, these prestige brands regained full brand consistency world-wide. Burberry now plans to offer only the highest-end products in Japan—such as its $1800 trench coat—and operate only in the most exclusive locations. The goal is to have 35–50 directly operated stores by 2018, according to Pascal Perrier, Burberry's CEO in the Asia-Pacific region. "The license has been suffering from overexposure. We will never do that again," he said.[30]

Using Existing Channels: Western Retailers

In industries like consumer packaged goods, with rare exceptions such as Nespresso boutiques, developing your own distribution outlets is not a realistic option. In Western markets, you can still coordinate your distribution strategy through such large and efficient players as Walmart, Tesco, Sainsbury, and Carrefour, some of which operate on a regional or global scale. These retailers have perfected their logistics and are often better informed about consumer needs than the global CPG companies.

Increasingly, global retailers are looking for GAM. Consider Walmart, the world's largest retailer with sales of around half a trillion dollars in 2016. In 2010, Walmart announced a drive to combine store purchasing across national frontiers, using four global merchandising centers. One of the manufacturers is P&G: Walmart accounts for one out of every seven dollars of P&G's revenues. A large customer team works on global

---

[30] Chu and Fujikawa (2015).

strategy at Walmart's headquarters, while the other P&G team members work in Walmart stores around the world to assist with order placements, inventory management, and marketing research.

The Challenge of Emerging Markets

As much as many brand manufacturers love to hate powerful retailers, they miss them wherever the retailers do not operate. That situation characterizes most emerging markets, where easily 80% of consumers buy their groceries from mom-and-pop stores, often no bigger than a closet. If Western brand manufacturers wait until a modern retail infrastructure forms, they would miss early branding opportunities among households with growing incomes and small business owners with plans to grow. Modern retailing has succeeded mainly in countries with good road networks, high or fast-rising car-ownership rates, a large middle class that enjoys decent wages and stable employment, and a high proportion of households with room at home to store groceries. In most emerging markets, only a small part of the market meets these conditions. Moreover, many small retailers own their storefronts, rely on family and friends for free labor, and fly under the radar screen of the taxman. While modern (foreign) retail chains often have considerable operating-cost advantages from better sourcing and supply-chain processes, customers and regulators hold them to a higher, costlier standards than mom-and-pop stores.[31]

As a consequence, the traditional trade has shown remarkable resilience against formidable global competitors. MNCs have to seek opportunities in a fragmented distribution channel. Branded manufacturers enjoy high margins by supplying small shopkeepers, who have little negotiating leverage. Shelf space is the critical factor in these closet-sized stores, and so MNCs secure shelf space strategically, one shelf at a time, one shop at a time. First movers have a strong advantage since few stores have the space to carry multiple brands in the same category. Consider the enduring performance of Unilever's brands in markets like Indonesia (present since 1933), Brazil (since 1929), and India (since 1888) where

---

[31] Child, Peter, Thomas Kilroy, and James Naylor (2015), "Modern Grocery and the Emerging-Market Consumer: A Complicated Courtship" *McKinsey Quarterly*, August, pp. 1–8.

it has developed fine-grained sales networks decades deep. Unilever provides discounted goods to small shop owners in exchange for prominent placement, and salesmen check in weekly to make sure everything is in stock and displayed neatly. Said a shop owner in Jakarta, "Competing products are in the back" pointing to the dusty, unlit shelves behind him. "You can't fight Unilever."[32]

IKEA's Global Marketing Strategy

IKEA has been successful with a highly integrated global marketing strategy. It uses the same brand name, logo, and signature blue and yellow colors around the world.[33] You immediately recognize from afar any of its 328 stores in 27 countries. The global product assortment is the base from which country managers choose the products they offer in their country. While there are some minor adaptations to individual products in individual countries (e.g., in the United States, beds and bedding are not made to metric measure but to King, Queen, etc.), in general the standardized assortment is so wide that there is the scope for every market to adjust by finding something that fits. Products are "branded" with the same fancy labels (like Billy or Pax) everywhere. While the global aim of IKEA is to deliver high value for a low price, country managers have considerable leeway to set their own prices, taking into account the strength of the competition, average income, and their spending priorities. Moreover, the low-price position is difficult to achieve in some countries such as China due to centralized sourcing which increases costs (e.g., import taxes). However, across all countries, it follows a strategy of cutting prices over time.

---

[32] Wuestner, Christian (2013), "Unilever: Taking the World, One Stall at a Time," *Bloomberg Businessweek*, January 7, pp. 18–20.

[33] IKEA's global marketing strategy is described in detail by Steve Burt, Ulf Johansson, and Asa Thelander (2011), "Standardized Marketing Strategies in Retailing? IKEA's Marketing Strategies in Sweden, the UK and China" *Journal of Retailing and Consumer Services*, 18, pp. 183–193; see also http://www.curbed.com/2014/10/8/10038294/how-ikea-became-americas-furnitureselling-powerhouse; and http://deredactie.be/cm/vrtnieuws.english/News/1.1826337; accessed February 24, 2016.

The catalogue is IKEA's most important marketing communication tool, accounting for more than two-thirds of its annual advertising budget. Over 200 million copies were published in 2015, in over 60 editions and 30 languages. The cover of the catalogue may change to some extent, and in markets IKEA entered more recently there is more information about the company and how to shop at IKEA, but these are relatively minor deviations from the core template.

IKEA controls the distribution channel—most stores are owned, others are franchised. While the location and layout of the stores has to fit local conditions and regulations, the stores are usually well out of the city center, with two floors, and parking outside the store. The in-store environment is basically the same in terms of core features: layout and design, number of departments, display and colors, service levels, restaurant. However, the room-setting displays are adapted to reflect local housing and living conditions. Service levels are intended to be the same around the world with similar staffing levels everywhere.

IKEA's highly integrated global marketing mix strategy resonates with customers. Its revenues grew from to €10.4 billion in 2001 to €32.7 billion in 2015, in which year net profits exceeded €3 billion.

Putting It Together

Table 4.5 summarizes dominant managerial practice and recommendations for various elements of the global brand's marketing program. Executives can integrate these insights with

- their assessment of the local and global environment for their global brand,
- the fit between environment and the global brand strategy,
- the type of industry they are in, and
- the ability of their firm to effectively execute the strategy (discussed in Chapters "Organizational Structures for Global Brands" and "Global Brand Management").

Table 4.5 Global marketing mix decisions: managerial practice and recommendations

Dominant managerial practice	Recommendations
Use of the same brand name and logo across the world	Use the same global brand name around the world unless it has undesirable local connotations or is impossible to pronounce If a different brand name has to be used, retain the sound of the global brand name (transliteration) and/or the meaning of the global brand name (translation); use dual branding when possible and use the same logo, etc.
Powerful forces pushing forward product standardization	Use core product standardization Use common, interchangeable modules or subsystems as building blocks Product components that are prime candidates for modularization (1) are out of sight (unless they can be modularized, too); (2) make up a considerable part of the total CoGS; and (3) are R&D intensive
Prices are often set locally Pricing policies are more integrated across similar countries Increasing need to harmonize prices across countries	B2B markets require higher price integration than B2C markets Pursue high degree of global price integration for luxury brands Develop global price band for list and transaction prices based on major markets Value-optimized pricing to differentiate between applications, not countries
Advertising increasingly integrated across countries to project a consistent brand image	Consider uniform advertising when the target segment has a strong preference for global brands and for fun and prestige brands Allow local managers to choose from among a set of global ads Distinguish between creative strategy and execution; creative strategy has a greater globalization potential than execution Search for a universal human motivation that will resonate anywhere in the world as basis for global creative strategy Use glocal advertising if customers do not care about or even reject global brands and in countries where unique local attitudes or customs make a global campaign ineffective

(continued)

Table 4.5 (continued)

Dominant managerial practice	Recommendations
Sales promotion set locally	Give local managers a high degree of freedom Use global sales promotion coordinator to facilitate worldwide learning of best local practices to reduce parallel imports and to protect global brand integrity
Predominantly set locally Global account management (GAM) on the rise	Give local managers a high degree of freedom Vary emphasis on output- and behavior-based sales management control systems based on country uncertainty avoidance and competition/compassion Use global sales coordinator to facilitate worldwide learning of best local practices and to evaluate proposed control systems in specific countries Assess whether GAM is appropriate for your company by answering four questions Evaluate major multinational customers on their prospect for GAM using Tool 4.2
B2B firms standardize their distribution strategy more than B2C firms Standardization potential lower in emerging markets	If feasible, develop your own channel, either through directly operating the channel or via contractual agreements If you distribute your brand using licensing, ensure that (1) any branded products developed by the licensee need to be approved by headquarters; and (2) the licensing agreement is limited to 5–10 years Leverage learnings from different countries to develop policies for modern retail chains Consider GAM with international retailers Develop micro-strategies to deal with thousands of mom-and-pop stores in emerging markets Early commitment to local channels in emerging markets makes it difficult for followers to obtain distribution

I conclude with several general observations about global program integration as opposed to global integration of specific marketing mix elements.

First, taking all evidence together, firms that integrate their global marketing program perform better on market metrics (market share, competitive position) and financial metrics (profitability, return on investment) than firms that pursue a localized marketing strategy.

Second, larger firms are more likely to employ integrated marketing programs than smaller firms because they can take greater advantage of economies of scale and scope. Their less flexible organizational structures also make it more difficult for large firms to effectively adapt their marketing strategy to local conditions.

Third, firms whose leaders centralize decision making at headquarters more often employ integrated marketing programs. HQ decision-makers prefer an integrated strategy to one of adaptation for better control over the subsidiaries' products and services.

Fourth, global program integration potential is higher for prestige and fun brands which cater to a relatively uniform global segment. It is also higher in high tech, durables, and new categories and lower in culturally grounded B2C categories such as foods.

Fifth, although you might expect global integration potential to be higher for B2B firms than for B2C firms, there is no consistent evidence that B2B firms actually integrate their marketing programs to a greater degree than B2C firms, perhaps because certain activities that are mission-critical to B2B firms such as sales typically exhibit low degree of integration.

Finally, MNCs tend to configure their marketing programs so that a higher degree of integration on one component tends to relate positively to the degree of integration on other marketing mix elements, as firms strive for internally coherent marketing strategies for their brands. However, the correlation between the degree of integration for the different marketing mix elements is fairly modest (in the range of 0.3–0.5); MNCs carefully consider the optimal degree of standardization for each component separately.

Managerial Takeaways

To standardize or to localize?—this question has vexed MNCs for many decades. Some have reframed the argument as global efficiency versus local effectiveness, but the dichotomy is too simplistic. Efficiency gains are illusionary if the global marketing program is misconceived, while local effectiveness ignores the dynamic spillovers between countries in a globalized world. Global integration—coordination of marketing activities across countries – not blanket standardization is the watchword. The task of the executive is to make informed decisions about each element of the marketing mix. Here are guidelines.

- Understand that global integration exists on a continuum, from local decisions within a common global branding framework to uniform around the world.
- Consider your context. The potential for high degree of marketing program integration is highest for prestige and fun brands, high tech, consumer durables, and new product categories without a long cultural history.
- The integration potential in B2B is higher than in B2C, but company practice shows that integration in B2B firms is only higher for distribution decisions. Global brand managers may be missing integration opportunities in product design, pricing, advertising, sales promotion, and sales management.
- Consider the optimal degree of integration for each marketing mix element. Table 4.5 provides the recommendations. Ensure the result is an internally coherent marketing program for your brand.
- Analyze your brand's major markets in depth before deciding whether to allow local adaptation. You may have to accept lower performance in minor markets to avoid negative spillovers to major markets (e.g., price).
- Understand that adaptation of any element of the marketing program entails out-of-pocket costs, lost profits due to delay, and greater organizational complexity. Weigh those against the expected higher local sales.
- Remember, local managers have their own agenda! Be prepared to dissuade more powerful local managers of large countries from demanding unnecessary localization.

5

Global Brand Building in the Digital Age

Some 20 years ago, before the advent of the public Internet and commercial use of the World Wide Web, building a global brand was a long and painstaking process: the brand had to secure physical distribution in key countries, and that meant cultivating strong relationships on the ground. Its price could differ substantially from country to country, with many consumers and purchase managers ignorant of the pricing differential. Communication was mostly unidirectional: firms told relatively passive consumers about their brands. Television and print advertising were the primary media to reach the widest possible global audience with the brand's promise. With the explosion of Internet users, however, growing from 360 million (5.9% of the world's population) in 2000 to 3.4 billion (46.4%) in 2016, the digital space is reshaping how organizations go global with their brands.[1]

Any chapter written about digital branding strategies runs the risk of obsolescence before it hits the printer. Specific digital platforms and tools for global brand building change rapidly over time. Just look at the roll-out of social media: LinkedIn in 2003, Facebook in 2004, YouTube in

---

[1] http://www.internetworldstats.com/stats.html; accessed March 31, 2016.

© The Author(s) 2017
J.-B. Steenkamp, *Global Brand Strategy*,
DOI 10.1057/978-1-349-94994-6_5

2005, Twitter in 2006, Tumblr in 2007, Weibo in 2009, and Instagram and Pinterest in 2010, to name but a few. Digital platforms not even invented, perhaps those on blockchain technologies, might replace these familiar global media brands. What will not change quickly are the underlying trends, such as the expansion of digital global distribution channels, co-creation of global brand components with your customers, market transparency of your global brand's activities, global connectivity among your brand's customers, and the Internet of Things. Therefore, in this chapter, I focus on how these fundamental shifts in the marketing environment affect global brand strategy. Table 5.1 summarizes the implications.

Digital Sales Channels

Global business-to-consumer (B2C) e-commerce sales exceeded $1.5 trillion in 2015 and are expected to hit $2.5 trillion in 2018. Business-to-business (B2B) e-commerce sales are even higher, exceeding $6 trillion in 2015, and projected to top $12 trillion by 2020.[2] Western countries are no longer primarily fueling this growth. For the first time in 2014, consumers in Asia-Pacific spent more on e-commerce purchases than those in North America, making Asia-Pacific the largest regional e-commerce market in the world. No surprise, China is the primary driver of growth in the region. Growth in B2C e-commerce sales comes primarily from the rapidly expanding online and mobile user bases in emerging markets, advancing shipping and payment options, and the push of major global brands into new international markets.

---

[2] http://www.emarketer.com/Article/Global-B2C-Ecommerce-Sales-Hit-15-Trillion-This-Year-Driven-by-Growth-Emerging-Markets/1010575 and http://ecommerceandb2b.com/b2b-e-commerce-trends-statistics/; accessed September 20, 2016.

Table 5.1 Global brand building in the digital age

	Global digital sales channels	Co-creation of brand strategy with your customers	Transparency of global brand strategy	Global connectivity among your customers	Internet of things
Existing global brands	Penetration of hitherto unreachable regions Favors trusted established global brands	Co-creation may clash with the firm's administrative heritage	Information asymmetry with customer reduced Need for globally consistent customer proposition	Shift in power balance to customer Success critically dependent on customers' opinions Sharing economy requires radical rethinking of business model	Privacy and confidentiality concerns favor established global brands Protection of data from unauthorized access is crucial
Emerging global brands	Every brand can be global in a keystroke Potential for niche brands targeted at global micro segments Reduces channel advantages existing brands Scaling to global level is faster	Meshes well with the mindset of new firms Difficult for SOEs Reduces resources disadvantage (R&D, marketing) vs. established players	Easier for new firms given lack of administrative heritage Difficult for SOEs	New brands can gain rapid acceptance through eWOM Opportunities for new global brands based on sharing economy	SOEs and brands from countries with a weak rule of law are at a disadvantage

(continued)

Table 5.1 (continued)

	Global digital sales channels	Co-creation of brand strategy with your customers	Transparency of global brand strategy	Global connectivity among your customers	Internet of things
Product	Global niche segments can be reached profitably Counterfeits greater problem	Facilitates geocentric NPD Potential to reduce R&D costs Increases NPD performance but specific conditions apply	Favors value and premium brands vs. mass brands Corporate scandals impossible to hide; you need to come clean fully and fast	Accelerate new product success by co-opting digital opinion leaders	Create value with service-transition strategies Reduces product commoditization Increases customer loyalty to the product offering
Pricing	Price comparison websites orient the market toward price Increased arbitrage			Special ("confidential") price deals become known	Increases pricing power by providing value that is difficult to duplicate or imitate

Communication	More targeted and time-relevant advertising Create the right mix of digital and offline advertising ROI of advertising can be readily calculated	Co-creation of ads Interactive marketing communication Potential to reduce advertising costs	Engage honestly with customers; minimize legalese Advertising adaptations to meet local requirements can create a global backlash	Manager no longer controls the brand narrative Monologue becomes multilogue Multiplier effect if brand advertising is taken up by social media
Distribution	Power shift to e-retailers D2C selling/dis-intermediation Online market-places offer great potential for smaller/new brands Omni-channel strategy Counterfeits favor Western e-retailers	Collaborative global selling with global e-retailers	Geo-blocking increasingly untenable	Peer-to-peer transactions create distribution channels over which the brand has no control

Opportunities for Global Brands and Local Brands Going Global

Digital channels allow global brand managers to reach consumers in parts of countries that they could otherwise not reach without physical stores. For example, in China, 600 million rural consumers have no easy access to modern distribution. With the Internet-connected smartphone, they are leapfrogging the brick-and-mortar phase, going directly to digital, and gaining access to every product, from tissue and shoelaces to appliances and weightlifting sets. To the delight of Kimberly-Clark, these consumers can purchase their first box of Kleenex.[3]

If customers buy the brand in a physical outlet, they can return to the store for redress if the brand falls short of its promises. But how can a customer get redress for an e-purchase? How can the customer tell whether the product or service is trustworthy? By buying a well-known brand, many of which are global. Recall that the global availability and acceptance of a brand instills customer confidence. Hence, the digital world favors strong global brands.

While the digital sales channel offers opportunities to existing global brands, the benefits for new brands, including brands from emerging markets, are even more profound. With the Internet, every brand is just a keystroke away from a local customer overseas. In an online survey conducted in 24 countries more than half of respondents—73% of Germans, 64% of Mexicans, 58% of Chinese, and 50% of South Koreans—said that they had made an online purchase from an overseas retailer in the past six months. Only 30% of US respondents had bought something online from another country, perhaps because of such home-grown giants as Amazon.[4] Because the digital channel allows them to grow fast, they can compete with established global brands without much warning.

The online market for razorblades barely existed in 2010. Along came Dollar Shave Club, an American company whose customers subscribe to monthly deliveries of razor blades and other personal grooming products. It positioned itself as a convenient, cost-effective alternative to expen-

[3] Clover, Charles (2015), "Delivering the Jack Ma Economy," *Financial Times*, September 15, p. 8.
[4] Nielsen (2016), "Global Connected Commerce."

sive blades sold through retail chains that often lock them up to prevent theft, thus increasing the inconvenience of the shopping experience. By 2015, 8% of the roughly $3 billion market for men's shaving gear had gone digital in the United States. This rise of online sales caught industry leader Gillette off guard; it sued the Club for patent infringement and launched its own club, and so Dollar Shave Club countersued.[5] The Club has already expanded to Canada and Australia and in July 2016, Unilever bought the company for 1 billion, which translates into roughly $300 per current subscriber. Regardless of Dollar Shave Club's ultimate success, it has changed the nature of the global competition for men's grooming budget. No more does the revenue automatically flow to companies with strong retail ties and deep pockets for prominent shelf displays and flashy packaging. As many brand managers have observed, digital technology has practically eliminated these barriers to entry. New brands do not need real estate or sales staff. They do, however, need top notch digital security, Internet expertise, customer service, low-cost delivery systems, quality design and manufacturing, patient venture capital, and excellent legal representation.

The digital channel also offers opportunities for traditional—typically local—brands to go global. Take cashmere company Sand River with its seven boutiques in Shanghai, one each in Beijing, Suzhou, and Tokyo, and a showroom in Germany. Its CEO Juliet Guo believes the brand's value proposition of authenticity and cutting-edge designs has global appeal but it lacks the resources to develop its own distribution channel. She has set her hopes on Internet sales. She has opened webstores for France, Germany, the Netherlands, the United Kingdom, and the United States. Her target is that Internet sales in overseas markets account for 20% of total revenues by 2018.

---

[5] Woolhouse, Megan (2015), "Gillette Sues Dollar Shave Club for Patent Infringement," *The Boston Globe*. December 17; Quirk, Mary Beth (2016), "Dollar Shave Club Files Countersuit Against Gillette In Patent Fight," *The Consumerist*, February 17.

Advertising and the Digital Channel

You may have heard the Buddhist expression "When the student is ready, the teacher will appear." The global brand marketer's equivalent is "When the customer is ready to buy, the brand will appear." Timing is everything, and that is why in-store advertising is so effective. Thus, along with the spread of the digital sales channel, advertising is shifting from traditional to online media (Fig. 5.1). In 2016, the Internet's share of advertising spending is estimated to top 31%, double the level of 2010. Internet advertising is far more targeted than traditional mass media advertising as it tracks an individual's online behavior to provide ads most relevant to the person's activity. It also reduces time between interest and action, since consumers can click immediately to buy. And importantly in an era of accountability, return on Internet advertising investments can be readily calculated.

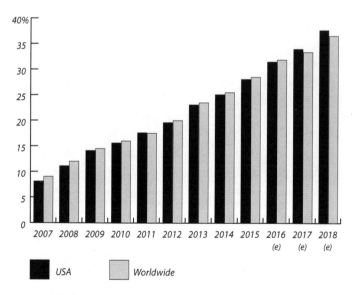

Fig. 5.1   Internet's share of ad spending (*Source*: Adapted from ZenithOptimedia. Internet includes mobile)

Table 5.2 Trust in Internet advertising media across generations

Internet advertising medium	Millennials (%)	Gen X (%)	Baby boomers (%)	Silent gen (%)
Branded websites	75	70	59	50
E-mails one has signed up for	57	56	53	54
Online video ads	53	50	37	27
Ads in search engine	52	50	41	33
Ads on social networks	51	47	35	26
Mobile advertising	48	45	31	20
Online banner ads	47	43	34	25
Text ads on mobile phone	41	38	27	18

Source: Adapted from Nielsen (2015)
Note: Reported is the percentage of respondents who completely or somewhat trust a particular Internet advertising medium. Results based on 30,000 consumers in 60 countries

As Internet advertising gains importance and becomes the proverbial "talk of the town," global brand managers must take care to not abandon traditional forms of advertising. Why? First, even in the United States, Internet advertising does not have the reach of TV advertising. TV plans can easily deliver unduplicated reach of 85% to 90%, but even the best digital plans struggle to exceed 60% and to achieve high levels of digital *video* (the closest analog to TV advertising) reach is even harder.[6] Second, reach of—and trust in—most Internet advertising media drops off sharply among the older generations around the world (Table 5.2). Finally, there are important synergies—a strategy that uses both online and offline on average yields 50% more "bang for the advertising buck" than when all the money is spent on online only.[7] Thus, for the foreseeable future, global brands are advised to use a mix of online and offline advertising.

---

[6] http://www.nielsen.com/us/en/insights/news/2015/uncommon-sense-thinking-of-going-all-digital-answer-these-10-questions-first.html; accessed November 13, 2015.

[7] Kumar, Ashish et al. (2016), "From Social to Sale: The Effects of Firm-Generated Content in Social Media on Customer Behavior," *Journal of Marketing*, 80 (January), pp. 7–25.

Digital Distribution Options for Global Brands

In nearly every generation, new technology has disrupted the distribution channel. In the mid-1800s, Macy's pioneered the concept of the department store, then in 1895, Sears leveraged the routes and stability of the US Postal Service to launch its mail-order business. Sears grew phenomenally by selling a range of merchandise at low prices to farms and villages that had no other convenient access to modern retail outlets. Sounds familiar, yes? Michael Cullen introduced the supermarket concept in 1930 by opening his first King Kullen inside a 6000-square-foot former garage in Queens borough of New York City. In 1961, Belgium's GIB group introduced the first hypermarket in Antwerp; and, in 1962, Sam Walton opened Walmart Discount City in Rogers, Arkansas. In 1976, Sol Price introduced his Price Club, the first members-only retail warehouse club for serious bulk buyers, and merged it with Costco in 1993. And in 1996, Jeff Bezos launched Amazon.com.

All these new distribution formats fundamentally changed how consumers shopped and how companies marketed and distributed their products. I have already written of Walmart's long-standing relationship with Procter & Gamble (P&G); that became Walmart's model for working with its suppliers. Now the digital distribution and online shopping are disrupting global brand strategies again, with profound implications for global brand manufacturers.

Digital Channel Options

For the global brand, the digital channel offers three broad options, not mutually exclusive. First, your corporation can establish its own brand website as companies from P&G (pgshop.com) to Apple (Apple.com) have done as a direct response sales channel, eliminating the middleman and preserving gross margin. Trust in branded websites is generally high among all generations (Table 5.2) and brand managers generally have full control over the marketing mix for their products, including website design, dynamic pricing, customer loyalty programs, sales promotion, and site traffic data capture. The threat of commoditization is relatively lower as it takes additional effort to compare prices and product specifications across competing brands.

However, order fulfillment adds complexity while the typical stand-alone website generates far fewer visitors than the other options. While little traffic is a serious limitation for most global B2C brands, it is less problematic for prestige brands and for established B2B brands. In these cases, the target segment is relatively small and purposefully looking for a particular brand. Order fulfillment is also less of a problem because the number of orders and the value/volume ratio is generally more favorable for these brands. Finally, branded websites collect a lot of information about their customers, which means that data breach can be an issue. Granted, any company that maintains some database that connects with any intranet is hackable. But sites that take consumer data are more vulnerable because of the interface and consumer protection laws in countries like the United States hold the website responsible for data breaches.

A second option is selling through an e-retailer like Amazon, which resells the products it purchased from the brand manufacturer to customers. This option is closest to the arrangement brands have with brick-and-mortar retailers. The global brand manager loses considerable control over the marketing mix, with potentially adverse consequences. Consider that 75% of people in a global study said they are suspicious of brands that appear to behave differently in different channels.[8] Loss of control over pricing is especially strong. E-retailers have moved to a dynamic pricing model, adjusting prices on items several times a day based on competitive conditions. Amazon, for one, adapts 2.5 million prices *per day*. To illustrate, during the course of a single day, Amazon changed the price for a GE microwave oven eight times, between a low of $744 and a high of $870.[9] To use price in your brand positioning is challenging in such a selling environment.

Commoditization is a distinct threat given that many e-retailers leave little room for unique brand presentation, facilitate side-by-side comparison of functional attributes of brands, and have a strong focus on

---

[8] Garforth, Celia (2014), "Build From the Inside Out," *Admap*, June, pp. 34–36.
[9] Abraham, Jorij and Kitty Koelemeijer (2015), "The Rise of the Global Marketplaces," Ecommerce Foundation.

price. Further, the margin e-retailers command can easily be 30%. But e-retailers generate tremendous traffic—for example Amazon had 188 million unique visitors *per month* in 2015—and they handle order fulfillment.[10] Channel conflict is always an issue if you sell the same brand through different channels, particularly when dealing with e-retailers. Increasingly, smartphone-toting shoppers "showroom" and simultaneously visit e-retailers to compare prices. Unless they need the item right now, if it is cheaper online, they can order it with a single click.

In between these two extremes is setting up a brand store on a marketplace platform, such as eBay, Tmall (Alibaba), Rakuten, and Amazon (which operates both as e-retailer and as marketplace). The brand manufacturer sells directly to buyers, that is, the platform does not take ownership of the products. If you want, though, you can hire the platform to fulfill orders. Consider the scope of Amazon's operations: it connects customers from 185 countries with two million suppliers from more than 100 countries, of which 65% use Amazon for order fulfillment.[11] Costs vary substantially between marketplaces. Amazon takes a 15% cut of every sale on its platform. Tmall takes a lower cut, 5% or less.[12]

The advantages and disadvantages of marketplace stores fall broadly between those of the other two digital channel options (see Fig. 5.2), with the exceptions of the ability to attract visitors, where the marketplace option can easily score as high as the e-retailer option, and of the potential for channel conflict, which is like that of standalone branded webstores. While you have more control over your brand marketing mix using a marketplace than when you sell it through e-retailers, the design of your webstore depends on marketplace format rules. For example, the image and display of products on major Chinese platforms tend to follow the same format; brands have little room to convey unique brand imag-

---

[10] http://www.statista.com/statistics/271450/monthly-unique-visitors-to-us-retail-websites/; accessed November 19, 2015. Note that this number includes visits to Amazon as e-retailer and marketplace platform.

[11] Abraham and Koelemeijer (2015).

[12] Barber, Tony, "Inditex's Tmall Deal Shows and Evolving Approach to China," *Financial Times*, October 30, p. 14.

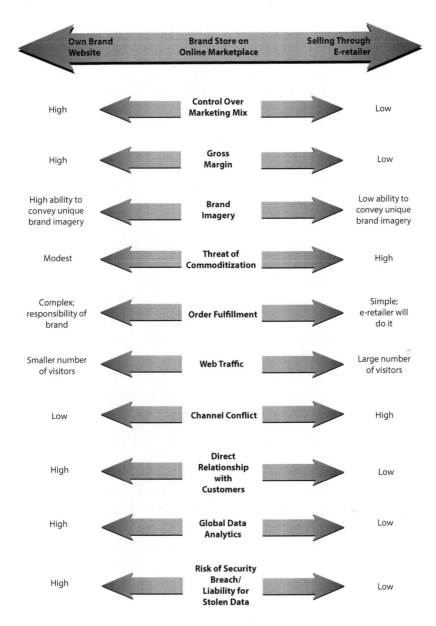

Fig. 5.2 Digital channel options for global brands

Table 5.3 Consumer preferences for distribution channel

Country	% of consumers preferring online shops with physical stores to pure e-retailer		% of consumers who, in the future, will shop in physical stores at least as frequently as they do now	
	16–21 years	22–65 years	16–21 years	22–65 years
USA	70	55	82	86
UK	73	60	72	75
India	74	68	78	69
China	70	65	62	50
South Korea	59	65	85	78

Source: Adapted from GfK (2015)

ery, and that's why Japan's Uniqlo shut its online shops on JD.com in 2015.[13]

Online marketplaces are not restricted to B2C players. There is a growing number of large online B2B marketplaces, including Alibaba, ThomasNET.com, and IndiaMART, where sellers can easily create their own homepage to showcase products and services, locate and liaise with global buyers, reply to "buying leads," and post "offers to sell." These B2B marketplaces attract traffic and, hence, are an attractive option for lesser-known B2B brands that desire to go global.

Omni-Channels

Digital technology has shifted power from traditional brick-and-mortar retailers like Walmart and Carrefour to e-retailers like Amazon and Alibaba. In response, traditional retailers have added a digital channel to their physical outlets; and most consumers prefer omni-channels to digital only (Table 5.3).[14] Walmart benefits from this synergy. While its online-only customers spend on average $200 a year with the retailer and

---

[13] Wang, Zhuoqiong (2015), "For Priests of High Fashion, Offline Is Better Than Online," *China Daily*, July 31, p. 14.

[14] Cama, Alessandra (2015), "How Young People Will Shop in the Future in India and China," CMO Round Table, August 21, GfK.

its average store-only customers $1400, those who buy online and in the store spend more than $2500 annually at Walmart.[15]

Since online prices change frequently to match the competition, physical-only retailers must learn to coordinate their prices across channels. For example, consumer electronics omni-channel big box retailer Best Buy uses its Price Match Guarantee to match the product price of key online and local retail competitors (including their online prices). Retailers like Nebraska Furniture Mart and department store Kohl's use digital price labels in their physical stores. In digital displays, the executive can now quickly update the chain's prices on thousands of products in multiple locations to beat the latest offers from competitors.

Counterfeits

Unfortunately, rogue actors can more easily offer counterfeit products over the Internet, especially in countries like China where, according to the Chinese State Administration for Industry and Commerce, four of every ten products bought online are either bad quality or outright fake.[16] Crappy counterfeits hurt the image of aspiring global brands but benefits established Western e-retailers that have cultivated reputations for selling only genuine products: they attract buyers from countries where intellectual property (IP) laws are poorly enforced. Consequently, cross-border B2C e-commerce in China stood at $41 billion in 2015, up 67% from 2014, with American e-retailers benefitting most. The most important reason to buy from abroad? Product quality. Overseas sales can cover a remarkably broad array of goods, not just durables and luxury items. Take Geng Xiaoyan, a 33-year-old marketing specialist in Shanghai; she purchases everything her son needs, from shampoo, toothpaste, toothbrushes and body lotion, to healthy food, underwear, and toys from Western websites.[17]

---

[15] Neff, Jack (2015), "Clash of the Titans," *Advertising Age*, November 9, pp. 12–13.

[16] Clover, Charles (2015), "China's Singles Day Buying Spree Puts Fakes in Spotlight," *Financial Times*, November 11, p. 16.

[17] Zhong, Nan and Shi Jing (2015), "Chinese Like Shopping on US Websites," *China Daily*, July 29, p. 3.

The presence of counterfeit goods inhibits the global ambitions of Chinese e-commerce giants like Alibaba. Counterfeit merchandise hurts the image of its global sales platform AliExpress with overseas consumers. Business groups and Western brands are increasingly scrutinizing AliExpress's activities, worrying that it will send counterfeits from Chinese factories straight into consumers' hands on a global scale, thus damaging their global brand equity.

Co-creation of Global Brand Strategy

In the preindustrial age, craftsmen usually made products to order and involved the customer in the process. Mass production in the industrial age left little room for co-creating goods with customers. With digital technology, we can have both. Nowadays, some customers like to participate in particular aspects of the brand program, such as brand positioning, new product development, and advertising.

Co-creation requires a change of mindset among executives whose livelihood depends on developing and executing brand strategies and keeping trade secrets. Many managers cannot imagine sharing control of the brand's future with outsiders. Co-creation flourishes in organizations with flat structures, cultures comfortable with trial and error, and permeable boundaries for collaborating seamlessly with partners. New firms often exhibit such traits, such flexibility and transparency, more than established firms; the latter are typically more bureaucratic, hierarchical, legalistic, and opaque. An exception is new state-owned enterprises (SOEs), especially in emerging economies such as China. They tend to be hierarchical and bureaucratic from the get-go. If they are looking to co-create, then they are likely talking with government bureaucrats rather than with customers.[18]

---

[18] For more information on SOEs, see Kumar, Nirmalya, and Jan-Benedict E.M. Steenkamp (2013), *Brand Breakout: How Emerging Market Brands Will Go Global*, New York: Palgrave Macmillan, chapter 8.

Customer Participation in New Product Development

The hope that firms can improve their innovation performance by tapping into customers' knowledge around needs and solutions has created great excitement among managers of B2B and B2C MNCs alike. Muji, a Japanese consumer goods brand, sold in almost 500 Muji stores in 22 countries, reported that sales of products from users' ideas were five times higher than sales of products built from professional designers' ideas.[19] Danish toy-maker Lego employs a four-step procedure to create new Lego sets. Anybody can create a model of their liking, which is posted. If your idea gets at least 10,000 supporters, it qualifies your project for review by the Lego Review Board of set designers and marketing people. Projects selected by the Board go into production and are released for sale around the world. You are featured in set materials, receive a royalty on sales, and are recognized as the product creator. Examples of products from users' ideas include *Doctor Who*, created by Andrew Clark and *Wall.E*, created by Angus MacLane.[20]

Company experience derived from 18,000 new product development (NPD) projects shows that customer participation in the NPD process increases new product performance (sales, profits) in the marketplace. Yet the effect of involving your customers is not always equally beneficial. Here are the key insights:

- Customer participation in the ideation stage in the NPD process improves new product performance. In this stage, customers provide a variety of needs-related input, comment on other customers' new product ideas, and often participate in selecting promising ideas for further consideration.
- Customer participation in the development phase generally reduces new product performance. Company experience shows that involving customers in the development phase significantly delays time to mar-

---

[19] Nishikawa, Hidehiko, Martin Schreier, and Susumu Ogawa (2013), "User-Generated Versus Designer-Generated Products: A Performance Assessment at Muji," *International Journal of Research in Marketing*, 30 (2), pp. 160–167.

[20] https://ideas.lego.com/; accessed March 14, 2016.

ket. Moreover, activities in this stage are highly interdependent, such that changing one component on the basis of customers' input may unintentionally affect other functions negatively. In particular, if the market is rapidly changing and interdependency among a product's parts is critical, engaging customers in the development stage should not be pursued because it can significantly delay time to market and cause firms to miss market opportunities.

- Customer participation in the launch stage improves new product performance. At this stage, customers provide their firsthand feedback on product usability, product performance, potential problems specific to the prototype, and the positioning and marketing mix of the new product. All this is crucial to new product success.

- Customer participation is more beneficial in low-tech industries than in high-tech industries. High-tech industries are often mentioned when it comes to co-creation but many companies struggle to transfer complex knowledge to the firm's NPD team. Low-tech industries pose much lower barriers to integrate and utilize knowledge from customers.

- Co-creation with business customers yields greater benefits than engaging consumers in NPD. Business customers typically possess more relevant knowledge and have a higher motivation to share that knowledge than consumers as they can expect more direct benefits from participation in the NPD process.

- The benefits of customer participation for small firms are greater than for large firms. A large firm's organizational inertia and large stock of extant knowledge inhibits acquiring knowledge from customers for NPD, whereas small firms are highly motivated to complement their lack of internal knowledge and R&D resources through customer participation.

- Firms in emerging markets benefit more from customer participation than firms in developed markets. Developed countries' firms tend to have more resources and knowledge about their products and market.

In contrast, many emerging markets' firms are relatively young or recently privatized, and possess limited knowledge resources.[21]

Crowdsourcing

Crowdsourcing, the gathering of ideas or information by enlisting a large number of people usually over the Internet, is among the most important types of co-creation. Global crowdsourcing facilitates truly geocentric NPD, by taking input from customers around the world, not just the home country. Companies have started to source input from a global crowd in many industries, from technology to packaged goods. Dell, for example, reported that, by 2016, the crowd has submitted more than 24,000 ideas to its IdeaStorm site, attracting around 750,000 votes and 100,000 comments. Dell turned approximately 549 of those ideas into reality.[22]

Mini-Oreo cookies while being a commercial success, did not have their own identity versus regular Oreo cookies. Kraft decided to engage consumers to explore positioning and communication ideas for Mini-Oreo. It worked with crowdsourcing firm eYeka's online community (see Table 5.4) to tell Kraft what they saw as unique to Mini-Oreo in a poster or a print ad. This format was chosen to force consumers to choose the single most important message they wanted to communicate, while allowing for visual expression. Kraft received more than 500 ideas from 42 countries and identified ten potential ideas for its new brand positioning. Several of the crowd's creations were of a high enough quality that Kraft could consumer-test them immediately. Their work inspired the new value proposition and global campaigns for Mini-Oreos around Bonding Moments. The success of Mini-Oreos helped Oreo in retaining its position as the world's best-selling cookie brand, with nearly $2.9 billion in annual revenues.[23]

---

[21] Chang, Woojung and Steven A. Taylor (2016), "The Effectiveness of Customer Participation in New Product Development: A Meta-Analysis," *Journal of Marketing*, 80 (January), pp. 47–64.

[22] http://www.ideastorm.com/; accessed March 28, 2016.

[23] See for an example of a Hong Kong ad: https://www.youtube.com/watch?v=VENEl6272mM; for the campaign in Malaysia to create one million minutes of bonding moments and its effect

Table 5.4 Crowdsourcing by eYeka

The Paris-based crowdsourcing company eYeka organizes creative contests for B2C brands and broadcasts them via the Internet to a community of over 330,000 registered members from more than 160 countries. Client companies typically approach eYeka with specific creative business problems, such as generating ideas for new products or services, product designs, brand positioning, or advertising campaigns. A team of strategic planners at eYeka transforms the business problem into a creative brief that is posted online as a contest and broadcasted globally. Every project is organized as a one-stage or multiple-stage contest with one or more potential winners; participants must submit their entries by a stipulated deadline. The member interface is available in a wide range of languages. Submissions can be in any of these languages, and are translated by eYeka community managers. Each contest awards multiple prizes for winning submissions, typically ranging from €1,000 for idea-submission contests to €15,000 for contests that require video production. At the end of a contest, the client company has access to all the submissions via a dedicated online platform. The client may award more prizes than was originally advertised so it can legally own the ideas embodied in the good submissions. Under eYeka rules, intellectual property rights in the submission are transferred to the client for those submissions that for which a prize is awarded and accepted by the member.

Source: Adapted from Yannig Roth, personal communication, February 29, 2016

Co-creation of Advertising

Kraft used global crowdsourcing to develop its global advertising campaigns for Mini-Oreos. Indeed, why not leverage the creative genius of the masses? Creative advertising ideas are scarce, and crowdsourced advertising is no longer just for the Super Bowl. As part of its "Make Love Not War" campaign, Unilever's Axe partnered with the advertising crowdsourcing community Tongal for "Kiss for Peace," an effort which solicited videos for the campaign.

Hyundai was looking to bring to life its global brand campaign "live brilliant" with fresh creative expressions that show that a car can create special experiences beyond transportation. It challenged the eYeka community to come up with an original, unique, and engaging story where people have a brilliant, memorable experience with a car, in the form of videos and print ads. In five weeks, they received 233 entries from around the world. The winning print ad design, from an Italian creator

brand metrics: https://www.youtube.com/watch?v=ZWjm-ujI74Q; accessed September 25, 2016.

called Federico Grosso, depicts a man sitting in his Hyundai, stopping by a majestic tree who decides to draw a tree house on the car window to complement it. Grosso was awarded €10,000 for his idea. It was adapted by Hyundai and its advertising agency into a series of ads showing how a cloud can turn into an ice cream when you hold a cone up to the car window, or how musical notes could be etched when passing by electrical power lines.[24] The campaign was rolled out in airline magazines as well as global publications such as *The Economist*.

Global Selling Collaboration

Brand manufacturers can also collaborate with digital channel partners to develop a business model that will take their brands global. Amazon is a leader with its collaborative model called "Global Selling with Amazon." Amazon's Global Selling enables the firm to list and sell its brand on any one of Amazon's websites in China, France, Germany, Italy, Japan, Spain, the United Kingdom, and the United States. It offers global order fulfill-ment and tools for online order management and it helps with customer support, international taxes and regulations, and registration requirements in key countries as the United States, European Union, China, and Japan.[25]

Many Chinese companies want to move from "made in China" to "branded in China," but executives lack the knowledge and channel exper-tise to export their brands to Western markets. Amazon has seized this opportunity by developing operating platforms in Chinese on Amazon. com and Amazon.co.uk Amazon.co.uk and unified seller accounts for fledgling Chinese MNCs, so that they can register and transact business on the websites of any EU country. Sebastian Cunningham, global senior vice-president of Amazon, explained, "My vision is that … it will become easier for Chinese businesses to open shops on Amazon and sell products

---

[24] For examples of the ads, see http://eyeka.pr.co/70295-hyundai-launches-global-brand-campaign-based-on-crowdsourced-idea; accessed March 28, 2016.

[25] http://go.amazonservices.com/rs/amazoneu/images/global-selling-with-amazon.pdf; accessed September 12, 2016.

all over the world. They just need to focus on quality, while we can help them with the difficult part like cross-nation logistics."[26]

Is Co-creation Right for Your Brand?

Co-creation with customers and other businesses can shore up geocentric new product development, advertising that engages customers, and even collaborative distribution models. However, if you let outsiders in, you give up some control over your brand. If you solicit input from customers and do nothing with it, then you have wasted your resources and theirs, thereby damaging your corporate reputation once the word gets out—and it always does. And there is no guarantee that all effort put into co-creation will lead to viable business propositions. To determine whether co-creation is right for your brand, consider discussing the following with your executive team:

1. Do we need co-creation or can we solve the creative challenge internally?
2. Do we have significant organizational resources and oversight capabilities for such an initiative?
3. Are we willing and able to experiment, even though the results may not be better than what we could do alone?
4. Can we engage external help without compromising our competitive advantage? Do we need outside parties to sign confidentiality agreements? If yes, then maybe co-creation is not appropriate: at an early stage, your competition can glean insight into your plans.
5. Is our organization ready to accept outside input? Do we suffer from the not-invented-here syndrome, or can we overcome internal resistance to external ideas?
6. Is our organization ready to take input from all parts of the world seriously, or do we have a strong home country bias?

[26]Xu, Jingxi (2015), "Amazon Plans More Business-Friendly Initiatives in China," *China Daily*, July 30, p. 17.

Transparency

In the industrial era, products grew ever more complex, so much so that customers had more difficulty assessing product quality and value. More brands started to travel internationally, but most customers did not; they bought locally and got their information locally. Information asymmetry was especially high for global brands, typically at the technological frontier. Brand managers could exploit the lack of cross-border flow of information among customers to charge higher prices and offer varying quality or customer service as they saw fit.

The digital age has minimized information asymmetry. E-retailers and price comparison websites are improving customer decision making. Online shoppers even in the remotest parts of countries like China know a lot about a global brand's attributes and pricing worldwide, without ever having seen the product in a physical store. Consumer access to information affects different types of global brands differently. It tends to favor global value and global premium brands and hurt global mass brands because excelling on price or performance is easier than occupying the middle ground. Fun and prestige brands are better in side-by-side comparisons because they have grounded their unique value proposition in intangible, emotional benefits.

Transparency Challenges of Established Global Enterprises

Full transparency about the global brand's activities, ranging from its supply chain to after-sales service, has become essential in the digital age. Prepare for constant scrutiny. The idea of opening the corporate kimono makes many business leaders blush, especially within established firms. Volkswagen A.G. struggled in the aftermath of its emission scandal. When the US Environmental Protection Agency (EPA) exposed VW's deliberate and systematic cheating on emission tests, the company was slow to acknowledge its efforts to mislead regulators and customers. Instead, it claimed technical problems, sparred with US regulators, and withheld information from German and EU officials, thereby turning a bad dream into a brand nightmare. It even continued to sell certain VW, Audi, and Porsche models that were also rigged to dupe emissions tests. According to New York attorney-general Eric Schneiderman, "Volkswagen's co-operation with the states' investigation has been spotty – and frankly, more of the kind one expects from a company in denial than one seeking to leave behind a culture of admitted deception." Volkswagen defended its foot-dragging: "Fundamentally, our statements are based on current knowledge of the relevant facts."[27] That is legalese, not the stuff of transparency.

Transparency Challenges of State-Owned Enterprises

Transparency is easier to achieve for new firms that have grown up naked, so to speak, than for established firms with an administrative heritage of confidentiality. However, like co-creation, transparency is a challenge for emerging market firms closely linked to the state. Nowhere is that more transparent (forgive the pun) than in China. The governance structure of the typical Chinese SOE is often unclear and if they have a stock market listing, close examination reveals that its stock filings may reveal that its stock pertains to part of the company. Controlling interest remains with the state, and its larger operations remain under veil.

Digital giant Tencent is a major player in the social media space with its WeChat (in China called 微信 or Wēixìn, meaning "micro message") messaging service, which combines—in a single app—the attributes of Facebook, Twitter, WhatsApp, Dropbox, Tinder, Uber, and Apple Game Center. Tencent's inner workings are rather murky. Customers wonder whether the Chinese government can see whatever Tencent can see. Its CEO Tony Ma does not help his brand by toeing the party line. At a tech conference in Singapore, he said, "Lots of people think they can speak out and be irresponsible. I think that's wrong."[28] This stands in stark contrast with Apple's CEO Tim Cook's refusal to grant the FBI backdoor

[27] Boston, William and Mike Spector (2015), "VW Draws Regulators' Ire," *Wall Street Journal*, November 19, p. B1; Milne, Richard (2015), "VW Admits to Second Defeat Device," *Financial Times*, November 24, p. 13; Chon, Gina and Andy Sharman (2016), "US Criticises VW Over 'Spotty' Progress With Emission Probe," *Financial Times*, January 9, p. 8.

[28] Elliott, Dorinda (2014), "Penguin Rising," *Fast Company*, May, pp. 80–85.

access to its iPhones. While lack of privacy may or may not be a problem in China, it does hurt Tencent's international ambitions. The Indian government has called WeChat a national security threat.

Transparency in Market Communication

Global brand managers should engage where customers are posting. Acknowledging feedback consistently and thoughtfully—not legalistically—over time demonstrates a willingness to learn from customers, and that may positively affect how customers interpret your brand messages. Yet in a world of different cultural values and regulations, marketing messages in one country can lead to a backlash in other countries. For example, IKEA airbrushed women out of the Saudi Arabian edition of its furniture catalogue. In response, people posted on Tumblr images where women had obviously been replaced by IKEA furniture. Starbucks also suffered a backlash for replacing its green female mermaid logo with a crown in the water in Saudi Arabia. "It's an extremely difficult position for a global brand to be in," said Saatchi & Saatchi's Adil Khan. "On the one hand, they have their value system as a global brand, but then on the other they have to be aware of local market sensitivities."[29] Brand managers must ask themselves not only whether a particular market communication is sensitive to a local audience but also how a global audience might respond.

Geo-blocking Exposed

Transparency has major implications for a common company practice known as "geo-blocking"—differential treatment of customers based on their geographical location or nationality. Geo-blocking can take different forms, such as denied website access, refused sale, no delivery options, or different prices or conditions of sale. Such practices will be exposed more fully and rapidly than ever before, something Disneyland Paris experienced. German consumers complained that they could not

---

[29] Hall, Camilla (2012), "Mideast a Minefield for Brands," *Financial Times*, October 6, p. 9.

access cheaper online deals that were available to residents of France, as they were directed to the theme park's national website, which did not have the same offers. Pricing data gathered by consumer organizations showed that one premium package cost €2447 on the theme park's German site, compared with €1870 on the UK site and €1346 on the French site. Another concern was that some payment options for annual subscriptions were only available to people with a French bank account. Internal research by EU officials showed a 15% difference between prices in pounds and euros for the same type of ticket. To avoid an investigation by the European Commission into its geo-blocking practices, the theme park operator agreed to ensure that non-French customers have fair access to its best offers on its website.[30]

Connectivity

People's social connections are no longer geographically restricted, usually to village or neighborhood. With the advent of Facebook, Twitter, Instagram, WeChat, Weibo, and other social media, customers can now exchange information about your brand with hundreds or thousands of people every day. Brands are both emotional and social constructs; their meaning emerges from everyday customer experience, cyclical media coverage, and cross-platform promotions. In other words, customer perception of your brand is beyond your control, but not beyond your influence.

Electronic Word of Mouth

The opinions of other customers are a key, if not the most important, factor driving brand purchase decisions. Customers communicate with others through social media, general review platforms (e.g., Yelp, Epinions), specialized review platforms that have a narrow focus on a particular product category (e.g., Movies.com, CarandDriver.com), e-commerce platforms (e.g., Amazon, eBay), and other platforms. The totality of these

---

[30] Brunsden, Jim and Duncan Robinson (2016), "Brussels to End Pricing Probe into Disneyland Paris," *Financial Times*, April 16, p. 3.

virtual communications is commonly called electronic word of mouth (eWOM)—Internet-mediated written communications (e.g., reviews, tweets, blog posts, "likes," "pins," images, video testimonials) between current or potential customers.

EWOM has profoundly shifted the balance of power between global brands and their customers. For example, in August 2013 Mondelez Australia quietly altered its Kraft Easy Mac microwaved snack formula, removing processed cheese and replacing it with flavored cheese sauce powder. The change spectacularly backfired; complaints to its website increased by 320%. After one year, Mondelez reverted to the original recipe after plummeting sales threatened the future of the product.[31]

Electronic Word of Mouth and Global Brand Sales

EWOM has become a key metric for brand success. A 1% improvement in the favorability of eWOM reviews (e.g., average rating given to a product) leads to 0.42% increase in sales, while 1% increase in eWOM volume (number of reviews, etc.) is associated with 0.24% increase in sales.[32]

A large body of research from around the world has identified those situations where eWOM is especially effective in increasing brand sales. Table 5.5 summarizes the actionable insights. The effect of eWOM on social media is nearly twice as strong as the effect of eWOM on e-commerce platforms; but, importantly, eWOM on all types of platforms affects brand sales. The effect of eWOM depends on the type of product you are selling. You should be especially keen on spending resources on stimulating eWOM—through, for example, frequent postings of messages and press-releases on the brand's own social media pages or a personalized, high-volume, moderately toned (not over the top) Twitter

---

[31] http://www.heraldsun.com.au/news/victoria/easy-mac-snack-recipe-goes-back-to-original-after-customer-backlash/news-story/1058f41168a45969f7bfe4ed5dae7509; accessed February 25, 2016.

[32] You, Ya, Gautham G. Vadakkepatt, and Amit M. Joshi (2015), "A Meta-Analysis of Electronic Word-of-Mouth Elasticity," *Journal of Marketing*, 79 (March), pp. 19–39; Babic, Ana et al. (2016), "The Effect of Electronic Word of Mouth on Sales: A Meta-Analytic Review of Platform, Product, and Metric Factors," *Journal of Marketing Research*, 53 (June), 297–318.

Table 5.5 EWOM and global brand sales

When is EWOM particularly effective?	Why?
EWOM on social media platforms (vs. reviews on e-commerce platforms such as Amazon)	Social media are seen as more trustworthy since they do not have an (obvious) incentive to manipulate consumer reviews
EWOM on social media when receivers can assess their similarity to eWOM senders based on e.g., username, profile page, or geographic location	The sociological principle of homophily—people tend to trust others that are more "like themselves" more than others
EWOM on specialized review platforms (e.g., Yelp) (vs. reviews on e-commerce platforms)	Specialized review platforms are seen as more trustworthy since they do not have an (obvious) incentive to manipulate consumer reviews and are higher on expertise
EWOM for durable goods and in more expensive categories	Costs associated with a wrong decision are higher, creating more consumer risk
EWOM for services (vs. goods)	The quality of services is more difficult to assess prior to purchase; thus, opinions of others are more informative
EWOM for products that are privately (vs. publicly) consumed	Because consumers cannot learn about product benefits by observing the consumption of privately consumed products, eWOM is more valuable
EWOM for products new to the market	Purchase risk is higher and knowledge about the product is less widely diffused in society compared with mature products

Source: Based on Babic et al. (2016) and You et al. (2015)

strategy—if your brand represents durable goods, expensive categories, all types of services, products that are privately consumed, and products that are new to the market.

Brand Communication in a Connected World

Advertisers like social-media platforms because they gather data on each user's age, consumption patterns, interests, and so on. They can aim their ads at customers with accuracy impossible through analogue media. For example, Chevrolet sends ads to the Facebook pages and Twitter feeds of people who had expressed an interest in, or signed up to test-drive, a competitor's vehicle.[33] That practice is already standard, albeit smart and targeted, use of an advertising medium. Savvy brand managers leverage the inherent connectivity of social media to develop advertising content that people want to share on social media, creating a multiplier effect, maybe even going viral. In 2012, the Dollar Shave Club founder launched his company with a hilarious video poking fun at over-engineered existing brands (read: Gillette) with expensive features people allegedly do not need. The video got 23 million views and created instant awareness for a new brand that lacked the resources for a large (read: P&G sized) advertising campaign.[34]

We have seen previously that negative eWOM forced Mondelez to go back to Easy Mac's original recipe. But how to regain the trust of their millennial customers? In an ironic turn of events, Easy Mac used the connected world for just that. Starting in October 2014, the brand shared a selection of crowdsourced videos on social media. The results surpassed expectations. Facebook delivered over 10 million impressions, YouTube delivered over 200,000 views, and most importantly, sales increased by 20%.

KLM Royal Dutch Airlines wanted to promote its one-stop mobile travel service, which allows passengers to research, plan, book, change and share their journeys entirely from their smartphones, to a young, tech-savvy audience across Asian markets. Antoine Peigner, Head of e-Commerce, Asia-Pacific, worked with eYeka to crowdsource humorous videos showing extreme situations that could happen due to smartphone addiction. Four videos were selected for amplification in a digital mix

---

[33] *The Economist* (2015), "A Brand New Game," August 29, pp. 51–52.
[34] The ad can be found at https://www.youtube.com/watch?v=ZUG9qYTJMsI; accessed September 26, 2016.

of media, editorial features, social influencers, promotions, ad units and engagements on various social websites such as Facebook, YouTube, Youku, Twitter, and blogs. The campaign achieved over 1.2 million views, which was 42% higher than the industry benchmark and generated an overall rate of engagement of 2.35% of viewers across 11 Asian countries.

Customers communicate directly with each other about the brand; the brand manager is, at best, one of the participants in the conversation and, at worst, left out. Monologue has become multilogue and multilingual. All the more reason for global brands to harmonize their communication across countries. Yet, even in multilogues, only a minority of brand users will be initiating discussions. For any given brand, most customers consume rather than produce brand information. Executives must identify digital opinion leaders through social network analysis techniques.[35] Effectively engaging digital opinion leaders and soliciting their opinions at an early stage, in new product development, in the development of new advertising campaigns, and in brand positioning will improve the likelihood that new products and marketing campaigns will meet with success.

New Global Brands for the Sharing Economy

One consequence of greater connectivity is sharing—the sharing economy, defined as a peer-to-peer, market-mediated activity of obtaining or sharing access to goods and services—on an online platform that aggregates supply and demand. This digital platform typically has an eBay-style rating or review system so that people on both sides of the transaction can determine whether they could trust the other. With the popularity of these services, many people choose to rent rather than buy. Sharing platforms have disrupted mature industries, ranging from hotels (Airbnb) to encyclopedias where Wikipedia's success forced the venerable Encyclopaedia Britannica to terminate publication of its print edition after 244 years in 2012.

---

[35] For an example of social network analysis for life sciences companies, see http://www.cognizant.com/InsightsWhitepapers/identifying-key-opinion-leaders-using-social-network-analysis-codex1234.pdf; accessed January 18, 2016.

Transportation network company Uber develops, markets, and operates the Uber mobile app: consumers with smartphones submit trip requests through the app which routes requests to available Uber drivers using their own cars. Uber is among the fastest-growing start-ups in history. Founded in 2009 in San Francisco, by 2016, it had more than one million (!) active drivers operating in 400 cities in 70 countries.

The transportation industry will never be the same. Even if companies like Uber, Lyft, or Didi Chuxing (China) were to fail, others will succeed. The economic and societal implications will be huge. Realizing the potential new market for car sharing, BMW started Drivenow, a joint venture with car-rental company Sixt, which provides car-sharing services in several cities in Europe. Drivenow is a paid car-sharing service where a user may book any of the designated cars randomly distributed throughout the city. When the user is finished, they may park the car anywhere within the assigned city area.

Some of the biggest hotel groups, including InterContinental Hotels and Wyndham, are taking tentative steps to tackle the threat of Airbnb and HomeAway, investing in rival home-sharing start-ups and launching digital initiatives that tap alternative forms of accommodation. These moves signal a belated change of tack for the hotel industry and the end of denial. The surge in merger and acquisitions in the industry can also be traced back to the emergence of home-rental companies.

Internet of Things

Tangible goods are more easily copied than intangible services. Thus, many leading goods firms have added services to their existing products. Experience from companies ranging from GE to Caterpillar has shown that augmenting the product with services makes the brand's value proposition more unique and valuable to customers. IBM for example holds over $100 billion in multiyear service agreements with its customers. Sweden's SKF no longer sells industrial bearings; it collaborates with customers to provide machinery up-time and productivity.[36]

The digital era has taken these so-called service-transition strategies to an entirely new level; the Internet of Things (IoT) is fast becoming a reality. The number of wirelessly connected products in existence (not counting smartphones or PCs) is expected to increase from five billion in 2015 to 21 billion by 2020. Stuffed with sensors and microchips, ever more products can communicate with each other and with human beings. Diebold, a leader in self-service transaction technology, monitors its cash machines for signs of trouble, either fixing problems remotely by a software patch or, if that does not work, by dispatching a technician. Agricultural machinery giant John Deere collaborates with Monsanto. Agronomic data from its machines in the field are transmitted to the agrochemical company to allow it to deliver farmers advice based on real time weather and crop information.

Nevertheless, the power of the IoT is only just starting to be explored. Companies in areas from manufacturing to energy, transport, and mining collect huge volumes of data, but use only a fraction of it. Firms that succeed in finding ways to use that information to cut its costs and raise the productivity of its products and services gain a critical competitive advantage over rivals.

Imagine the following scenario: high above the Atlantic Ocean, on a flight from New York to New Delhi, the jet is struck by a bolt of lightning. This is usually harmless but in this case, it caused some problems in one of the Rolls-Royce engines. While the plane is still in flight, immediately after lightning hit the engine, a stream of data is beamed from the plane to Derby, England where Rolls-Royce engineers get into action. The question is whether the plane will need full engine inspection after it lands in New Delhi, which is the normal practice but causes delays and is expensive. The engineers in Derby are able in real time to analyze the problem and conclude that there is no problem in this case. No engineers are necessary to examine the engine in New Delhi and the return flight takes off on time. Everybody benefits—the airline, the passengers, and the

---

[36] Fang, Eric, Robert W. Palmatier, and Jan-Benedict E.M. Steenkamp (2008), "Effect of Service Transition Strategies on Firm Value," *Journal of Marketing*, 72 (September), pp. 1–14; Zeithaml, Valarie A. et al. (2014), *Profiting from Services and Solutions*, New York: Business Expert Press.

supplier. In fact, Rolls Royce earns up to seven times the revenue from services over the lifetime of an engine than it does from selling the engine.[37]

McKinsey estimates that IoT will create up to $1.1 trillion of economic value per year by 2025 for suppliers; the impact on customers is even greater.[38] Yet not every brand is equally well positioned to profit from IoT. The types, amount, and specificity of data gathered by billions of devices create concerns among individuals about their privacy and among organizations about the confidentiality and integrity of their data. Providers of IoT enabled products and services will have to create compelling value propositions for data to be collected and used, provide transparency into what data are used and how they are being used, and ensure that the data are appropriately protected. This benefits established brands with a track record of protecting customers' interests (think Apple or Google) while it puts brands owned by SOEs and brands from countries with a weak rule of law at a decided disadvantage. If many Americans do not trust the US government with their data, how many would trust Huawei with their data, knowing that it is a Chinese SOE? Even when the company is privately held, if it is located in a country characterized by a weak rule of law—think about Mexico, Russia, China, and Turkey[39]—the brand's customers may have serious doubts about the privacy and confidentiality of the data. To illustrate, when I gave an executive seminar in China, a participant from Taiwan argued forcefully that the software used in privately held Xiaomi smartphones contained a backdoor, allowing the Chinese authorities to monitor activity. So she used a Samsung device.

IoT in B2C

As a child in the 1960s, I got my first exposure to an IoT-enabled home when I watched the animated sitcom *The Jetsons*. I was exposed to such

---

[37] This example was taken from Bryson, John R. and Peter W. Daniels (2015), *Handbook of Service Business*, Cheltenham (U.K.): Edward Elgar.

[38] Manyika, James et al. (2015), "The Internet of Things: Mapping the Value Beyond the Hype," McKinsey Global Institute Report, June.

[39] http://worldjusticeproject.org/rule-law-around-world; accessed March 4, 2016.

clearly fanciful products as videophones, machines that can respond to spoken commands, vacuum cleaners that guide themselves, and domestic robots to assist in food preparation. *The Jetsons'* world is now fast becoming a reality, and brands that will effectively use IoT to provide value to consumers will dominate the future.

Korea's LG has programmed a line of smart refrigerators that can sense their own contents and track inventory through barcode or radio-frequency ID scanning. P&G's Oral-B launched the Oral-B SmartSeries 7000—based on insights obtained in partnership with eYeka—the world's first connected electric toothbrush, which connects via Bluetooth Smart technology to the Oral-B app. The app acts like an oral care personal trainer, providing real-time guidance while you brush, and recording brushing activity that you can share with dental professionals, helping to create smarter and more personalized brushing routines. The invention won a German Design Award in 2015. Founded in 2007, Fitbit has grown into a major wellness brand offering an array of wireless-enabled wearable technology devices that collect data such as the number of steps walked, heart rate, quality of sleep, steps climbed, and other personal metrics.

Arguably the most exciting area of application is self-driving cars. Some of the world's strongest brands, including automakers BMW, Mercedes, Ford, Nissan, and Tesla, as well as tech companies like Google and Apple are spending billions of dollars to build or plan electric, self-driving cars made of lightweight composites. The stakes could not be higher. Global passenger car sales exceeded 75 million units in 2016, and six car brands had a brand value exceeding $10 billion. It is becoming increasingly clear that their future will be determined by the ability to develop and own the hardware as well as the software of the car of the future. There is reason to be concerned. Google and Tesla could have self-driving vehicles on the road by 2021, a decade before major automakers say they can do it.[40] Uber plans to launch a fleet of autonomous vehicles as soon as they become available. According to Uber's founder Travis Kalanick, "When there is no other dude in the car, the cost of taking an Uber anywhere

---

[40] Dumaine, Brian (2016), "The Ultimate Driving Machine Prepares for a Driverless World," *Fortune*, March 1, pp. 125–136.

becomes cheaper than owning a vehicle. And then car ownership goes away."[41]

IoT in B2B

IoT-enabled developments in the consumer world have captured the imagination. Who would not be excited by the prospect of a Jetsons' World? Yet B2B applications are expected to generate about 70% of economic value created by IoT. Few companies have staked their future as strongly on IoT as General Electric, which according to CEO Jeff Immelt is being transformed into a "digital industrial company." GE's products such as aero engines, power generation equipment, locomotives, and medical scanners are being made part of IoT and the company is building new capabilities in software to understand and manage those machines. If GE can succeed in finding ways to use that information to cut its costs and raise the productivity of its products and services, it could gain a critical competitive advantage over rivals such as America's United Technologies, Germany's Siemens, France's Schneider Electric, Britain's Rolls-Royce, and Japan's Mitsubishi. It also aims to create a new source of income from cutting costs and boosting productivity for other companies, even if they are not using GE equipment. The company is investing heavily in digital capabilities, hiring 1000 software engineers and data scientists, and setting up a new data analytics center in San Ramon, California.

In setting itself up as a software business that can help other industrial groups reap the benefits of IoT, GE—one of the world's strongest brands (2016 brand value: $54.1 billion)—is drag-racing with Amazon, IBM, Microsoft, and SAP, all of which are (like GE) among the 25 most powerful global brands in 2016, according to Millward Brown. But it may have no choice. Frank Gillett of Forrester Research explained, "GE is in a race to capture customers before the likes of Amazon get better at meeting industrial requirements, and before customers get comfortable about using them." If it succeeds, the GE brand will soar. But if the costly

[41] Chafkin, Mark (2015), "What Makes Uber Run?" *Fast Company*, October, pp. 110–124, 141–142.

bet on the industrial internet fails, a future of deeper cost cuts, lower levels of investment, declining brand strength, and perhaps a further break-up would await.[42]

Managerial Takeaways

Digital technology has disrupted the analogue rules of branding. But let's not confuse the means with the end. Successful global brands still deliver a clearly differentiated customer proposition to the global target segment, with the right integrated global marketing strategy. What *has* changed is how MNCs create and deliver brand value. Here are the key changes.

- Established global brands can reach hitherto unserved parts of countries through the digital channel. Niche brands can garner sufficient scale by aggregating demand across countries.
- The boundary between local and global brands becomes permeable. In fact, any local brand can become global at the touch of a keystroke.
- Digital has reduced the window of response to new global entrants from decades to a year or less. Global brands will emerge faster and from unexpected directions. Incumbent brands must constantly surveil the marketplace and react quickly to emerging threats. This requires vastly increased organizational agility.
- Rapid information flows, connectivity, and market transparency render brand consistency across countries ever more important. Customers and competitors will quickly notice differences in customer proposition, pricing, quality, service, and advertising messages. Containing the fallout of corporate or brand crises to one country will be impossible. All this calls for increased global integration of brand strategies to maintain brand trust.

---

[42] Crooks, Ed (2016), "General Electric: Post-Industrial Revolution," *Financial Times*, January 12, p. 7.

- The pendulum of power has decisively shifted to the customer, who is more demanding and better informed than at any time in human history. Engage customers via co-creation strategies. Identify digital opinion leaders and engage them in the product development and marketing process.
- eWOM volume and valence need to be tracked. Develop strategies to improve eWOM performance. Engineer customer advocacy, even if you cannot control it.
- Digital channel partners are the new Walmart. However, they can also provide invaluable services in the quest to go global, especially for smaller firms.
- Assess whether the sharing economy can disrupt your business too. If so, engage in creative destruction yourself as you can be sure that a new entrant, not burdened by legacy costs, will emerge soon.
- IoT is the new frontier in service transition strategies. Brands that own a platform and have the ability to communicate and coordinate across people and machines will capture future brand value. Traditional goods manufacturers are drag-racing with the best software companies to capture the value generated by IoT. Lose that battle and you will be relegated to original equipment manufacturer status, with commensurately dismal profit margins.
- You share control over your brand with customers: this is something you have to accept.

Part II

Structures and Processes for Global Brand Building

A strong brand can tumble not because its customer proposition and marketing program are weak but because the organization fails to implement the strategy. In this part, I turn to the organizational structure and management processes that enable the global brand to deliver on its promise to its customers, the firm, and other stakeholders. While global brands benefit the MNC, their complexity increases costs. That's the global brand paradox. The MNC must achieve four goals:

1. maintain brand consistency and capture economies of scale and scope across borders;
2. differentiate goods and services where necessary to suit the needs of local customers;
3. leverage learnings and share knowledge among all parts of the company;
4. while managing to prevent complexity from hindering speed and agility.

Of course, there are tensions and tradeoffs among these goals. The MNC must act like the elephant, the chameleon, the owl, and the flea all at once. It needs the size, the range, and the power of an elephant, the adaptability to local environments of the chameleon, the learning capabilities and the wisdom of an owl, and the speed and agility of a flea—by design. If it can combine these anatomies and physiologies, the MNC creates a tiger brand – strong, fast, smart, and flexible. If combined poorly, the MNC creates a snail brand –slow, cautious, imperceptible. Chapter, "Organizational Structures for Global Brands," discusses the structural solutions to the global brand paradox, while Chapter, "Global Brand Management," complements the structural hardware with managerial software. Many local managers believe that their context is unique and that consumer insights "not discovered here" and best practices "not invented here" are "not relevant here." How does a global brand manager retain brand integrity and enlist local managers in the global brand strategy?

In the twenty-first century, effective and efficient are no longer sufficient. Customers increasingly expect the firm to behave responsibly in the world. MNCs must contribute to solving environmental and social problems linked to what they sell and how they do business. This is the topic of Chapter, "Corporate Social Responsibility." Companies ranging from Ikea to Google have infused corporate social responsibility (CSR) in firm-wide activities. But how can you to transfer corporate CSR activities to your global brand? The chapter introduces a procedure for imbuing your brand with CSR connotations.

6

Organizational Structures for Global Brands

"They always say time changes things, but you actually have to change them yourself," said Andy Warhol. If organizational design is a product of our imagination—and it is—then we cannot change it without changing our thinking about it. Yet, too often, executives would rather fiddle with business models than grapple with the elephant in whose room they sit.

And so organizational structure should be as much a global brand consideration as strategy in facilitating global brand growth and innovation, speed to market, and ability to adapt and respond to local environments. The key is to change deliberately. That's what Procter & Gamble has done over its history of international expansion.[1] It has designed and redesigned its global organizational structure to achieve the four goals that constitute the global brand paradox—maintaining brand consistency and capturing economies of scale and scope across borders, differentiat-

---

[1] The description of P&G's journey through organizational designs is based on Piskorski, Mikolaj Jan and Alessandro L. Spadini (2007a), "Procter & Gamble: Organization 2005 (A)," Harvard Business School case 9-707-519; Piskorski, Mikolaj Jan and Alessandro L. Spadini (2007b), "Procter & Gamble: Organization 2005 (B)," Harvard Business School case 9-707-402; Bartlett, Christopher A. (2003), "P&G in Japan: The SK-II Globalization Project," Harvard Business School case 9-303-003; and on in-company discussions.

© The Author(s) 2017
J.-B. Steenkamp, *Global Brand Strategy*,
DOI 10.1057/978-1-349-94994-6_6

ing products where necessary to suit the needs of local customers, and leveraging lessons and sharing knowledge without letting complexity get in the way of speed and agility.

Procter & Gamble's Deliberate Design of Organizational Structure

After World War II, P&G established a geographical structure for its international activities based in Brussels, Belgium, consisting of small self-sufficient subsidiaries, each structured like the US organization and situated in a viable country of Europe. Autonomous country managers adapted P&G technology, sourced from its R&D labs in Cincinnati, and applied US marketing expertise to local markets. This highly decentralized model worked well in a world of trade barriers, national regulations, and an emerging European middle class. Consumers were just beginning to use laundry detergent, disposable diapers, and other P&G stalwarts. Some brands were global (e.g., Pampers diapers), others were regional (e.g., Ariel laundry detergent), and still others local (e.g., Dreft liquid soap). Country managers did not coordinate brand positioning and strategy, and Brussels did not insist upon brand coordination. As long as each country met its sales and profit targets, regional HQ did not interfere with local operations.

But these local subsidiaries were slow to launch some of P&G's most proven and popular brands. For example, P&G launched Pampers in America in 1961, but P&G Germany took another 12 years to introduce German parents to the disposable diaper, and the French rollout took 17 years, even though the product itself required little local customization. And so P&G lost years of sales and profits, while competitors like Sweden's SCA got years to develop and launch their own brands.

P&G had not standardized manufacturing across countries, and so each subsidiary reinvented its own wheel. Local manufacturers tweaked product designs for no valid business reason; these tweaks added significant cost to manufacturing, significant complexity to the supply chain, and very little value to consumers. At one time, there were 69 variants of the feminine protection brand Always across Europe! Operations became expensive, unreliable, not scalable, and no longer competitive.

Starting in the late 1980s, P&G restructured into a matrix consisting of global categories (e.g., detergent), global functions (e.g., R&D, manufacturing, supply chain), and country product-category managers (e.g., general manager detergent Germany) who were responsible for local product and brand management, distribution, advertising, and sales. This structure eliminated redundancies, pooled knowledge and best practices, and accelerated global product launches. By the early 1990s, P&G took only four years to roll out a new initiative globally. For example, in the late 1980s, the beauty-care global technical center in Cincinnati developed the revolutionary two-in-one shampoo-and-conditioner technology. By the early 1990s, the hair-care global category president had rolled it out globally under the Pantene brand with a consistent worldwide marketing message and identity.

But accountability within matrix organizations is typically not symmetrical. At P&G, regional managers had the sole responsibility for financial results, and so they had to choose whether to launch whatever the global category manager was pushing, be it a new laundry detergent or an improved diaper. Global category managers still had to get each regional manager or country manager's buy-in to launch a new product in that manager's territory. Regional managers often hesitated to launch a particular product because it could weaken their upcoming profit-and-loss statement, even though the product could strengthen their long-term profitability. As a result, the company's globalization of brands and innovation stagnated. For example, P&G acquired the US cosmetics brand Cover Girl in 1989 but did not globalize it until the late 1990s. As the company diversified, the number of country product-category management positions proliferated. By the mid-1990s, Germany alone had more than ten category general managers. The bane of the matrix, complexity, became ever more pernicious.

In the late 1990s, P&G began restructuring again, replacing its matrix with three independent, yet interdependent types of organizations: all product-based activities were located in *global business units* (GBU) which responsible for product development, brand strategy, and new business development; all of the geography-based, product customization activities were in the *market development organizations* (MDO), which were responsible for tailoring the company's global programs to local markets and using local knowledge of consumers and retailers to inform P&G's global marketing strategies; and all of the globally shared functions were in *global business services* (GBS), which was responsible for streamlining and standardizing where possible such processes, systems, and IT platforms as HR, purchasing, logistics, and facilities management across GBUs and MDOs. Importantly, none of these three types of organization reported to each other and none was superior to the others. The only place where their lines of responsibility met was at the CEO level.

This structure was designed to achieve three goals—globally integrate brand strategies and speed-up global product rollouts, differentiate brand strategies where necessary, and achieve scale economies within shared functions. The C-suite was keenly aware that these goals often are at odds with each other, but also that top-down and centralized decision making for every brand in every category in every country in every time period was unworkable either. Instead, it delegated decision rights to middle managers who were tasked to resolve tradeoffs between these goals dynamically as they arose.

Initially, P&G compensated GBUs on profitability, MDOs on sales growth, and GBS on cost management. However, these one-dimensional performance metrics led to unintended outcomes: major innovations take several years to take off, something that would not be attractive for MDO leaders with a time horizon of one to three years. And so P&G executives added more sophisticated performance metrics such as cash flow and margin. Similarly GBS pushed for the highest level of standardization to achieve lowest costs, but GBUs and MDOs wanted a high level of customization. So P&G added GBU and MDO customer-service ratings as a GBS performance metric.

Sales and profits increased in subsequent years, and the company was better able than ever before to tap into local insights and innovations for global success. For example, in collaboration with R&D labs in Cincinnati and Great Britain, Japanese technologists developed a new lip product involving a durable color base and a renewable moisturizing second coat. Recognizing that this two-stage application would result in a more expensive lipstick, the global cosmetics category executive asked

Max Factor Japan to be the global lead market. The Japanese product management team developed the marketing approach—concept, packaging, positioning, communications strategy, and so on—that led to the new brand, Lipfinity, rolled out in Europe and America within six months of the Japanese launch. Many other new product ideas and marketing concepts emerged from local markets.

With this network structure in place, P&G then launched its Connect + Develop program to harness the ideas of external innovators and companies. Its website features past successes, current needs, and what P&G looks for in its innovation partnerships. P&G currently relies on outside collaboration for a full 50% of its innovations.[2] This culture of openness, collaboration, and learning is a far cry from P&G's past internally focused culture.

With greater global integration, P&G has been able to concentrate its marketing power with retailers and its advertising expenditures of 10 billion dollars behind its global brands. In 2016, P&G had over 20 brands with sales exceeding one billion dollars annually, nearly all of them global. Two of its brands (Pampers and Gillette) were among the world's 100 most valuable brands in 2016 while Olay, Pantene, Crest, and Oral-B were among the world's 15 most valuable personal care brands, according to Millward Brown.

Four Organizational Models for Global Brands

Over the last five decades, P&G deployed three of four organizational models—geographical, functional, matrix, and network—that MNCs use to support their global brands. These organizational models vary in the tradeoff between global integration of brand activities versus local autonomy (Fig. 6.1). Of course, in practice, firms will blend elements from different organizational models as P&G did, although you should be able to identify your dominant organizational model.

---

[2] http://www.pgconnectdevelop.com; accessed January 1, 2015.

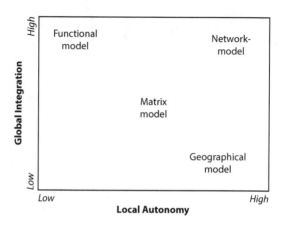

Fig. 6.1 Global organizational designs (*Source*: Adapted from Bartlett and Ghoshal (1989))

You can use these organizational models for the marketing function alone or for the entire corporation. Since market-oriented companies should organize all their activities around their global brands, I focus on the entire organization in this chapter. I do not recommend functional silos. Marketing organizations ought not to operate separately from the rest of the firm. To be effective, they must fit into the overall organizational structure. Suppose you centralize your marketing organization in a geography-centric model, then your global plans could fizzle at the local level under strong regional managers who control profit and loss.

As Table 6.1 shows, the four generic models use three coordination mechanisms to varying degrees: centralization, formalization, and normative-cultural control.[3] To understand how the organizational models work, we first need to understand how these coordinating mechanisms work.

---

[3] Ghoshal, Sumantra and Nitin (1989), "Internal Differentiation within Multinational Corporations," *Strategic Management Journal*, 10, pp. 323–337; Nohria, Nitin and Sumantra Ghoshal (1994), "Differentiated Fit and Shared Values: Alternatives for Managing Headquarters-Subsidiary Relations," *Strategic Management Journal*, 15, pp. 491–502.

Table 6.1 Organizational models

	Geographical model	Functional model	Matrix model	Network model
Rank order of use of coordinating mechanisms	Normative-cultural control (weak) Formalization Centralization	Centralization Formalization Normative-cultural control	Formalization Centralization Normative-cultural control	Normative-cultural control Formalization Centralization
Ability to address global brand paradox:				
Global consistency and efficiency	Low	High	Medium	Uncertain
Local responsiveness	High	Low	Medium	Uncertain
Worldwide learning and innovation	Low	Low/Medium	Medium	High
Speed and agility	High for local opportunities and threats Low for global opportunities and threats	Low for local opportunities and threats High for global opportunities and threats	Low	High

(continued)

Table 6.1 (continued)

	Geographical model	Functional model	Matrix model	Network model
Conditions favoring its use	Products with deep local cultural heritage Customer needs differ significantly across countries Low economics of scale and scope Heavily regulated and politically sensitive industries	New product categories Global need segments dominate country segments Universal agreement what constitutes "best" products Home country is lead market in the industry High economies of scale and scope	Products for which there are significant cross-national differences in customer needs but where COMET factors require global integration	"Millennial" companies Companies involved in the "Internet of things" Digital firms
Weaknesses	Brand anarchy Diseconomies of scale and scope Not-invented-here syndrome	Loss of local opportunities Slow in responding to global potential of local threats Ethnocentric focus may create animosity overseas	Complex Costly Conflicting objectives Compromise solutions that fail to excel	Unproven Is normative-cultural control sufficient? Clash between cultural glue and national norms Lack of diversity in senior management English proficiency Challenges in cross-cultural communication
Global brand types	Value brands, mass brands	All five types of global brands	Mass brands, premium brands	All five types of global brands
Examples	Kimberly-Clark, Costco, Haier	Samsung, IKEA, LMVH, Catholic Church	Philips, Campbell's Soup, Schlumberger	IBM, Bharti Airtel, Airbnb

Coordination Mechanisms

Centralization: "Who Decides?"

Centralization is a governance mechanism whereby the C-suite organizes global branding decisions hierarchically. It is the least expensive governance mechanism: headquarters often makes most of the crucial strategic and tactical decisions and coordinate subsidiaries by fiat and continuous monitoring.[4] It requires few resources to institutionalize but many administrative resources to maintain. While it solves the issue of control in a straightforward way, brand decisions reflect the competencies at headquarters and underutilize the competencies of subsidiaries. And if a subsidiary has strong leadership, deep marketing talent, and large resources, it can push back.

Formalization: "How Is the Decision Made?"

Formalization is the routinization of decision making and resource allocation. Formalization decreases the power of both the headquarters and the subsidiary by replacing decision making with an impartial set of rules. When codifying these decisions, the parties involved must specify worldwide rules, policies, and operating procedures, global budgets for global initiatives, global performance review and compensation systems, and monitoring mechanisms so that neither headquarters nor subsidiaries could or would want to override the system.

Formalization is more expensive to institutionalize because executives devote considerable time and effort to develop a comprehensive set of decision-making rules and templates. But once established, the mechanism takes relatively little administrative resources to maintain—so little that inertia can set in. In times of uncertainty and ambiguity, it may constrain the brand from rapidly adapting to changing conditions in local environments.

---

[4] The term "headquarters" is used in a generic sense. It can refer to the company or to the business unit—dependent on the exact organization.

Normative-Cultural Control: "What Binds Us Together?"

Centralization and formalization are similar in that they achieve global brand integration through administrative control mechanisms. Normative-cultural control constrains action by linking all brand decisions to common values and objectives. It works with a strong corporate culture that pervades headquarters as well as local subsidiaries. Corporate culture is a system of shared assumptions, values, and behavioral norms that shape how people do things in the organization. By recruiting the right managers and socializing them to the firm's culture, a brand team minimizes divergent interests and reinforces mutual interests. Alphabet (Google), for example, puts a lot of effort into hiring the right people. In the hiring process, the hiring manager looks for culture fit with the team and the organization. Alphabet sees culture rather than centralization or formalization as the main coordinating mechanism.

Normative-cultural control is the most costly mechanism to develop. It involves significant investment for both initial socialization and continued cultural fidelity. The online shoe store Zappos offers $3,000 to new hires to leave the company after four weeks. While costly, it is money well spent: those that accept the offer it considers mis-hires in the first place, and it invigorates the rest with a sense of purpose, intensifies their commitment, and generates free publicity.

Diagnosing the Use of Coordinating Mechanisms by Your Company

These three basic control mechanisms are not mutually incompatible. For example, most firms will exhibit some centralization, while normative-cultural control cannot operate without some formalization. And so MNCs will use multiple control mechanisms to some degree. Tool 6.1 helps you determine which control mechanisms your company uses. This tool has three primary purposes.

Score each item, tally the scores per section, then use the key at the bottom to gauge the use of each coordination mechanism by your company.

A. Centralization   Score (1-7)

Indicate the relative influence of headquarters and local subsidiaries over elements of strategy on a scale from 1 (local managers make decisions on their own) to 7 (HQ makes decisions for subsidiaries):

1. Introduction of a new product

2. Changes in product design

3. Changes in manufacturing process

4. R&D program and project priorities

5. Brand name, targeting, and positioning

6. Marketing mix: pricing, placement, package, promotions, advertising

Score Subtotal A (items 1-6)

B. Formalization

Indicate the extent to which you agree with the following statements about your company's governance on a scale from 1 (disagree strongly) to 7 (agree strongly):

7. We use the same standard operating procedures and common manuals worldwide

8. We follow the same detailed common rules and policies worldwide

9. We work with global budgets for global product introductions and marketing campaigns

10. We use the same performance review and compensation system for all brand managers, no matter where they are based

11. Headquarters monitors brand management worldwide to make sure everyone plays by the same rules and followes the same policies and procedures

12. Our company culture is bureaucratic and responds slowly to change

Score Subtotal B (items 7-12)

C. Normative-Cultural Control

Indicate the extent to which you agree with the following statements about your company on a scale from 1 (definitely false) to 7 (definitely true):

13. Our corporate culture is global and appeals to potential employees around the world

14. Our company's senior management includes a significant percentage of people from countries around the world

15. Our company truly emphasizes collaboration, synergy, and mutual interdependence

16. Our company recruits and promotes employees regardless of nationality

17. Our corporate culture acts as glue among subsidiaries and gives direction to our behavior

18. Our company rotates managers from all countries through headquarters

Score Subtotal C (items 13-18)

Total Score per Section	Use of the Coordinating Mechanism Is
<19	Low
19-30	Moderate
31-42	High

Tool 6.1 Diagnosing the use of coordination mechanisms by your company

1. You can administer it to managers at headquarters and at the local subsidiaries and compare the scores. A survey among executives working for a wide variety of global companies showed that there is often a disconnect between the perceptions of HQ and executives working in the field.[5] Stark differences should serve as a warning sign for senior leaders. As the battleground shifts from strategy to execution, the ability to bridge this gap is becoming ever more important.
2. You can compare your company's scores with those of your competitors, using your own insights and input from colleagues who are former employees of the competition. Administer the questionnaire during new employee onboarding while the previous employment experience is fresh. Where are there gaps in usage between you and your key competitor? Are they ahead of you, or do you feel their approach is misguided, and why? You can also compare your scores to a successful new competitor. Are they adopting a different set of control mechanisms, which could be an early warning signal that times are changing?
3. You can benchmark your firm's relative use of the three coordinating mechanisms versus that of four generic organizational models (Table 6.1). Is the rank order the same or different from the generic model that most closely resembles your organization? If it is different, why? Is it a deliberate choice?

Geographical Model

As brands go global, executives often organize marketing and operations by geography, by regions or countries depending on the potential of the market (Fig. 6.2). This structure is highly decentralized; the C-suite vests most decision-making power in regional or local business units and then monitors their sales and profits. Country managers possess considerable autonomy. They can experiment and respond rapidly to changes in local market conditions. In such a structure, a shared corporate culture can

---

[5] Khanna, Dinesh et al. (2015), "The Globalization Capability Gap," The Boston Consulting Group and IMD.

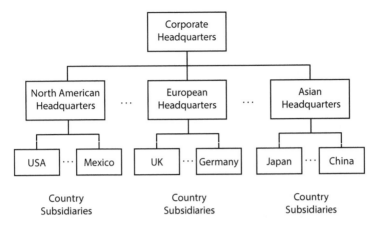

Fig. 6.2 Geographical model

act as coordinating mechanism for global branding activities, such as introducing new products, developing consistent value propositions, or launching global advertising campaigns.

However, if local business culture does not mesh with headquarters HQ culture, then global brand managers may struggle to coordinate strategic initiatives. If local managers do not fully endorse corporate goals and the global brand identity, then local experimentation can lead to brand anarchy, diseconomies of scale and scope, and even the not-invented-here syndrome. You can mitigate such a situation by delegating decision-making authority to regional units, but increasingly COMET factors such as economies of scale, transnational innovation, and rapid rollout of new products supersede not only countries but also regions, and thus the geographical model.

Therefore, in terms of the global brand paradox, the global geographical model will help you differentiate products and services to suit the needs of local customers but you will forgo economies of scale and scope, brand consistency across borders, and knowledge sharing between units. The geographical organization is fast and agile when spotting local opportunities and threats such as a multi-cooker for preparing local recipes like Borscht in Russia but not global ones such as the rise of new Chinese competitors.

In industries where local tastes are deeply ingrained, geography may well be the most effective organizational model. Consider retailing, especially food retailing. Although Costco can centralize certain elements of its brand strategy (e.g., size of stores, private label brand name, membership club, bulk sizes), 65% of its assortment—mostly foods—caters to local tastes. To avoid balkanization, Costco uses normative-cultural mechanisms. According to Jim Murphy, executive vice president of Costco's international division, the company spends considerable effort communicating Costco's history, values, ethics, and merchandising strategies to all 189,000 employees worldwide so that they are aware of its business goals.[6]

SABMiller, the owner of global brands like Foster's, Grolsch, and Peroni, differed from its more centralized competitors AB InBev and Heineken in that it gave its managing directors in each country responsibility for all in-country operations. Its decentralized structure fit its management philosophy that global brands play only a modest role in selling beer. In 2015, AB InBev acquired SABMiller for $106 billion. For this price tag to make economic sense, AB InBev needs to achieve cost savings of at least $1.4 billion per annum, and that does not bode well for SABMiller's decentralized approach.

Functional Model

The polar opposite of the geographical model is the functional model (Fig. 6.3). Where the former emphasizes localization, the latter emphasizes globalization; while the former deputizes local managers, the latter reserves power in the head office; while the former espouses decentralization, the latter uses centralization, as well as some degree of formalization, but we should interpret common rules, policies, and procedures as mandates from the head office. Marketing managers within the local units take their instructions from the chief marketing officer or executive vice-president of marketing at global headquarters.

---

[6] *The Costco Connection* (2015), "Worldwide Warehouses: Costco's Message of Value Translates Well around the Globe," July, pp. 28–32.

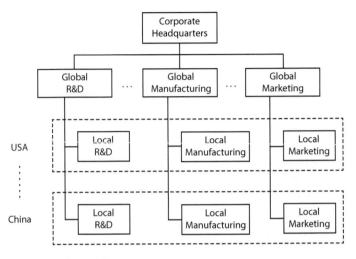

Fig. 6.3 Functional model

Functional organizations develop a single brand strategy, minimizing local differences and emphasizing global commonalities. Corporate HQ sets global R&D strategy and budgets underpinning the brand and tightly integrates product development around the world. Brands have strong global identities, and their managers set up global marketing programs. Senior managers in subsidiaries are often expatriates from the MNC's country of origin, and this management talent facilitates a consistent brand strategy around the world. While highly creative local marketers and product managers can find this model quite rigid, especially in its ideal type, it ensures brand consistency, is highly efficient, and allows for rapid new product introductions. These advantages likely outweigh its lack of local adaptation if the home country is the lead market in the industry or if customer tastes and needs do not differ significantly across borders. The functional model allows for top-down learning, but much less so for truly worldwide learning without rotation of global talent, both creative and operational. Its centralized decision making allows for speed and agility to fulfill unprecedented global needs such as the need for simple, durable, well-designed furniture at a low price uncovered by IKEA. However, it is slow to respond to local opportunities and threats such as the Chinese startup Huawei, founded in 1988. Western telecom equipment giants like Ericsson and Cisco ignored the special needs of the Chinese market and underestimated Huawei's ability to grow beyond its strong base in China to become the second largest firm in the industry in only two decades.[7]

The Catholic Church is the oldest still existing functional organization in the world. It is also the only functional organization that claims infallibility for its "CEO." IKEA largely follows the functional model. Its brand strategy originates in its Scandinavian homeland and travels well across countries. Most senior managers hail from Sweden or Denmark, they develop products primarily in Sweden, and they have standardized 95% of the product assortment. In other words, you will find nearly the same furniture in Parnas, Russia, as in Paramus, New Jersey. Many Chinese, Japanese, and South Korean companies also tend to follow the functional model. They tend to appoint country nationals as managers in foreign markets as Huawei did in Western Europe, Canada, the United States, and India, and these foreign managers may struggle to attract the best local talent.

Matrix Model

The geographical model sacrifices global efficiency for local responsiveness while the functional model does the opposite. The matrix model combines these strengths by giving equal power and responsibilities to functions and geography (Fig. 6.4). In a matrix, the global vice-president of marketing oversees the global marketing budget as well as influences the decisions and career of the marketing manager in the local business unit, whereas the general manager of the local business unit allocates the local marketing budget and likewise influences the decisions and career of the local marketing manager. Thus, middle managers have a functional and a geographic boss. The global VP of marketing manages global marketing strategies while local marketing managers implement local

---

[7] Steenkamp, Jan-Benedict E.M. (2014), "Huawei: Taking a Chinese Brand from B2B to B2C amidst Political Resistance," The Case Centre Case #514-043-1.

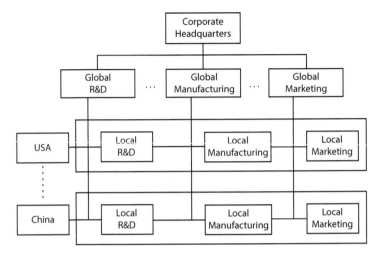

Fig. 6.4 Matrix model

marketing strategies. The global and local managers reconcile their plans through strategic planning meetings.

The matrix internalizes the pressures for global brand consistency and efficiency, local responsiveness, and synergies among business units. Formalization coordinates these initiatives. Moreover, since the matrix explicitly infuses the global element (not: home-country dominance) into the organizational design, it provides normative-cultural control as well. The "dual boss" hierarchy helps where strategic planning fails to reconcile differences between global and local marketing plans.

Netherlands' Royal Philips, a consumer lifestyle and healthcare corporation, recently reconfigured itself into a matrix.[8] It views as its key strength its ability to offer locally relevant innovations. For example, in response to milk contamination in China, its consumer division pioneered the soy milk appliance so that people could produce their own milk from soybeans. According to its CEO Frans van Houten, "To truly satisfy customer needs, you cannot just offer a global [standardized] solution because you over-simplify the differences between regional markets and

---

[8] Mocker, Martin, Jeanne W. Ross, and Eric van Heck (2014), "Transforming Royal Philips: Seeking Local Relevance While Leveraging Global Scale," MIT: Center for Information Systems Research case 394.

individual customers." To obtain economies of scale and scope, Philips chose to standardize its processes and platforms, not its products, around the world. Its managers believed that its globally recognized brand name and logo, and the new tagline "Innovation and You," allow it to compete successfully with the big Asian companies and with agile local players. It identified three core processes—idea-to-market, market-to-order, and order-to-cash—that it could use to create standardized models for four business models—products, services, software, and systems—that encompass most of its global operations. Although its leaders have imposed standardization on these core processes, they permit exceptions within its 400 newly created business-market combinations (BMC). Philips augmented this structure with a number of additional roles—such as business model owners, business process owners, and business process experts—to take an enterprise-wide perspective on the trade-off between long-term and short-term effects of these exceptions to process standards.

Gordian Knot of a Matrix

Matrix structures have several disadvantages. First, the matrix can become so complex as to become unmanageable. Only time will tell whether Philips' new matrix structure will prove effective; it is certainly more complex than Philips' old geographical model.

Second, the matrix is anything but fast and agile. For a matrix to work properly, you need to install numerous costly conflict resolution mechanisms, particularly committees, meetings, and task forces. Decisions take a long time, sometimes because no one knows who is supposed to make which decision. Some analysts have criticized P&G management for responding too slowly to market changes, a symptom of matrix complexity. The Gillette brand team apparently had an idea for a shaving club before Dollar Shave Club, but parent P&G's internal processes stalled its launch, and Gillette is having to play catch-up.[9]

Third, the two bosses will frequently have conflicting objectives. Their direct reports will do whatever the more powerful of the two instructs. In

---

[9] Whipp, Lindsay (2015), "Plot Twist in the Soap Opera," *Financial Times*, October 21, p. 6.

that case, the matrix collapses under its own weight. Or, to satisfy their two bosses, managers may compromise, satisfying neither the demand for global efficiency nor the need for local responsiveness.

Thus, none of the three established organizational models totally solves the global brand paradox. Increasingly, MNCs have begun to create global networks, with normative-cultural control as the coordination mechanism.

Network Model

The most distinctive characteristic of a network is the principle of reciprocal dependencies: people from all units at all levels communicate meaningfully.[10] Theys learn from each other and from their touchpoints up and down the value chain, and they share brand lessons and innovations (Fig. 6.5). Network design addresses the inherent tendency of matrix structures to gravitate toward one dimension. In networks, all roles have market intelligence and capabilities that are critical for competitive success; and so neither function nor geography dominates.

Networks seek efficiency as a means to achieve global competitiveness; harness local responsiveness for greater flexibility in international operations; and regard brand innovations and best practices as the outcomes of organizational learning. Some MNCs have extended their network to other companies, suppliers, distributors, and customers. For example, India's mobile phone company Bharti Airtel outsourced hardware, software, and IT services requirements to IBM. This included all customer-facing IT applications, such as billing and data warehousing. In addition, IBM serviced the company's internal-facing applications such as the intranet, email, and online collaboration, and consolidate the company's data centers and IT help desks. This agreement supplemented another agreement with Ericsson and Nokia to help develop and manage Bharti Airtel's telecom network. So what was left? Everything what Bharti Airtel

---

[10] Palmisano, Samuel J. (2014), *Re-Think*, New York: Center for Global Enterprise; Lasserre, Philippe (2012), *Global Strategic Management*, New York: Palgrave Macmillan.

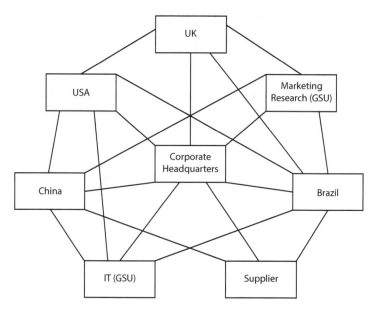

Fig. 6.5 Network model (*Note*: *GSU* global service unit)

considered as its core competence. Bharti Airtel's Manoj Kohli explained the thinking: "We have kept to ourselves our core competence … customer management, branding, people management and motivation, financing is our job…. Everything else is done by our strategic partners, who have better domain knowledge, skills, and capabilities to help us."[11]

This approach served the company when it expanded internationally, acquiring telecom operators in Sri Lanka in 2009, in Bangladesh in 2010, and most importantly, when it acquired the African assets of Kuwait's Mobile Telecommunication Company, known as Zain, for $10.7 billion. The acquisition gave the company a foothold in 15 countries across Africa. One of the immediate challenges was integrating the 15 companies, all rebranded to airtel, its global brand name with a newly designed logo, which had operated as stand-alone units. The company did not need to reinvent the wheel in each country—it created offices serving multiple countries. This accelerated the pace at which Bharti

---

[11] Palmisano (2014), p. 72.

Airtel could enter the markets and begin offering solutions to customers. Although the company subsequently faced financial challenges due to taking up (too) much debt, requiring it to sell off some assets, airtel was the second most valuable Indian brand in 2016, with a brand value of $10.0 billion.[12]

Networks are characterized by a clearly defined and tightly controlled set of operating systems—in particular a transparent global management information system—and inter-unit decision forums with active participation of global and functional managers in subsidiaries' boards. A lot rides on normative-cultural control mechanisms, including good interpersonal relationships, ability to communicate effectively across borders, strong corporate values, and a culture of sharing and willingness to collaborate.

Networks as a Sign of Our Times?

The network model resonates with our use of social media and our increasing wariness of authority vested by hierarchy rather than by ideas. Millennials have great respect for inspirational leaders but not necessarily for people in positions of authority "just because." At Facebook—the first Fortune 500 company built by millennials—managers encourage even low-level employees to question and criticize management. Executives give employees unusual freedom to choose and change assignments, even outside their areas of expertise. "You get zero credit for your title. It's all about the quality of the work, the power of your conviction and the ability to influence people," said Don Faul, a manager at Facebook and former Marines Special Forces commander. As with Royal Philips, time will tell how Facebook's management system will evolve as Facebook's young employees age and work alongside even younger colleagues.[13]

Thriving in the era of the Internet of Things requires that other firms, developers, and customers can have access to your platform. That requires an organizational model and culture that is comfortable with risk taking,

---

[12] Millward Brown (2016), *BrandZ Top 50 Most Valuable Indian Brands*.
[13] Albergotti, Reed (2014), "At Facebook, Boss Is a Dirty Word," *Wall Street Journal*, December 26, p. B1.

putting app development in the hands of autonomous teams. These requirements are best met with the network model.

The network's culture of openness to intra- and extra-organizational learning fits with the trend toward crowdsourcing, which brand managers can do externally and internally. Internal crowdsourcing avoids such concerns as IP ownership and protection that firms have about external crowdsourcing. Internal crowdsourcing is a powerful tool to share information among employees to achieve a joint purpose within the workplace. Employees can contribute, comment, and vote on ideas about how to improve business processes and services. An example is Cemex, the Mexican cement company. It taps into the collective knowledge of its 4000 staff in 50 countries using its "Shift" internal social network to share best practices and increase collaboration. "Shift" also includes a function called "Think & Build," for engaging its suppliers online to improve Cemex's procurement process. While cement is a tough business to be in, Cemex's brand value in 2015 stood at $3.0 billion, up 11% from 2014.

This democratic approach increases staff buy-in, motivates employees, and aligns teams better, provided managers are willing to test ideas they may not always personally believe will succeed. Continuous managerial override of the ideas of the firm's own employees has the exact opposite effect—making tapping into the community knowledge yet another management fad, which can really backfire.

IBM's Global Network Model

IBM is among the companies that have moved toward the network model. The depth and breadth of its global operations had made traditional organizational designs unwieldy. It had 60 to 70 major product lines, more than a dozen customer segments, and clients in 170 countries, yielding more than 100,000 product-segment-country combinations for which IBM had to close out P&L statements every day, take strategic decisions, allocate resources, and make trade-offs. Then-CEO Samuel Palmisano described IBM's predicament, "I recognized that trying to manage every one of those intersections centrally would drive people crazy. It would also be highly inefficient."[14]

Palmisano's team realized that IBM had to empower its middle managers to make decisions. But IBM also needed to ensure that middle management made the right decisions. How to achieve this? It used to be that "people don't do what you expect; they do what you inspect." But with its current complexity, IBM could not inspect everyone. It needed to create a management system that would empower people. Crowdsourcing employee input, IBM defined three new corporate values: "dedication to every client's success," "innovation that matters – for our company and the world," and "trust and personal responsibility in all relations [both internal and external]."

IBM eliminated layers of bureaucracy and pressed for more decision making in local markets and less at HQ. It moved managers out into local markets, where they could execute closer to clients. It changed financial incentive systems to reward work with clients better. These and other changes flattened IBM's hierarchies, eliminated redundancies, and improved productivity. It turned all its support functions (e.g., human resources, finance, legal) into globally integrated support functions, which any local unit could source from anywhere. It centralized global procurement in China, back-office finance operations in Brazil, data center delivery in India, and intellectual property management in the Netherlands. IBM Japan sources its human resources function from Manila, accounts receivable from Shanghai, accounting from Kuala Lumpur, procurement from Shenzhen, and customer service from Brisbane. While IBM continues to face challenges, its shift to this network model has strengthened its brand. Its brand strength score was a decidedly modest two (out of 5) in 2006, in 2016, it was an impressive four, according to branding consultancy Millward Brown.

---

[14] More information on IBM's transformation into a global network company can be found in Palmisano (2014).

Challenges to the Effectiveness of Global Network Model

While in theory, the network model does not favor the functional (global) or the geographical (local) dimension, the network needs global vigilance and strong governance like the matrix model. Cemex's CEO Zambrano acknowledged that the company continuously had to avoid the risk of tilting towards one extreme or the other. Another obstacle is a lack of diversity in the senior management of multinationals. CEO Samuel Palmisano commented, "If you are going to truly be a globally integrated enterprise…your top talent should be whatever the top talent of the world is." Presently, few companies fit that description. Despite globalization, an analysis of the top management teams of the world's 500 largest corporations reveals that only 15% are not from the corporation's home country. US companies fall close to the global average (12%), while South Korea (1%), India (2%), China (4%), and Japan (5%) have the fewest senior nonnative top executives.[15] This is actually less surprising than it seems. At the end of the day, almost all companies have an identifiable nationality. Coca-Cola is American, Daimler-Benz German, and Samsung Korean. How many companies have genuinely shed nationality? Michael Skapinker in the *Financial Times* could come up with only one: engineering giant ABB.[16]

The organizational culture necessary to make networks a success is egalitarian rather than hierarchical. While that may be congenial to executives from the United States, Canada, Australia, and Northwestern Europe, executives from Japan, South Korea, India, China, Nigeria, and Russia may feel more comfortable with clear lines of authority.

Intensive lateral communication between local business units at all levels of the network requires widespread proficiency in English, the only truly global language. But English proficiency varies dramatically across countries (Table 6.2). While in many countries that rate low on proficiency, the elite will speak English, the global network requires lateral

[15] Ghemawat, Pankaj and Herman Vantrappen (2015), "How Global Is Your C-Suite?" *MIT Sloan Management Review*, 56 (Summer), pp. 73–82.
[16] Skapinker, Michael (2016), "Companies Cannot Escape Nationalities and Borders," *Financial Times*, April 14, p. 10.

Table 6.2 English proficiency around the world in 2015

Very high	High	Moderate	Low	Very low
Sweden	Austria	Spain	Peru	Sri Lanka
Netherlands	Germany	Slovakia	Chile	Turkey
Denmark	Singapore	South Korea	France	Kazakhstan
Norway	Malaysia	Italy	Russia	Egypt
Finland	Argentina	Vietnam	Mexico	Iran
Slovenia	Belgium	Japan	Brazil	Colombia
Estonia	Czech Republic	Taiwan	UAE	Venezuela
Poland	Switzerland	Indonesia	Costa Rica	Thailand
	India	Hong Kong	Pakistan	Saudi Arabia
	Hungary	Ukraine	China	Cambodia

Source: http://www.ef.edu/epi/
Note: Native English-speaking countries are obviously not included. Within each proficiency category, countries are ranked from highest to lowest. Not all countries are included

communication also among lower levels of management, where proficiency is more in line with general proficiency in that country as a whole. In other words, you may be unintentionally excluding business units in parts of the world with low English proficiency from your company's lateral conversations. And even when everybody is able to converse in English, cross-cultural communication is fraught with misunderstanding, a topic that will be discussed in the next chapter.

Networks de-emphasize hierarchy. Pushed to its radical endpoint, internal hierarchy in a network yields to a Zappos-like *holacracy* where organizational founders bestow authority and decision making in self-organizing teams rather than in a management hierarchy. Yet there is pervasive evidence that organizations—biological, technical, and social systems—need hierarchy to survive. Indeed, Nobel Prize laureate Herbert Simon noted that hierarchy makes complexity possible.[17] Even in the flattest of networks, we can be confident that connections and company politics will be at least as important for securing company rewards as job performance.

---

[17] Pfeffer, Jeffrey (2013), "You're Still the Same: Why Theories of Power Hold Over Time and Across Contexts," *Academy of Management Perspectives*, 27 (4), pp. 269–280; for a compelling historical overview how since 6000 BC, increased complexity and increased hierarchy of communities moved in lockstep, see William H. McNeill's (1991) monumental work *The Rise of the West: A History of the Human Community*, Chicago, IL: University of Chicago Press, Chapters 2 and 3.

Finally, you might wonder how strong the normative-cultural glue is. In a study of corporate values of the FTSE 100 companies, three values crop up over and over again—integrity, respect, and innovation.[18] How do these values create employee attachment to one company over the other? Which company would ever claim *not* to espouse integrity, *not* to respect people, or *not* to want to innovate? Do you actually know your firm's core values?

A Look Ahead

To design the organization of tomorrow, consider what your structure will need:

- *Speed.* Cycle times are shorter and faster than ever before. Digital technology is a main driver. It is not about big eating small; it is about fast eating slow.
- *Economies of scale and scope.* With low-cost competitors, some from emerging economies like China, others from anywhere through digital channels, you must control costs more tightly than ever before.
- *Consistency.* Customers and competitors will point out brand inconsistencies across countries and channels, in terms of pricing, sourcing, labor, quality, service, government lobbying, handling of scandals, or anything else that matters to your constituents.
- *Collaboration.* Most firms lack the necessary expertise to compete in fluid conditions such as the Internet of Things. They need to move from "pipeline thinking"—ordering supplies, fashioning them into products, and then pushing them at customers—to a "gardener mindset"—maintaining an ecosystem which attracts and retains other firms and customers.[19]

---

[18] Kellaway, Lucy (2015), "Hands Up if You Can List What Your Company's Values Are," *Financial Times*, October 5, p. 12.

[19] *The Economist* (2015), "Does Deutschland Do Digital?" November 21, pp. 59–61.

What does that mean for the organizational model of the future? The network model excels in meeting the fourth dictate but its ability to meet the others is relatively untested. For many firms, the functional model may be the safest bet, provided adaptations are made, especially by managing the global brand with a top management team, which will be discussed in the next chapter. Adaptations are necessary since the functional model's proclivity toward top-down hierarchy and organizational boundaries do not mesh well with developments in the digital arena such as co-creation and the fluid collaboration demanded by the Internet of Things.

In response, companies like sporting goods retailer Decathlon and tire-maker Michelin are experimenting with smaller units, inspired by Isaac Getz's philosophy for "liberated" companies. While smaller units are more expensive to run, they are easier to manage and motivate. Getz maintained that what you get is greater "agility, creativity, innovation, engagement, and customer satisfaction."[20]

Other companies are starting to experiment with various "accelerators" to incubate new business ideas and work with other parties. Experience indicates that to be successful it is advantageous that the "accelerator" be physically and organizationally separated from the mother organization, whose culture is often hierarchical and relatively risk-averse. And importantly, locate the "accelerator" at a place popular among IT specialists and creative people. So, when Klöckner, a large independent distributor of steel, supplying the European and North American markets, set up its incubator for internal startups, it chose hip Berlin, far away from its headquarters in dour Duisburg.

Nestlé has established an "innovation output" in Silicon Valley as well as "digital acceleration teams" in 13 markets to help deepen relationships with consumers in the digital world and respond to their needs more quickly. The innovation outpost aims to enhance existing partnerships with the world's largest technology companies while seeking future partners among the thousands of small technology startups. Mark Brodeur, global head of digital-marketing innovation explained

---

[20] Carney, Brian M. and Isaac Getz (2016), *Freedom, Inc.*, New York: Argo-Navis; Hill, Andrew (2016), "Toppling Bureaucracy," *Financial Times*, April 15, p. 7.

Nestlé's thinking: "You can't underestimate the importance of having an external presence in high-innovation, rapid turnaround places like Silicon Valley. It's both energizing and humbling, and in a short time we've built invaluable relationships with many of the players setting the tempo."[21]

Managerial Takeaways

To determine the suitability of the current organizational structure, executives can follow the following approach using Table 6.1 as benchmark.

1. Identify which organizational model comes closest to your own (marketing) organization based on your overall qualitative insight.
2. Identify whether there is a fit between the organizational model and the conditions favoring its use as outlined in Table 6.1. If not, why is there a disconnect?
3. Assess whether your organization addresses the global brand paradox better or worse than the benchmark model. If there is a discrepancy, why?
4. Evaluate whether the benchmark weaknesses indicated for your ideal-type model apply to your organization as well. Or are you doing better or worse? On which aspects?
5. Rate your organization on the use of various control mechanisms using Tool 6.1. Compare the ranking of the three control mechanisms with your benchmark model. Focus especially on the #1 control mechanism.
6. Use this analysis to pinpoint aspects where your organization is found wanting. To help you locate elements for improvement, benchmark against your leading competitor and a successful new entrant (if applicable), by scoring them on the use of various control mechanisms (or hire a consultant to do this).
7. Develop a remedial action plan.

---

[21] Visser et al. (2015, p. 9).

8. To prepare for the future, consider smaller teams or add "accelerators" to your organization or invest in startups. Locate accelerators away from headquarters, preferably in places like Silicon Valley or other places where "geeks" want to live and where new (digital) developments take place.

7

Global Brand Management

If the organizational structure is the anatomy of the firm, the management processes are its physiology. Thus, effective global brand management is as integral to a multinational's success as its short-term capital management and long-term investment plan. Failure to do so inevitably leads to clotting, weakening, and mediocrity. Yet only 10% of companies believe they have the full complement of executional capabilities required to win overseas.[1] Global brands without effective management are truly vulnerable to globally integrated powerhouses and nimble local brands. The Dutch Philips Electronics' name-sake was managed on a country-by-country basis. When Japanese competitors entered world markets with a global strategy, Philips saw the threat but was too feeble to mount an effective response. Within a decade, it had lost market leadership to Sony and Panasonic, never to regain it.

To manage global brands effectively, companies need to take the process seriously and make it a strategic priority. They should (1) assign global brand responsibility and leadership; (2) develop a global brand

---

[1] Khanna, Disnesh et al. (2015), "The Globalization Capability Gap," The Boston Consulting Group.

© The Author(s) 2017
J.-B. Steenkamp, *Global Brand Strategy*,
DOI 10.1057/978-1-349-94994-6_7

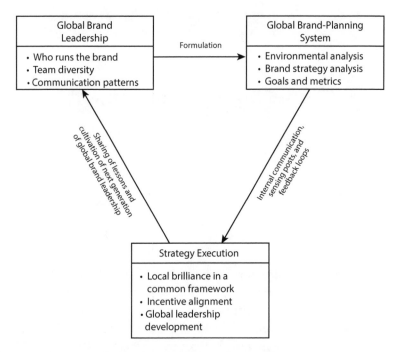

Fig. 7.1   Elements of effective global brand management

planning system; and (3) execute global brand strategies in local markets
within a common framework (Fig. 7.1).

Assign Global Brand Responsibility and Leadership

Managing global brands across countries sometimes creates chaos rather
than synergies. Why? Because local managers believe that their context is unique, their in-depth knowledge is irreplaceable, and consumer
insights, competitive analyses, and best practices from other markets
are largely irrelevant. To suggest otherwise is to threaten their position.
Moreover, many local managers think they make their mark by taking
their own actions rather than merely executing a strategy developed else-

where (often at headquarters). So how do you retain brand integrity *and* motivate local managers?[2]

Brand Management Team: The Least Disruptive Option

Consider creating a *brand management team*, consisting of country and/or regional managers and managers at corporate headquarters. The team shares best practices and uses the team as platform to negotiate local brand positioning between headquarters and country managers and among country managers. Those are the basic coordinating mechanisms. Teams work well in firms that organize by geography, have strong country managers, and traditionally tailor products to local market conditions. While the team approach gives the MNC maximum local responsiveness, negotiations take time and rollout of new products is slow.

Kimberly Clark, the owner of well-known brands like Huggies, Kleenex, and Kotex has manufacturing facilities in 38 countries and sells products in 175 countries. Its customer needs do differ across countries, and so it has organized along geographical lines. The company uses brand management teams whose primary role is to transfer and apply best practices; the teams have no line authority over regions or countries. A global brand director explained the rationale: "[O]ur major competitor globally is Procter & Gamble…and they tend to operate their brands much more globally than we do … We feel like they lose some effectiveness by doing [so], so they're just not quite as nimble at a local level, and so I think that's … part of the reason that drives our competitive advantage."[3] Yet the brand strength of P&G counterparts like Pampers and Always is higher than Huggies and Kotex.[4]

---

[2] The three options to manage a global brand were introduced by Aaker, David A. and Erich Joachimsthaler (1999), "The Lure of Global Branding," *Harvard Business Review*, vol. 77 (November–December), pp. 137–144.

[3] Matanda, Tandadzo, and Michael T. Ewing (2012), "The Process of Global Brand Strategy Development and Regional Implementation," *International Journal of Research in Marketing*, 29 (1), pp. 5–12.

[4] According to Brand Finance, in 2016 the brand strength of Pampers, Always, and Huggies was AAA-, AAA-, and AA+, respectively. Kotex was not even rated.

Brand Champion: The Ambitious Option

Consider appointing a *brand champion* responsible for building and managing a brand worldwide. This person monitors the consistency of the brand's positioning in international markets, has sign-off authority on all major brand strategy aspects, and authorizes brand extensions to other products and businesses. According to Saatchi and Saatchi's Vaughan Emsley, a successful brand champion has seniority, is committed and strong, and makes clear early on that he or she can and will provide leadership and makes tough decisions. Weak brand champions are harmonizers and peace makers.

The brand champion must be familiar with local contexts and local managers to weigh the validity of their requests for local adaptation. The champion can be a country manager or a senior manager at corporate headquarters. If the brand champion is the CEO, CMO, or VP marketing, this person has the organizational power to push through decisions. In other situations, their success will largely depend on personal credibility as a successful (past) manager of important brands. Brand champions do well in firms that organize by function (and so the champion could be a member of the C-suite) or by geography (where the champion's effectiveness derives from persuasive power rooted in personal credibility as successful brand manager).

Samsung implemented the brand champion model when it appointed Eric Kim as executive vice president and CMO in 1999. At the time, the Samsung brand lacked a unified, compelling customer proposition; it used 55 advertising agencies worldwide and 20 different slogans. Not surprisingly, the Samsung brand languished far behind industry leader Sony. Kim's assignment was to unify and strengthen the proposition so that the brand could rival Sony in brand value. Within five years, Kim accomplished his mission. Samsung's brand value increased from $5.2 billion in 2000 to $15 billion in 2005, the year it surpassed Sony on the Interbrand Top 100 list of most valuable global brands. The gap widened in subsequent years. In 2015, Samsung ranked seventh globally with a brand value of $45.3 billion, whereas Sony ranked

58th at a value of $7.7 billion, according to Interbrand.[5] Kim had the right stuff:

- Strong support of Samsung's chairman Kun Hee Lee and vice chairman Yun Jong Yong.
- Control over Samsung's above-the-line brand-building budget (40% of Samsung's worldwide advertising expenditure).
- Personal credibility in terms of rank, prestige—including a master's degree in engineering at UCLA and an MBA from Harvard Business School (important in an education-obsessed society)—and expert power grounded in the creation of a corporate global marketing operations unit.[6]

This shows that to be successful, a brand champion needs a strong mandate from the C-Suite, a large own budget, and personal credibility. If any of these is lacking, think twice before taking the job.

Top Management Team: The Best Option

For most MNCs, I think the best option is the third: a top management team (TMT). The TMT consists of powerful senior regional (or large-country) managers, with deep knowledge of local conditions and chaired by a member of the C-Suite (CMO, CEO, or VP Marketing). Since not even the veteran CMO will live and breathe the nuances of local markets, the MNC must rely on regional experts. Creating a TMT also increases the likelihood of local buy-in into global branding strategies: local managers typically rate the quality of decisions higher if they have some influence over the process.[7]

---

[5] I use Interbrand for the comparison because Millward Brown BrandZ does not go back to 2000.

[6] Quelch, John A. and Anna Harrington (2008), "Samsung Electronics Co.: Global Marketing Operations," Harvard Business School Case 9-504-051.

[7] Pfeffer, Jeffrey, Robert B. Cialdini, Benjamin Hanna, and Kathleen Knopoff (1998), "Faith in Supervision and the Self-enhancement Bias: Two Psychological Reasons Why Managers Don't Empower Workers," *Basic and Applied Social Psychology*, 20 (40, pp. 313–321; Pfeffer, Jeffrey (2013), "You're Still the Same: Why Theories of Power Hold Over Time and Across Contexts," *Academy of Management Perspectives*, 27 (4), pp. 269–280.

P&G reorganized itself in the early 2000s (Chapter, "Organizational Structures for Global Brands") into seven global business units (e.g., beauty care, fabric & home care), each of which was run by a TMT called Global Leadership Team (GLT). Each GLT comprises the business general managers from several regions, representatives from key functions such as R&D, consumer research, product supply, HR, and finance, and chaired by the president who directly reported to the CEO. The GLT is in frequent contact and meets formally a number of times per year. Its key responsibilities include:

- To define the brand identity and positioning for global brands in the category. Country brand and advertising managers are really implementers of strategy at P&G.
- To nurture local brand-building excellence that can become the basis of new global brands when possible.
- To manage product innovation by planning category-identifying technologies that can be used to build brands and determining which brands will get which technologies.[8]

This approach led to results. For example, P&G's premium skin care brand SK-II was an outcome of the beauty-care GLT.

When Is TMT Most Effective?

To get the most from your TMT, you need to meet several conditions. First, while the TMT is a deliberative body—members share and evaluate information—the team's chair must have ultimate responsibility for making decisions. Despite the best of intentions, "shared responsibility" is all too often "nobody's responsibility," a problem that plagues matrix organizations. As Stanford Professor Jeffrey Pfeffer put it, "Both internal and external agents want to be able to see 'who's in charge' to assign accountability."

---

[8] Aaker, David A. and Erich Joachimsthaler (2000), *Brand Leadership*, New York: Free Press.

Second, the TMT needs functional and gender diversity; it must consist of top managers with a background in different functional areas and gender. Empirical evidence shows that functional and gender diversity lead to better firm performance, measured as return on assets. As the brand is the ultimate compression of the firm's efforts to create value, be sure to factor in various value-adding activities, not just marketing.

Third, the TMT should have a diversity of nationalities. Leaders from neighboring large markets, even if they all have deep knowledge of markets on other continents, lack a diversity of thinking, feeling, and acting. The culture, institutional frameworks, and economic conditions of the country in which managers grew up have an enduring impact on their mindsets and their interpretation and response to strategic issues. As multinational teams strive to integrate and reconcile their diverse experiences, they discuss issues deeply, consider various alternatives, and generate new and creative ideas. As a result, nationally diverse TMTs solve complex tasks better and arrive at more innovative solutions than homogenous groups. Again, empirical evidence shows that nationality diversity in TMTs leads to better firm performance; and the more international the firm, the more important the diversity of the brand team. Firm internationalization intensifies managerial complexity and poses new challenges, such as information-processing, coordination, and governance. In terms of rapidly changing contexts, MNCs need the team's diverse experiences and cultural aptitudes to overcome difficulties inherent in competing everywhere in the world.[9]

Failure to embrace nationality diversity can have serious consequences. For example, the number of Japanese companies in the Fortune Global 500 fell from 81 in 2005 to 54 in 2015, the largest percentage decline among all large developed countries, and only four Japanese brands made the 2016 BrandZ Top 100 list of most valuable global brands. While there are multiple explanations, among them the rise of Chinese companies, national homogeneity in top management teams is a major factor. A survey of some 3400 major Japanese companies revealed that 99% of corporate boards lack a single foreign member, and the typical Japanese

---

[9] Nielsen, Bo Bernhard and Sabina Nielsen (2013), "Top Management Team National Diversity and Firm Performance: A Multilevel Study," *Strategic Management Journal*, 34, pp. 373–382.

executive has never held an international assignment. Such Japanese companies as Toyota are scrambling to shore up this weakness, but analysts wonder whether cultural change will come fast enough.[10]

The Culture Map: Comparing Teams Across Multiple National Cultures

Nationality diversity of TMT may come at cost for team dynamics. As culture heavily affects communication patterns and interaction styles, multinational TMTs may experience increased interpersonal tensions, less cohesion, and slower decision making. What we say, how we say it, and what we mean, is highly culture-dependent, regardless whether we communicate in English or in another language.

When Danish multinational pharmaceutical company Novo Nordisk purchased a new operation in Tokyo, Harald Madsen Senior VP Marketing found himself heading a group of Japanese marketing managers. He began his first meeting by telling his team, all younger than him, that he wanted them to feel comfortable challenging his ideas so that they could arrive at the best solution for their market. He presented a few ideas and asked for input. The response? Silence. What was the problem? In Japan, asking people for their opinion can feel confrontational. What if my ideas go against those of the others? Moreover, you certainly do not disagree openly with higher management, and you do not disagree with older people either.[11]

Many conversations in multicultural teams go awry because managers do not realize the extent to which communication is shaped by culture. To help managers decode cross-cultural communication challenges, INSEAD professor Erin Meyer has developed a tool called the Culture Map. It is made up of eight scales representing the management behavior where cultural gaps are most common. The eight scales are:

---

[10] *The Economist* (2010), "From Walkman to Hollow Men," November 6, p. 79; Iwatani, Naoyuki, Gordon Orr, and Brian Salsberg (2011), "Japan's Globalization Imperative," *McKinsey Quarterly*, June, pp. 1–11; Kubota, Yoko (2015), "In First, Toyota Taps Foreigner for Big Job," *Wall Street Journal*, March 5, p. B2.

[11] Meyer, Erin (2014), *The Culture Map*, New York: Public Affairs.

1. Communicating: low-context (precise, simple, explicit, and clear) vs. high-context (sophisticated, nuanced, and layered).
2. Evaluating: direct negative feedback (frank, blunt, and honest) vs. indirect negative feedback (subtle and diplomatic with negatives being wrapped in positives).
3. Persuading: principles-first (preference for beginning an argument or a report by building a theoretical argument before moving to the practical conclusion) vs. applications-first (discussions are approached in a practical concrete manner, avoiding theoretical or philosophical discussions).
4. Leading: egalitarian (the distance between the boss and a subordinate is low, the best boss is a facilitator) vs. hierarchical (large distance between the boss and a subordinate, the best boss is a strong leader).
5. Deciding: consensual (decisions are made in groups through preferably unanimous agreement) vs. top-down (decisions are made by individuals, usually the boss).
6. Trusting: task-based (trust is built through business-related activities which show that the manager does good work consistently) vs. relationship-based (trust is built through social activities and getting to know the manager personally).
7. Disagreeing: confrontational (disagreement and debate are positive for the team, open confrontation is appropriate and will not negatively impact the relationship) vs. avoid confrontation (disagreement is viewed negatively and open confrontation will break group harmony and harm work relationships).
8. Scheduling: linear (project steps are approached in a sequential fashion, sticking to the schedule is valued over flexibility) vs. flexible (project steps are approached in a fluid fashion, flexibility is valued over promptness).

The Appendix to this book provides the scores of many countries including the world's major economies on these dimensions. A question I have frequently encountered is whether stereotyping national cultures in this manner is useful. Aren't all people different? While this argument sounds valid, the human condition is less enlightened. Indeed, Erin Meyer argues that this view has kept countless managers from learning what they need to know to meet their objectives. If you go into every business meeting assuming that culture does not matter, your default mechanism will be to view others through your own cultural lens and to judge or misjudge accordingly. This is not ill will—it occurs largely unconscious. If your business success relies on your ability to work successfully with people from around the world, you need to have an appreciation for cultural differences as well as respect for individual differences.

I concur with Meyer. It is my experience that general cultural tendencies are usually remarkably accurate, especially when you ask people from other countries. For example, while many Dutch managers may not consider themselves to be particularly blunt or frank—this by itself is already a matter of perspective—(scale 2), wait till you hear what Americans, let alone Japanese have to say. One other example. Sometime ago, a prominent annual marketing conference was organized by a top Chinese university. The conference schedule was finalized a few weeks before the conference and underwent changes afterwards. The year thereafter, the Germans were in charge of the organization. Eleven months in advance, the schedule had been set to the minute, including that the bus would leave at 2:45pm on a specific day after the conference to transport the interested conference goers to Berlin for sightseeing (scale 8). You better not show up at 2:50pm because the bus will be gone.

Tool 7.1 helps you analyze the positioning of cultures relative to each other. By comparing the position of one nationality relative to another on each scale, the user can decode how culture influences collaboration. The tool will increase your effectiveness in managing your TMT as well as in dealing with overseas partners.

As an example, Tool 7.1 plots the culture scores of France and the United States.[12] What can we learn from these scores? You will notice that managers from both countries are comfortable with the boss making decisions as long as the team has input (scales 4 and 5). The French are more flexible with time (scale 8) and are less prone to wrap positive messages around the negative feedback (scale 2). But the largest differences occur on the other scales. French managers are trained to set a conceptual

[12] The interpretation of the differences is based on the interactive tool developed by Erin Meyer: http://erinmeyer.com/tools/interactive-culture-map-exhibit/; accessed March 18, 2016.

framework (scale 3), conduct a spirited debate (scale 7), and then come to the conclusion. The American tendency to jump right to the point, bypassing conceptual discussion, may seem lacking in necessary rigor to the French. Americans are simpler and more precise in their communication than the French (scale 1) and can trust their French colleagues without having socialized with them (scale 6).

So, what can be done to bridge these gaps? Being aware of them is a good start. But more can be done. Start the engagement with a social event, and reserve time for a dinner with (French!) wine. Build a fixed time for debate into your meeting agenda. During that time encourage the group to play devil's advocate and pull each other's ideas apart, and allow for broader, philosophical discussion. When the debate time is up, the decision gets made and the group moves on. When I discussed the French–US culture map in my executive MBA class, one of the managers said that he now understood why his French colleagues were always so argumentative. They were simply following the time-honored model taught in the French school system of thesis (building up one side of the argument), antithesis (building up the opposite side of the argument), and synthesis (coming to a conclusion).

Newly formed and truly diverse TMTs are vulnerable to inter-cultural communication gaffs. With time, they develop the trust and rapport of the bridge on the starship *Enterprise*. After spending time working together, they establish norms of interaction, reducing affective conflict and friction even in diverse teams. Moreover, diverse teams form a common identity over time. As a result, their effectiveness increases.

Global Brand-Planning System

Some years ago, I worked with a global CPG company on developing a strategy to counter the rise of its store brands' competitors in the UK, Germany, Spain, Italy, and France. As part of the strategy development, we organized fact-finding sessions with country managers. We discovered that country managers used their own vocabulary, their own surveys and metrics to collect consumer data, their own templates, and their own set of competitors to benchmark, sometimes including store brands and

The Culture Map Tool is designed to improve your effectiveness in managing cultural differences in international teams, and with overseas suppliers, customers, nongovernmental organizations, and government officials. It is made up of eight scales representing the management behavior where cultural gaps are most common. By comparing the position of one nationality relative to another on each scale, the executive can decode how cultural influences international collaboration. For this, follow the following four steps:

Step 1: Construct the Culture Map
Plot the positioning of two (or more) cultures relative to each other on the eight scales of the culture map. The Appendix to this book provides the location of all major economies on these dimensions. Here is an example involving the United States and France:

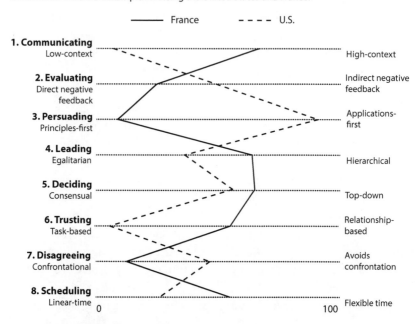

Step 2: Identify Areas of Common Ground
On which scales are the differences between countries minor? These scales provide a common ground from which to start the multi-cultural collaboration.

Step 3: Identify Flashpoints
Potential flashpoints are scales on which the differences between the countries is substantial.

Step 4: Develop Strategies
Develop strategies to deal with potential flashpoints. If unaddressed, painful situations are likely and may derail the international collaboration.

Tool 7.1   Culture map

sometimes not. No wonder the company's flagship brands were flailing on store shelves!

This absence of coherence is far from unique. Firms that come closest to practicing effective global brand management have implemented a global brand planning system specifying the same strategic analysis inputs, the same structure, and the same outputs across markets and products. The team (brand champion, or brand management team) should condense this information in a template, get input from local managers, and maintain it. While global brand-planning systems can take many forms, they should include a systematic analysis of the environment, a brand strategy analysis, and setting of goals and specification of quantifiable metrics (Fig. 7.1). In what follows I will outline key dimensions you should consider for each element.

Analysis of the Environment

The TMT should discuss and capture answers to the following questions:

Customer Analysis

- Segmentation: How should we segment the global marketplace? What is their relative size and geographical distribution across countries? What are the key global segments for our brand? How do we expect our target segment to evolve in size over the next few years?
- Trends: What are the trends in the marketplace? Which are opportunities or threats? How might we turn a threat into an opportunity? Do these trends signal new needs?
- Technology: How does the rise of digital affect customer behavior, especially in our target segments?
- How does the Internet of Things shape customer preferences? Can we move faster than competitors to make customers loyal to our brand?
- Account management: Do we see a shift toward global account management? By whom?

Competitors

- Current competitors: Who are the main global competitors? How do our core competencies stack up against theirs? Do they follow a globally integrated brand strategy? What are their strengths and weaknesses? Can we use their weaknesses to our advantage?
- New competitors: Do we see new competitors on the horizon? Do any local players have international ambitions? Should we try to fight them early on and how? What about purely digital players?
- Business models: Can we envisage a business model (e.g., based on the sharing economy) that could disrupt our business model and possibly turn the entire industry upside down? If so, should we introduce it ourselves?

Supply Chain

- Sourcing: How dependent are we on our suppliers? Are our suppliers consolidating? Do we have alternative sources of supply or can we develop them if necessary? Are new low-cost locations emerging?
- Outsourcing: Do we outsource more or less than our competitors? Why?
- Forward integration: Are there indications that our suppliers want to develop their own brands in direct competition with us?
- Backward integration: Do we see our competitors securing exclusive supply arrangements with suppliers? Does that threaten our sources of supply?

Brand Strategy Analysis

- Brand breadth: Are our brand's target segments growing or declining? For which regions/countries? Can we stretch the brand to cater to growing or emerging segments without diluting the brand's value proposition?
- Value proposition: Does our customer proposition still resonate with the market? Should we refresh it or even radically change it? If so, how and will it be believable?

- Innovation: Are we satisfied with the output of our R&D efforts? Do our new products reach their sales targets? Are we able to introduce genuinely new products that make life better for our customers? Do we leverage innovative ideas from different parts of the world?
- Advertising: Are we satisfied with the creativity and effectiveness of our advertising? Are we using digital advertising effectively? Do we have the right mix of online and offline advertising?
- Social media: Do we have a strategy in place to stimulate social media and leverage electronic word-of-mouth?
- Price arbitrage: Are customers or third parties arbitraging or parallel-importing our brand? What evidence? Between which countries?
- Digital channel: Do we use the digital channel effectively without creating conflict with physical channels? Do we use digital channels to reach hitherto unserved regions? How does our digital channel success compare to that of our competitors?
- Sales: Should we consider GAM? For which customers?
- Local input: Are there signals from local subsidiaries that lack of integration of our marketing mix program causes problems in major country markets? Or that high integration of our marketing mix program causes problems in major country markets?

Goals and Metrics

- Revenues: What are the sales, market share, and profit goals for our brand globally, for different regions, and for major countries? Have we met them? If not, what are the reasons?
- Pricing: What are the sales price goals for our brand globally, for different regions, and for major countries? Have we met them? If not, what are the reasons? Do our list prices differ significantly from our transaction prices? If so, does the size or the strategic importance of the accounts justify the difference?
- Loyalty: What goals are set for customer loyalty? How willing are they to pay a price premium for our brand?

- Electronic word-of-mouth: Do we have explicit goals for eWOM-volume and valence? Are they met? How does eWOM for our brands stack up against that for our competitors?
- Mindset metrics: What are the goals for brand awareness and customer perceptions of the brand?
- Equity: What are the goals for global brand value in dollars and in rank?

Strategy Execution

German Field Marshal Helmuth von Moltke ("Moltke the Elder") said that no battle plan survives contact with the enemy. While it will not be as extreme for brand plans, there is much truth to it. At the end of the day, any carefully developed global brand strategy disintegrates when poorly executed in local markets or against superior execution of competitors. To ensure and sustain effective execution, you need to put several elements in place—local brilliance within a common framework, alignment of incentives, and global talent development.

Local Brilliance Within a Common Framework

Any global strategy has many moving parts, from target segment and advertising to sales and distribution. Not only do you need to choose them; you need to figure out how they move together. We can trace a lot of confusion in execution back to lack of clarity over who decides on what within which parameters. In a global survey of senior executives, barely half thought that their companies communicated strategy clearly to the workforce in the markets where they operate.[13] As a consequence, some local managers adapt the marketing strategy less than they could, while others adapt it more than they should. Voilà, we have brand bumbling.

---

[13] Dewhurst, Marin, Jonathan Harris, and Suzanne Heywood (2012), "The Global Company's Challenge," *McKinsey Quarterly*, 3, pp. 76–80.

To minimize these problems, the TMT should agree on and socialize a decision matrix which indicates for each element of the global brand's marketing program whether it is:

- globally imperative—local managers can provide input during strategic planning but cannot change or adapt the component, once the TMT has determined its role;
- locally adaptable—local managers can adapt the component locally, within the limits set by the TMT; or
- locally discretionary—local managers can do whatever they want with the brand (Fig. 7.2).

When socialized and applied, the decision matrix as a shared tool actually frees people to shine locally. It is well-designed globally imperative constraints that lead to creativity in local execution by shaping and focusing problems and providing clear challenges to overcome. When she was a Google executive Marissa Mayer put it as follows, "creativity thrives best when constrained."

Aligning Incentives

The execution of many global strategies goes awry because board members or the C-suite agree to executive performance metrics and bonus systems that do not distinguish between local success and global success. In a survey among executives working for a variety of MNCs, 57% said that performance incentives were not aligned to deliver global strategy.[14] For example, one electronics manufacturer decided to enter the international market by introducing a new product through its strongest division. But it compensated that division head on worldwide sales. If he made his sales target, he got his bonus. So he drove sales through his strongest and most developed markets, primarily the home market. So even though the firm got the numbers it wanted, its international expansion failed. Worse, it didn't learn anything about global markets in the process. Let's hope it

---

[14] Khanna et al. (2015).

Brand Strategy Component	Globally Imperative	Locally Adaptable (indicate boundaries)	Locally Discretionary	Comments/ Exceptions
Brand name				
Logo, symbols				
Target segment				
Value proposition				
Physical product				
Advertising theme				
Adv. execution				
Digital strategy				
Pricing strategy				
Sales promotion				
Supply chain				
Distribution				
After-sales service				
CSR				
...				

Fig. 7.2 Global brand strategy coordination matrix

learned this valuable lesson: people will do what you ultimately reward them for doing, even if it's not what you asked them to do.

You need to set rewards, especially bonuses, to reinforce the company's global objectives and the desired and acceptable behavior. The ends never justify the means, like cheating on emissions technology, bribing local officials, or corporate social media abuse, maybe using consumer data without their permission, let alone their knowledge. An industrial controls business changed its compensation system to base a portion of incentive compensation for its managers on worldwide achievement. Indeed, firms should award country managers not just on their performance but on that of their region or the world. For example, Unilever's performance in Europe drives a large portion of the bonuses payable to Unilever's senior executives in Europe. Why should they care about brand performance outside Europe? For your global brand strategy to take off, your executives have to have skin in the global game, not just the regional or the local one.

Global Leadership Development

Just as great generals like Alexander the Great and Julius Caesar cut their teeth in the trenches, so too must our global brand leaders cut their teeth in local markets. Evidence indicates that companies often drop the ball here. A global survey among senior HR executives showed that fewer than one-third of the executives in global companies felt their organization had a strong leadership pipeline and less than 20% thought that corporate leadership was satisfied with their company's bench strength.[15] In other words, over 80% of current leaders do not see future leaders among the rank and file. Clearly, responsible global brand managers should devote more attention to developing global brand talent. In the same survey, over 90% of the global firms regard developing globally competent leaders as vital to the long-term success of their organization. But which types of global competencies do you need? How can your firm develop the necessary competencies? And whom should you select for global competency development?[16]

Which Type of Global Competencies Does Your Firm Need?

Social scientists have identified more than 160 competencies relevant for global leadership. Many of these competencies overlap conceptu-

---

[15] Human Capital Institute/UNC Kenan-Flagler Business School (2015), "Compete and Connect: Developing Globally Competent Leaders."

[16] Reiche, B. Sebastian (2015), "An Integrative Approach to Cross-Border Expansion: The Role of Global Leadership," working paper, IESE.

ally. Semantic differences aside, these are among the most BASIC global competencies:

- **B**rilliance in local execution, that is, a **B**ias for action, to meet or exceed one's targets in a variety of markets.
- **A**wareness of one's own prejudice—cultural, political, and legal assumptions, views, and attitudes—with an **A**bility to work with people from different ethnic, national, gender, and religious backgrounds.
- **S**ynthesis of globally imperative elements of the brand's strategy with locally adaptable/discretionary elements, combined with **S**ympathy for and identification with the global world and local differences.
- **I**ntegrity amid often dramatically different institutional environments, and **I**ndependence enough to walk away from unethical deals or local practices that violate international treaties, human rights, and environmental protocols.
- **C**ross-cultural and multilingual communication skills; the ability to make human **C**onnections with local and global stakeholders (suppliers, customers, non-governmental organizations, governments, and colleagues).

How Can the Firm Develop the Necessary Competencies?

According to one survey of senior executives, only 7% believe their organizations are effective in developing global leadership capabilities. In another global survey, the number one area for improvement was to develop leaders who are culturally and functionally proficient across regions.[17] International exposure to, even immersion in, other markets remains the best way.

International exposure can include studying at an overseas business school, short-term postings, global virtual teamwork, often combined with

---

[17] Ghemawat, Pankaj (2012), "Developing Global Leaders," *McKinsey Quarterly*, 3, pp. 100–109; Aquila, Kate et al. (2012), "Managing at Global Scale," report, McKinsey & Company.

international business travel, cross-border project work, task forces, and international volunteering assignments. Citigroup uses conference calls, web chats, and international projects, supported by talent management programs and mentoring relationships across geographies. GlaxoSmithKline launched an international volunteering program a few years ago, which entails sending around 100 employees annually for three to six months to NGOs in mostly emerging countries. Participating employees continue to receive their full salary and benefits. In addition to directly benefiting the NGOs involved and GSK's corporate social desirability image, the program has been found to help develop cultural competences such as cross-cultural awareness and empathy among GSK's employees.[18]

The strongest version of international exposure is regular multi-year rotations across geographies. Although this is costly—expats can cost two to three times what they would in an equivalent position back home—firms that really wish to prioritize global leadership development need to allocate the required resources to manager rotation. Schlumberger requires managers to rotate jobs every two to three years across business units and corporate functions. It expects that senior executives will spend 70% of their total careers working outside their home countries. A leading mining company requires its managers to have experience in at least two different geographic regions and two different economic environments (e.g., high and low growth) before they can move into senior-leadership roles.[19]

Cultural training and mentoring can also help building global competencies, especially if they accompany an individual's international assignment. Some firms use specialized agencies such as THT. THT ("Culture for Business") specializes in cultural training to help develop individuals to improve their intercultural competence and teams to improve their performance by connecting different points of view.[20] French tire giant Michelin is one company that uses customized cross-cultural training programs, including training on how to develop relationships cross-

---

[18] Human Capital Institute/UNC Kenan-Flagler Business School (2015).
[19] Dewhurst, Martin, Matthew Pettigrew, and Ramesh Srinivasan (2012), *McKinsey Quarterly*, 3, pp. 92–99.
[20] http://www2.thtconsulting.com; accessed March 16, 2016.

culturally and etiquette. For the executives as well as their families, it offers cultural awareness and language training programs.

Who Should You Select for Global Leadership Development?

Some training centers aim to develop transcultural leaders, people who can manage effectively anywhere in the world as soon as they step off the plane. One person who fits this description well is Carlos Ghosn, the French-Lebanese-Brazilian Chairman and CEO of France-based Renault, Japan-based Nissan, and the Renault-Nissan Alliance, and Chairman of Russia-based AvtoVAZ. There are few executives like him.

To better understand the cultural complexities of multiple identities, let us consider the concepts of national and global identity. A national identity means that the manager feels he or she belongs to a particular country and identifies with that country's ways of life, whereas a global identity means the manager feels he or she belongs to the global community, identifies with a global lifestyle, cares about constituents everywhere, and understands how global politics, ongoing conflict, health crises, and environmental crises impact global operations and economics and, ultimately, the viability of the global brand. Combining these two dimensions gives four possibilities shown in Tool 7.2.

Transculturals regard themselves first and foremost as members of the global community. They have only a weak identification (at best) with their home-country culture—possibly regarding it as old-fashioned or backward. At first sight, transculturals look ideal for global strategies. However, your organization likely has few of them. Indeed, scholars of cross-cultural management regard the idea of transcultural leadership as unrealistic.[21] The evidence is overwhelming that, unless they deliberately work at changing how they think, adults fall into the home-country cultural patterns of thinking developed in early childhood. Moreover, we still live in a world of differences. Transculturals may not necessarily score high on the BASIC dimensions of global competencies if they deny or underestimate the real differences between countries in many industries.

---

[21] Ghemawat (2012).

This tool is designed to classify managers on their local and global identity and to identify managers who are the best prospects for global leadership development. For this, take the following two steps:

Step 1: Collect Information
Collect information about a manager's local and global identity.

Instructions: Circle the response that most closely reflects your opinion. If you score another person, adapt the items to refer to manager X.

Statement	Response Options		
1. My heart belongs to my own country	(a) not really	(b) largely true	(c) strongly agree
2. I have deep respect for the traditions of my home country	(a) not really	(b) largely true	(c) strongly agree
3. I strongly identify with my home country	(a) not really	(b) largely true	(c) strongly agree
4. I care about knowing events that are going on in my home country	(a) not really	(b) largely true	(c) strongly agree
5. I typically spend my vacations in my home country	(a) not really	(b) largely true	(c) strongly agree
6. My heart belongs to the whole world	(a) not really	(b) largely true	(c) strongly agree
7. Even when I am not working, I enjoy being with people from other countries to learn about their unique views and approaches	(a) not really	(b) largely true	(c) strongly agree
8. I see myself as a global citizen	(a) not really	(b) largely true	(c) strongly agree
9. When traveling, I like to immerse myself in the culture of the people I am visiting	(a) not really	(b) largely true	(c) strongly agree
10. I believe people should be made more aware of how connected we are to the rest of the world	(a) not really	(b) largely true	(c) strongly agree

Step 2: Assign Manager to One of Four Cells
Assign -1 for each (a) answer, 0 for each (b) answer, and +1 for each (c) answer. To obtain scores for national and global identity on a scale from -1 to +1, average the scores on items 1-5 (national identity) and average the scores on items 6-10 (global identity). Use these scores to assign the person to one of the four cells.

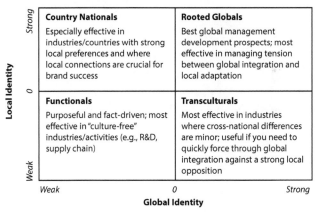

Tool 7.2 Assessing a manager's local and global identity

Rooted globals can navigate the global marketplace: they have affinity for other cultures and roots in their own culture. Unilever's Dutch CEO Paul Polman is an example—he studied in the Netherlands and in the USA, lived for protracted periods in other countries, and combines a deep understanding of global markets and commitment to worldwide sustainability with strong moral fiber grounded in Dutch Calvinist culture. An organization will have more rooted globals than transcultural managers, just as far more consumers embrace both the local and the global culture than only the global culture.[22] Rooted globals are especially suited for global management development programs. They understand the importance of local contexts and characteristics within a global context.

Country nationals strongly associate with their home country but not with the global world. One example is Huawei's founder Ren Zhengfei who said in a rare public appearance at the World Economic Forum in Davos in 2015, "We are a Chinese company. We definitely advocate for the Chinese Communist Party. We love our country. Having said that, we will not compromise the interests of other countries."[23] Country nationals likely have deep ties to the local community, ties especially valuable for MNCs in industries or countries where:

- local customer preferences are strong;
- local institutional networks and political connections matter, as they do in construction, extractive industries, utilities, and pharmaceuticals;
- government involvement in the marketplace is substantial, as in China, Vietnam, or Russia.

While this patriotism makes them effective managers at home, their relative lack of affinity with the global community renders them less attractive candidates for global development programs. A challenge is to ensure consistency between their local activities and the overall brand strategy. The global brand strategy coordination matrix can help to

[22] Steenkamp, Jan-Benedict E.M. and Martijn G. de Jong (2010), "A Global Investigation into the Constellation of Consumer Attitudes toward Global and Local Products," *Journal of Marketing*, 74 (November), pp. 18–40.

[23] http://www.ibtimes.com/huawei-founder-ren-zhengfei-dismisses-chinese-military-connec-tions-1791228; accessed March 16, 2016.

achieve this. Perhaps most challenging is that in a country like China, some country nationals may be more loyal to the Party than to your company, which vastly complicates your efforts to keeping trade secrets from Party members at your local and global competitors.

Finally, *functionals* identify strongly with neither their home country nor the global community. These managers are purpose- and fact-driven. You find them more often among tech firms and oil companies. You can deploy them fruitfully for the development of culture-free solutions— think about technology or some B2B industries, especially in R&D and product development.

Use Tool 7.2 to assess where your team (headquarters and local managers) stand on national and global identity. You can administer the questionnaire to managers and their bosses.[24] Completing this survey will take five minutes at most. Look for cases where the supervisor's assessment and the self-rating of a manager sharply deviate. This difference indicates a potential friction point that you may want to address.

Beware of the Similarity Principle

Don't forget to select managers for global competency development from outside the MNC's home country. That seems obvious but it is actually not standard company practice, especially in the most intensive forms of training, such as expatriation. Western MNCs largely send out people from their own country (or region) as expatriates.[25] Not only are they not grooming a nationally diverse cadre of future leaders, but they are signaling to locals, "Your career chances are not as bright as those of your Western colleagues." In the past, local high potentials in emerging markets may have had few alternatives. Nowadays, if you do not promote your gems in emerging markets, then big local firms will snap them up. Why be a second-class citizen in a Western company when you can take

---

[24] I use a relatively crude 3-point scale which sets a relatively high bar for agreeing with an item. I do this on purpose as the norm in many MNCs will be toward embracing not only the home country culture but also the global world. This gives rise to socially desirable responding, which is reduced by this asymmetric response scale.

[25] Sanchata, Mariko and Riva Gold (2013), "In Asia, Locals Hit Western Ceiling," *Wall Street Journal*, August 14, p. B6.

a front seat in a firm from your own country or region? In 2006, the top ten ideal employers for Chinese university students included only two Chinese companies and eight Western firms. In 2015, seven of the top ten were Chinese companies—Baidu (1), Alibaba (2), State Grid (5), Huawei (6), Industrial and Commercial Bank of China (7), Lenovo (9), and Bank of China (10). As one executive said, "Local competitors' brands are now stronger, and they can offer more senior roles."[26] With such a home-country bias, it is not surprising that many global companies say that retaining local talent is one of their top challenges.

Why do companies sometimes engage in such obviously ethnocentric behavior? The primary cause is the *similarity principle*. Most humans are simply more comfortable around people who look and sound similar to themselves. This principle is as old as life on this planet. It biases people to identify those who are similar to them and to extend more help to those who are like them. This bias is an almost automatic, unconscious response, and so the preference for similar others influences actions and choices even in unlikely circumstances. This principle applies with equal force in business contexts. According to consultancies and executive search firms, "Leaders tend to promote people in their own image and culture, perpetuating a cycle of white, male bosses."[27]

But, for more complex life to form, atoms needed both positive and negative charges. So underneath the similarity principle is the attraction of opposites: they need each other to remain stable. We need leaders who see others as members of the same species that needs all types.

Managerial Takeaways

Effective global brand management processes can substitute to some extent for organizational inadequacies. The converse is also true. Bad management can kill a good strategy and enfeeble an appropriate organizational structure. So, what should you do? Here are guidelines.

---

[26] http://cn-en.kantar.com/business/brands/2015/2015-ideal-employer-survey/, accessed December 15, 2015.
[27] Sanchata and Gold (2013).

Global Brand Leadership

- Assign clear global brand responsibility and leadership. A TMT is the preferred option, the brand champion is second best, and the brand management team third, although it may be the only feasible option for organizations with very decentralized structures.
- Ensure functional, ethnic, gender, and nationality diversity in your TMT.
- Expect initial cross-cultural communication challenges in diverse teams and watch for steadily increasing effectiveness of such teams over time. Use Tool 7.1 to accelerate this process.

Global Brand-Planning System

- Develop common brand planning templates.
- Assign the TMT or brand champion responsibility for managing, maintaining, and socializing use of the template.
- Structure the global brand planning template around three components—environmental analysis, brand strategy analysis, and goals and metrics.
- Conduct the analysis around a number of questions, and use the results as entries in the template.

Strategy Execution

- Facilitate local execution within the global, common framework using the global brand strategy coordination matrix.
- Align incentives for local managers with the global strategy. Reward local managers on both local accomplishments and contributions to meeting regional and global goals.
- To ensure great global brand management now and in the future, make sure to develop the next generation of global brand executives. Despite all good intentions, by their own admission, many companies fall short in this respect. What should you do?

- Identify and define global competencies that your company and your brands need. Use the BASIC framework to define those needs.
- Start or maintain a program to develop these BASIC competencies. Consider multi-year rotations in foreign countries, and require managerial candidates to work abroad before moving into senior executive roles.
- Select rooted globals who have proven themselves effective in executing brand strategies in their home country.
- Fight the similarity principle; give every high potential rooted global has an equal chance to participate in global brand management development.

8

Corporate Social Responsibility

Public opinion of the roles of companies in society has shifted dramatically in recent decades. Producing high-quality goods and services is no longer enough. Constituents expect corporations to address environmental and social problems linked to whatever they sell and however they conduct business. Corporate social responsibility (CSR) refers to voluntary actions—that is, actions not required by law—that attempt to further some social good, counter some social ill, or address the externalities of their operating in the world. The voluntary nature of CSR means that these activities can be viewed, broadly, as gifts to the community.

CSR as a corporate function has gone from a nominal commitment to a strategic necessity. Stakeholders no longer view these activities as a gift but as the neighborly thing to do in our global community. Increasingly, CSR is seen as a license a firm needs to be allowed to operate in society at all. Some go even further and see CSR as just compensation for the negative externalities associated with the economic transactions. Brands have an impact on people and the planet. A survey among 2500 executives from 113 countries revealed that the number of companies that have CSR as a top management agenda item jumped from 46% in 2010 to 65% in 2014, while the number of companies without a CSR policy

Table 8.1 CSR reputation and stakeholder support

	Firm CSR reputation		
Stakeholder metric	Poor (%)	Average (%)	Excellent (%)
Would buy products	9[a]	35	84
Would say something positive	8	30	83
Would trust to do the right thing	8	27	77
Would welcome into the local community	9	31	78
Would work for	11	31	73
Would invest in	7	24	67

Source: Adapted from 2016 Global CSR RepTrak100, based on 187,877 interviews in the world's 15 largest economies
[a]To be read: 9% of the respondents who rated the company's CSR reputation as poor said they would buy products from that company

declined from 42% to 23%, and for good reason.[1] A company's reputation for taking social responsibility drives stakeholder support (Table 8.1). Yet, in the same survey, only 10% of the executives thought their company was doing enough about social and environmental matters.

Most firms attempt to do "good" (societal contributions) and to do "well" (business value). Firms direct their array of CSR activities at diverse stakeholders, including legislators, local communities, nongovernmental organizations (NGOs), consumer activists, potential and current employees, the press, the investment community, and customers. Table 8.2 provides the ten companies with the best CSR reputation among the various stakeholders in the world.

In this chapter I focus on particular group of stakeholders—customers—the individuals and organizations that buy their goods and services for households, other corporations, and government and not-for-profit institutions. A corporation's global brands represent its various relationships with these customer groups. Customers increasingly expect the brand to behave responsibly. Companies are keenly aware of this because customer sentiment affects brand sales and ultimately, share price. In the aforementioned global survey, 78% of the executives indicated that

[1] Kiron, David, et al. (2015), "Joining Forces: Collaboration and Leadership for Sustainability," *MIT Sloan Management Review* & Boston Consulting Group.

Table 8.2 Companies with the best CSR reputation in the world

Company	Rank 2016	Rank 2011
Rolex	1	(not reported)
The Walt Disney Company	2	3
Google (Alphabet)	3	1
BMW Group	4	4
Daimler (Mercedes-Benz)	5	7
Lego	6	5
Microsoft	7	11
Canon	8	8
Sony	9	6
Apple	10	2

Source: Adapted from Global CSR RepTrak100

reputation and brand building are important reasons to do right by local communities, because these communities hold globally visible brands to higher ethical standards than local brands.[2]

Despite all CSR buzz, executives do not always understand its role in global brand building. Imbuing a global brand with positive social associations can be more complicated than simply operating responsibly in the world. Firms must understand the multiple facets of CSR, how to operationalize CSR in the brand's customer proposition, and how to leverage these associations to influence customer behavior. I will address these issues in this chapter.

A Framework for CSR Branding

Figure 8.1 presents a framework for CSR branding. It starts with the MNC's CSR activities. It is a strategic decision whether or not to associate the global brand with social responsibility. Executives need to search their souls—how committed are you really to operating responsibly? Do the firm's organizational structure and global brand management systems allow you to take social responsibility for your actions consis-

[2] Kiron et al. (2015); Holt, Douglas B., John A. Quelch, and Earl L. Taylor (2004), "How Global Brands Compete," *Harvard Business Review*, 82 (September), pp. 68–75.

tently around the world? Digital media will otherwise quickly expose inconsistent CSR. Once a firm has established its ability to act conscientiously, it needs to communicate what it is doing to the brand's target segment. Success of CSR branding critically depends on customer awareness (Do customers know about it?) and customers' attributions to the brand's motives (Do customers think the efforts are self-serving or other-serving?).

Customer response to CSR branding can be transactional (purchases) and relational (attachment and loyalty). Transactional outcomes matter to the short term bottom line, but the real value of CSR branding comes from its contribution to the brand's reputational capital over time. Let's look at the process through which CSR activities influence customer behavior (Fig. 8.1).

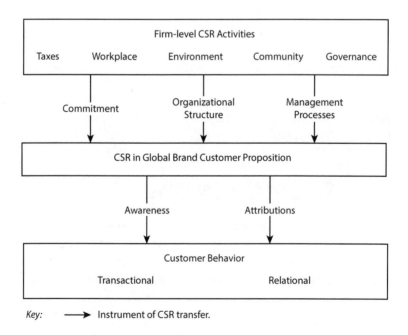

Fig. 8.1 Framework for CSR branding

CSR Activities

CSR has different meanings for different people and stakeholders. To structure the myriad of CSR activities, I distinguish between five domains of CSR activity: taxes, workplace, environment, community, and governance.

Taxes

Paying taxes is perhaps the biggest elephant in the room when executives sit down to discuss their firm's social responsibility. If you Google the phrase, "corporate tax dodger," you will get various sites such as Citizens for Tax Justice and Americans for Tax Fairness that track and report on corporate tax policies and practices. Among the more upsetting practices, they say, is the sheltering of profits in off-shore tax havens: members of the Fortune 500 simply declare that they will permanently reinvest profits in their overseas markets rather than repatriate and pay taxes on billions of dollars of income in their countries of origin. These groups argue that companies are not paying their fair share to support the very legal frameworks and social and economic institutions that foster innovation, protect intellectual property, and support entrepreneurial risk.

Not surprisingly therefore, an increasingly important aspect of CSR is that a company pays its share in local and national taxes. Executives do make choices regarding the extent to which their firms engage in moving investments through offshore financial hubs, relocating operations to low-tax countries, lobbying against any legislative measure that eliminates existing corporate tax loopholes, and tax planning that reduces the amount of taxes actually paid.

As governments around the world tighten their budgets and impose austerity on their citizens, these citizens are paying more attention to corporate tax avoidance. Aggressive tax avoidance can lead to serious reputational damage. Take Starbucks, well-known for its commitment to fair trade practices and green development. Its aggressive tax avoidance has started to hurt the company. Its highly successful British subsidiary ran persistent losses, while making large operating profits. How is that possible? Because it was "required" to pay high royalties to the (low-tax) Dutch subsidiary. The public started to take offense. Polls by YouGov found that a third less people rated Starbucks as their preferred coffee shop than they did before the tax-avoidance allegations came to light. To repair its brand reputation, Starbucks transferred its European headquarters from Amsterdam to London in 2014.[3] Starbucks is not alone. Other companies that have been accused of evading taxes include such famous brand names as Apple, Boeing, Microsoft, Facebook, FedEx, Fiat, Google, Honeywell, and Pfizer among others.[4]

There are signs that big investors are becoming more sensitive to the risks of aggressive tax planning at the companies they invest in. They are rightly concerned that the financial advantages of tax avoidance are not sustainable and lead to reputational and commercial risks with customers, governments, and regulators. Leon Kamhi at Hermes Investment Management, one of the largest institutional asset managers in the United Kingdom, explained, "Our stance is quite straightforward—we want companies to pay an appropriate level of tax. The normal person on the street sees [excessive tax avoidance] as an issue and there is an increasing consumer backlash."[5]

So do firms include paying their fair share of the tax lawfully collected in whichever country they are operating as part of CSR or do they try to separate it? The evidence is mixed. One study among Australian companies showed that corporations that scored high on CSR exhibited a lower level of corporate tax aggressiveness (i.e., paid on average a higher tax rate). However, a study among US companies found the opposite. Firms in the top 25% of CSR scores pay 1.7 percentage points less (as percent-

[3] *The Economist* (2015), "Starbucks in Britain: A Loss-Making Machine," February 14.
[4] Barker, Alex (2014), "Brussels in Crackdown on 'Double Irish' Tax Loophole," *Financial Times*, October 9; http://www.politicususa.com/2016/01/29/bernie-sanders-terrifies-wall-street-exposing-top-10-corporate-tax-dodgers.html; accessed March 30, 2016.
[5] Marriage, Madison (2014), "Aggressive Tax Avoidance Troubles Large Investors," *Financial Times*, November 9.

age of pretax income) in taxes than other firms and are more than twice as likely to lobby on tax.[6]

Workplace

If taxes are the African elephant in the room, then treatment of workers is the Asian elephant. Workplace conditions include paying fair wages, setting reasonable working hours, offering health benefits, seeking and supporting diversity, providing equal opportunities, and protecting employees from physical harm and sexual harassment. It also involves culture: corporate leadership has a responsibility to foster a culture of inclusion and respect for individual differences. If the firm does not succeed, the consequences can be severe. For example, in 2013, Bank of America and its Merrill Lynch unit settled a sex discrimination class action with female brokers for $39 million and agreed to pay another $160 million for discriminating against African-American brokers, the largest class-action settlement ever in a race-bias case.[7]

Google rates highly on workplace conditions. The company's compensation strategy includes high salaries and various incentives and benefits, such as free meals and flexible workflows. Google's facilities are also fun workplaces where workers can exercise, play games, and enjoy sharing ideas with each other. The company indirectly addresses the working conditions of its suppliers' employees through the Google Supplier Code of Conduct, which addresses employment practices and occupational health and safety.[8]

Workplace conditions extend to the supply chain, even though an MNC has limited control over its network of suppliers, potentially

---

[6] Lanis, Roman and Grant Richardson (2012), "Corporate Social Responsibility and Tax Aggressiveness: An Empirical Analysis," *Journal of Accounting and Public Policy*, 31, pp. 86–108; Davis, Angela et al. (2016), "Do Socially Responsible Firms Pay More Taxes?" *The Accounting Review*, 91 (1), pp. 47–68

[7] https://www.propublica.org/article/the-impact-and-echoes-of-the-wal-mart-discrimination-case; accessed March 17, 2016.

[8] Meyer, Pauline (2015), "Google Stakeholders & Corporate Social Responsibility (CSR)," August 22, Panmore Institute; http://panmore.com/google-stakeholders-corporate-social-responsibility-csr-analysis; accessed August 23, 2016.

located in distant countries with different cultures. For the last 20 years, Nike has been dogged by accusations of bad labor conditions in its supply chain. Reports of slave wages, child labor, and forced overtime in Pakistan and Bangladesh have given new meaning to "Just Do It." Apple and Samsung faced similar criticism of unacceptable labor practices in their Chinese suppliers and of unacceptable sourcing practices in their African suppliers of minerals like tantalum and tungsten, mined under horrible conditions from sites controlled by violent African militias.[9]

What constitutes acceptable workplace conditions differs across countries. Nike asserts that it commonly pays double the minimum wage in host countries, but the low absolute wage still strikes many Westerners as exploitive. China's labor laws allowed IKEA to require the workers at its Chinese suppliers to work a maximum 60 hour per week, high by Western standards. In 2015, IKEA reduced the limit to 49 hours including overtime, while maintaining wage levels.

Environment

Extreme weather events and the political instability sparked by the effects of global warming have put production waste, consumption waste, and environmental degradation at the top of many CSR discussions. IKEA has promised to go "all-in to tackle climate change."[10] By 2020, it intends to be 100% renewable. It has plans to use wind farms, solar panels, and biomass generators to produce as much energy it consumes in its operations.

Firms whose operations harm the environment are more likely to lose the public-relations fight against NGOs. In 2010, Greenpeace launched a social media attack on Nestlé's Kit Kat brand. In a YouTube video parodying the "Have a Break; Have a Kit Kat" slogan, it highlighted the use of unsustainable forest clearing in production of palm oil used in Nestlé's products including Kit Kat. The video went viral. Nestlé's responded by

[9] Banjo, Shelley (2014), "Inside Nike's Struggle to Balance Cost and Worker Safety in Bangladesh," *Wall Street Journal*, April 22, p. A1; Bradshaw, Tim (2014), "Apple in Supply-Chain Purge at Africa Mines," *Financial Times*, February 14, p. 17; Mundy, Simon (2014), "Samsung Hit by New Claims of a Supplier Using Child Labour," *Financial Times*, July 11, p. 18.

[10] IKEA Group Sustainability Report (2015), http://www.ikea.com/ms/en_US/img/ad_content/2015_IKEA_sustainability_report.pdf; accessed March 18, 2016.

forcing the video's withdrawal from YouTube, citing copyright infringement. This led to a viral outbreak of criticism on social media—Facebook users, for example, were irritated by its threats to remove posts on its fan page containing Kit Kat logos that had been altered to read "Killer". The antipathy soon gained expression in mainstream media around the world, and the threat of reputational damage was real. Nestlé threw the towel into the ring, suspended its relationship with its palm oil supplier and worked with The Forest Trust to audit its suppliers and establish "responsible sourcing guidelines."[11]

Community

MNCs, if only by their very size, have always had an outsized impact on the national and local communities in which they operate. Numerous MNCs give back to local communities not just by hiring locally, sourcing locally, and paying taxes locally but also through policies of social contribution, community participation, culture sponsorship, support of employees' volunteer activities, and education. SABMiller, for example, is engaged in teaching basic business skills to 500,000 small enterprises, mostly shops which sell its beer, in helping farmers use water more efficiently, and in sponsoring anti-drunkenness and road-safety campaigns aimed at its own customers.[12]

Pharmaceutical giant Pfizer and its peers still have much work to do. For example, on its home page, Pfizer claims to be "working to improve the health of people around the world through access to medicines."[13] Yet, in the United States for example, 73% of all Americans said the price of prescription drugs is "unreasonable," and 76% blamed drug companies for setting prices too high, according to a 2015 Kaiser Health Tracking Poll.[14] Several states have introduced ballot initiatives to require phar-

---

[11] *The Economist* (2013), "Less Guff, More Puff," May 18; http://www.ft.com/intl/cms/s/0/90dbff8a-3aea-11e2-b3f0-00144feabdc0.html#axzz42qKIJsgu; accessed March 18, 2016.

[12] *The Economist* (2014), "A New Green Wave," August 30, p. 63.

[13] http://www.pfizer.com/responsibility/workplace_responsibility/human_rights_statement; accessed 14 March 2016.

[14] http://kff.org/health-costs/poll-finding/kaiser-health-tracking-poll-june-2015/; accessed March 4 2016.

maceutical firms to justify the high prices. Pfizer and its rival Johnson & Johnson have contributed almost $6 million each to defeat such a transparency initiative in California.

In 2016, the State of North Carolina adopted the Public Facilities Privacy & Security Act ("the bathroom bill") regulating single-sex multiple occupancy bathroom and changing facilities in schools and public agencies. Opponents described it as the most anti-LGBT legislation in the United States. In protest, PayPal canceled its plan to open a new global operations center in Charlotte, NC. Dan Schulman, PayPal's CEO explained PayPal's community involvement, "[These] principles of fairness, inclusion and equality are at the heart of everything we seek to achieve and stand for as a company. And they compel us to take action to oppose discrimination."[15] Laudable words, but Schulman did not mention that PayPal's international headquarters are based in Singapore, where homosexual acts—even those done privately—are punishable by up to two years in jail. And PayPal's values didn't keep the company from opening and maintaining a global operations center in Malaysia, where homosexual acts are punishable by public lashings and jail sentences up to 20 years. There may be more than a hint of hypocrisy here. Take a stand when it gives you good publicity, do not take a stand when it is bad for business.

Governance

Good corporate governance is the capstone of various CSR efforts. It involves balancing the interests of various stakeholders in a company within the context of broader ethical considerations. Good governance requires the firm to square shareholder goals with the need to reduce externalities that impact other stakeholders. Corporations are expected to be attuned to public, environmental, and social needs.

Executive pay has emerged as an increasingly important governance issue in recent years. Fifty years ago, the typical US chief executive made $20 for every dollar a worker made; now, that gap is more than $300 to

---

[15] https://www.paypal.com/stories/us/paypal-withdraws-plan-for-charlotte-expansion;   accessed June 11, 2016.

$1. Put in real dollars, the average CEO at an S&P 500 company makes about $12 million a year to the average employee's $36,000.[16] The US Securities and Exchange Commission adopted a rule in August 2015 that requires a public company to disclose the ratio of the compensation of its CEO to the median compensation of its employees. There are also initiatives to pass laws to limit executive compensation in several US states, as well as some other countries such as Switzerland.

Stakeholders are starting to take note. In a series of online experiments, researchers found people were much more willing to buy a range of products, like towels and televisions, from companies that pay their CEOs salaries closer to what they pay their average employees.[17]

There is also pushback from the investment community. When supermarket giants Royal Ahold and Delhaize decided to merge in 2015, part of the deal was a large bonus—equal to a full-year salary—for their top executives. This created a barrage of criticism by investors and the proposal was withdrawn. In April 2016, a 20% pay rise for BP's CEO Bob Dudley was rejected by an unprecedented 59% of the shareholder votes cast. One top 20 investor said: "There is growing feeling that the quantum is too much for some chief executives, particularly when you factor in that Mr. Dudley is earning more than 100 times the average pay of employees."[18]

Today executives—agents of corporate owners—must not only prove themselves trustworthy stewards of corporate brand value but also treat employees, customers, communities, and the planet similarly, if not equal, to investors. Stakeholders expect corporations to establish governance mechanisms and processes that ensure transparency and accountability, engage all stakeholders and reconcile their interests, and minimize externalities. Such mechanisms include contracts, codes of conduct, CSR

---

[16] https://www.washingtonpost.com/news/on-leadership/wp/2015/08/04/this-new-rule-could-reveal-the-huge-gap-between-ceo-pay-and-worker-pay/;   https://hbr.org/2014/09/ceos-get-paid-too-much-according-to-pretty-much-everyone-in-the-world/; both accessed March 30, 2016.

[17] http://www.pbs.org/newshour/making-sense/high-ceo-pay-push-consumers-away/;   accessed March 30, 2016.

[18] Oakley, David and Kiran Stacey (2016), "BP Faces Revolt over Chief's 20% Pay Rise," *Financial Times*, April 8, p. 14.

board-level committees, non-financial reporting practices, and channels for stakeholder dialogue including whistleblowing.[19]

Integrating CSR into the Brand Proposition

The company can decide to treat CSR as a purely corporate activity. It may regard CSR as necessary to remain in the good graces of the authorities, to ward off attacks by NGOs, and to be eligible as investment by funds that have a CSR mandate—such as Parnassus Fund, TIAA-CREF Social Choice Equity Fund, and Allianz Global Sustainability Fund.

The firm can also take a bolder approach and integrate CSR into the global brand's customer proposition. A minority of brands such as The Body Shop, Ben & Jerry's, or supermarket chain Whole Foods are what we might call "CSR natives," brands born of the CSR movement. The essence of their customer proposition is the corporation's commitment to behave responsibly in social, economic, and environment terms. Another CSR native is Israel-based Netafim, a B2B brand that identified the lack of corporate responsibility as a business opportunity. Water is a scarce resource in large parts of the world, and agriculture wastes much of it. In response, Netafim developed drip irrigation, on orders of magnitude more efficient than flood or sprinkle irrigation. It is the world's largest drip irrigation company: it sells its innovative solutions to more than 110 countries. To educate small farmers in emerging markets, Netafim works with government partners, NGOs, and financing organizations such as the World Bank.

But most brands are not CSR natives. Their raison d'être is not to do "good" but to do "well." Yet, they can be strengthened by integrating CSR into their customer proposition. The rest of this chapter deals with how to do that. Rather surprisingly, many MNCs do not appear to have a well thought-out strategy how to use CSR initiatives to augment the global brand. Said one senior executive of a UK-based global distributor of safety clothing and equipment, "[B]randing is not a feature that

---

[19] Gill, Amiram (2008), "Corporate Governance as Social Responsibility: A Research Agenda," *Berkeley Journal of International Law*, 26 (2), pp. 452–478.

will be considered by the CSR committee.... We just accept if we've got enough [CSR activity,] it will benefit the brand."[20] This firm hopes that the positive effects of firm-level CSR will trickle down to the brand. If the link between MNC and brand is obvious to customers (e.g., when they bear the same name, such as Apple), perhaps goodwill will trickle. Perhaps it won't. But if it doesn't, why bother? That's the whole point. The firm's most effective socially responsible efforts are those that do good *and* become associated with the brand in the minds of constituents. Firms should select a socially responsible element to integrate into the global brand's value proposition. Before you choose one, answer the following questions:

- *CSR commitment*: Is acting with social responsibility truly integral to our corporate strategy? Do we want to engage in CSR initiatives beyond doing right by our community, even if those initiatives do not increase return on investment and shareholder value? Or do we talk the talk but not really walk the walk?
- *CSR delivery*: Are we able to operate responsibly around the world? That is, will we be able to coordinate activities across different countries, target segments, supply chains, and distribution channels? CSR initiatives can cost real money. If profit & loss is a local responsibility, how do you accommodate these efforts? Global CSR favors the global functional organization, and strong, effective global brand management at the highest level, using a top management team or a brand champion.

The answer to both questions should be an unambiguous *yes* if your firm wants to incorporate CSR elements into your brand's customer proposition. The specific social initiatives chosen (e.g., finding more sustainable means of production in countries that do not require it) may vary across countries as societal needs and aspirations are hardly uniform but all these local activities must fit under the comprehensive global promise to operate with a social conscience.

---

[20] Lindgreen, Adam et al. (2012), "Corporate Social Responsibility Brand Leadership: A Multiple Case Study," *European Journal of Marketing*, 46 (7/8), pp. 965–993.

Which CSR Aspect to Include in the Customer Proposition?

Once you have decided to include CSR in your brand's value proposition, you must determine which CSR aspect to associate with the brand. Executives can use the following criteria to select the CSR aspect:

- What would be most relevant to the global target segment? For example, Unilever's global research found that only 2% of women considered themselves beautiful. In response, its personal care brand Dove chose to fight distorted views of female beauty.
- What would fit best with our product category that would increase our credibility and minimize the likelihood that stakeholders view our efforts as a PR stunt? Luxury watch brand Omega supports Orbis International's Flying Eye Hospital. Participants in my Executive MBA class unanimously thought this was PR pure and simple.
- What would distinguish us from competing brands? Early movers have an advantage in claiming a social cause or changing policies or practices for social good. Dove's positioning and its use of real women who do not look like Gisele Bündchen or Penelope Cruz has set itself apart in its industry.
- Could we summarize it in a single, memorable tag line? Warby Parker, a US-based brand of prescription eye- and sunglasses, developed an innovative program, where for every pair of glasses a customer bought, Warby Parker donates a pair to people in need, mostly in developing countries. It communicates this program with the tagline "Buy a Pair, Give a Pair".
- Could we quantify its societal impact? For instance, since the program was initiated, Warby Parker has distributed over a million pairs of glasses to people in need.

Customer propositions that effectively leverage CSR should at a minimum aim to address the first three questions. The last two are "great to have"—they help in making communicating the CSR aspect of the value proposition easier.

Communicating CSR to Customers

To have any effect on customer attitudes and behavior toward your brand, you need to communicate your CSR initiatives as you would any other aspect of your brand's proposition. Low customer awareness and skepticism are the two communications challenges. Your communication strategy needs not only to raise customers' awareness but also to convince skeptics your motives are genuine.

Awareness

MNCs communicate their CSR activities through voluntary annual corporate responsibility reports, press releases, and brand websites. While these channels may create awareness of NGOs, investors, and legislators, they do not reach customers as advertising does. For example, Unilever promoted Dove's "Real Beauty" with print advertisements, billboards, and TV ads. Yet, Dove is an exception. Research shows that customers are generally unaware of most brands' CSR initiatives.[21] What can the brand team do to increase awareness of your efforts beyond spending more on mass-media advertising? Here are three cost-effective ways.

Packaging

Too few brands use their packaging—especially important at the point of purchase—as medium to communicate their promise to society. A Nielsen study of 1319 local and global brands in 13 consumer product goods categories revealed that only 21% of the brands communicated their efforts on their product's label or packaging. On average, the package-savvy brands experienced year-on-year sales growth of 4.5%

---

[21] Du, Shuili, C.B. Bhattacharya, and Sankar Sen (2007), "Reaping Relational Rewards from Corporate Social Responsibility: The Role of Competitive Positioning," *International Journal of Research in Marketing*, 24 (3), pp. 224–241.

Table 8.3 Use of on-pack CSR claims in 13 consumer packaged goods categories

Consumables	On-pack CSR claims (%)	Non-consumables	On-pack CSR claims (%)
Water	48	Laundry detergent	18
Tea	74	Household cleaner	13
Coffee	79	Paper towels	8
Soft drinks	0	Bath tissue	19
Snacks	61	Diapers	23
Cookies	17		
Breakfast cereal	49		
Baby food	88		

Source: Adapted from Nielsen (2015)
Note: Percentage refers to percentage of category dollar sales that is sold by brands using on-pack CSR claims

compared with 4.1% growth of those that did not use their packaging to spread the word.[22]

The low overall usage of on-pack communication hides large differences between product categories. Table 8.3 compares on-pack use by product category. In general, on-pack claims are much less prevalent among nonconsumables than on consumables (i.e., food stuffs). This is puzzling. First, most are low-involvement goods: customers consider product information primarily at the point of purchase. Second, many nonconsumables have significant externalities (e.g., environmental impact). More nonconsumable brands should be exploring the use of on-pack CSR claims.

Social Media

We have seen the impact of electronic word of mouth (eWOM). People are more likely to talk about CSR than about any other aspect of the global brand if it has broad societal relevance and because the heaviest users of social media (Millennials) are among the most socially-conscientious customers. Ice-cream business Ben & Jerry's—a born-social brand owned by Unilever but independently operated—has benefited enormously from consumers who act as brand ambassadors; they rave on social media about

[22] Nielsen (2015), "The Sustainability Imperative," October.

the brand's advocacy of mandatory genetically modified food labeling and what it calls "climate justice" to minimize carbon emissions. This kind of eWOM is more credible than any brand-mediated communication.

Your Own Workforce

Global brands underutilize their own employees in carrying the message. If your company takes great care of its people, then you should consider ramping up your internal communications to engage employees as CSR advocates. Better yet, find out what they care about, and connect their values with the brand's values. This serves multiple purposes. First, it equips employees to answer the toughest customer question of all: does your company really take its social responsibilities seriously? Second, employees typically have a wide reach among other stakeholder groups, including customers through their social ties. Research has found that about a third of employees have recommended their company's brand to another person because it had acted responsibly.[23] Outsiders often consider the views and experiences of frontline workers as more credible than advertising slogans. Third, engaging employees in social good increases employee motivation and retention.

Ben & Jerry's does this well. Its workplace practices, including its policies on livable wages work-life balance, and leave have turned its own employees into the brand's most ardent advocates.

Attribution

Romans were in the habit of asking *cui bono*? (who profits?). Customers exposed to claims of social initiatives ask this question as well. Why does this global brand engage in costly CSR activities? How you answer this question shapes how the customer responds to your CSR branding. The motives customers ascribe to CSR activities are of two kinds:

---

[23] Du, Shuili, C.B. Bhattacharya, and Sankar Sen (2010), "Maximizing Business Returns to Corporate Social Responsibility (CSR): The Role of CSR Communication," *International Journal of Management Reviews*, 12 (1), pp. 8–19.

self-interested and altruistic. Self-interested firms seek to use CSR to increase global brand performance (e.g., image, sales, profits), whereas altruistic firms seek to do good, fulfill their obligations as members of communities and society, and perhaps atone for past deeds. Branding activities that customers perceive to be authentic and altruistic tend to build reputational brand capital, whereas branding activities that customers deem self-serving are less likely to produce reputational capital because they align with the brand's profit-making motive. However, self-interested and altruistic attributions are not mutually exclusive. Customers can attribute a brand's CSR actions to both types, and different customers can hold different attributions. Thus, we can segment customers based on their CSR attributions toward the global brand (Tool 8.1).[24]

"Brand Idealists" believe that the brand's motives to pursue socially responsible goals are largely altruistic. They are likely to be brand ambassadors because they see the brand as doing something genuinely good for society.

"Skeptics" believe the opposite. They regard the CSR banner as a way to burnish the brand's image, to increase sales, or to charge higher prices, perhaps to deceive or manipulate the public. CSR can easily backfire among these customers. Touting the brand's CSR credentials could even harm the brand's image more than if these customers were unaware of its CSR activities.

"Integrators" understand that a brand must be both financially and socially responsible. CSR plays a role in achieving this, but integrators believe that the firm really cares for the social cause it champions. That and their sheer numbers are why they are an important group for the global brand. To communicate with this group, you should acknowledge that the brand has both selfish and altruistic motives. For example, if a brand that emphasizes its green credentials as part of its value proposition, it might communicate something like: "Brand X stands for energy conservation. We save money, which allows us not only to keep our prices low and but also to fight global warming." This frankness—combined

---

[24] Items used in this tool are adapted from Du et al. (2007).

This tool is designed to segment customers based on their attributions as to why your brand engages in CSR activities.

Step 1: Collect Information Among Your Customers
Administer the following two statements (possibly as part of a larger survey to save costs) to a sample of your customers. Use a scale from 1 (strongly disagree) to 7 (strongly agree).

Score (1-7)

1. This brand works for XX (the brand's CSR claim) because it is genuinely concerned about being socially responsible.

2. This brand works for XX (the brand's CSR claim) because it feels compelled to do so because of competitive pressure or pressure from society.

Step 2: Assign Customer to One of Four Cells
The first item measure altruistic motives, the second item self-interested motives. Customers are classified as low on a particular motive if they score four or lower, and are classified as high if they score five or higher.

	Low	High
High	**Skeptics** Contribution of CSR to brand reputational capital: 0/+	**Integrators** Contribution of CSR to brand reputational capital: ++
Low	**Unaware/Disinterested** Contribution of CSR to brand reputational capital: 0	**Brand Idealists** Contribution of CSR to brand reputational capital: +++

Self-Interested Motives for Global Brand CSR Activities (vertical axis)
Altruistic Motives for Global Brand CSR Activities (horizontal axis)

Tool 8.1   Classifying customers on their CSR attributions

with transparency in investments and results—enhances the credibility of its CSR message.

Finally, the "Unaware/Disinterested" are either oblivious of or apathetic to the brand's CSR activities. Many of your brand's customers may fall into this cell, especially if awareness of your brand's activities is low in general.

Customer Response to Brand-Related CSR Activities

Transactional Outcomes

Transactional responses refer to the effect of CSR-related brand associations on customer purchase behavior. In one study, 87% of American respondents said they were likely to switch from one brand to another (price and quality being equal) if the other brand were associated with a good cause. That's an increase from 66% in 1993. Consumer surveys in other countries also routinely find that the percentage of people who claim to take CSR into account when deciding between brands can easily reach 60% or higher. The aforementioned Nielsen study reported that 66% of respondents indicated they were willing to pay more for sustainable products, up from 55% in 2014, and 50% in 2013. While these results are encouraging, they do not involve concrete purchase situations where customers have to make tradeoffs in brand attributes. For example, one study of a specific product category (yogurt) found that the perceived quality of the brand was eight times more important than the brand's CSR in brand choices.[25] Moreover, any such general responses contain a considerable amount of socially desirable responding. Who wants to project an image of social callousness?

This does not mean that CSR does not matter in customer purchases. Rather, we should have a realistic expectation about CSR's transactional outcomes. More specifically, the effect of brand-related CSR on brand purchases is larger to the extent that you meet the following conditions:

- The product itself is of high quality. All evidence shows that few customers are willing to compromise on quality to purchase a CSR product.
- The brand's CSR meets the key criteria for inclusion in the customer proposition outlined above—the issue central to the brand's CSR

---

[25] Du et al. (2007).

efforts resonates with the target segment, fits the brand, and differentiates it from its competitors.

- The price premium charged is small. In artificial situations (surveys, experiments), people tend to overestimate the price premium they are willing to pay. Based on my experience in this kind of research, I use as a rule of thumb that the actual amount people are willing to pay morewhen real money is involved is about one-third to half of the price premium people claim to be willing to pay.
- The brand's primary target segment are Millennials. Millennials are on average considerably more CSR-minded than older generations.

These conditions explain why executives who have overly positive expectations about sales or price premium as outcome metric for their global brand's CSR efforts are setting themselves up for disappointment. Yet, CSR branding efforts can still affect transactional outcomes. To explain how, I turn to Herzberg's two-factor theory of motivation. In his work, dissatisfiers cause dissatisfaction if they are absent but rarely create satisfaction when they are present, while satisfiers create satisfaction. For example, airline safety is a dissatisfier. Presence of this factor will have little effect on demand. Few people will prefer an airline because it is safe. Everyone expects safety as part of the product or service. However, an airline with a bad safety record will see demand fall dramatically. I believe that, for many people, CSR acts as a dissatisfier rather than as a satisfier. Absence of brand-related CSR causes people to turn away from the brand but presence of CSR efforts does not mean that they are more likely to buy it or pay more for it.

Relational Outcomes

The basic strategic dividend of CSR turns out not to be transactional but relational. CSR efforts deepen brand-customer relationships over time, creating brand attachment, loyalty, and even advocacy. Loyal customers are less sensitive to competitive moves such as price promotions or new product introductions, and they tend to be more profitable, if only because attracting a new customers costs more than retaining existing customers. These relationships make for more stable cash flows and higher firm value.[26]

CSR as Long-Term Insurance Policy

Perhaps the strongest relational outcome of brand-related CSR is how the customer behaves when something bad happens to the brand—think about Whole Foods' overstating the weights of pre-packaged products and overcharging customers as a result. Think of Samsung's exploding smartphone batteries, contamination of Nestlé Purina pet food with salmonella, Chipotle's food poisoning scandal, BP's Deepwater Horizon oil spill, Shell's Brent Spar disaster, Cadbury's recall of Chinese chocolates over melamine concerns, JP Morgan misleading investors about mortgage backed securities, sweatshop conditions in factories making clothes for Gap and Disney, or accusations that H&M uses child labor in the Philippines. In these brand-threatening circumstances, CSR investments may yield their greatest dividend. CSR is like a long-term insurance policy that the brand team can draws upon when the firm behaves irresponsibly, illegally, or criminally.[27]

To understand how this works, let's turn to the basic psychological principle of cognitive consistency (Fig. 8.2). People strive to maintain cognitive consistency among themselves, the brand, and behavior of the brand. Cognitive consistency exists when the product of the signs of the three relations is positive. For example, "I love Nike" (+), "I hate child labor" (–), and "Nike hates child labor too" gives: (+) x (–) x (–) = (+).

So far so good. But what if the brand I love does something bad ("brand transgression")? It creates inconsistency in the mind of the cus-

[26] Luo, Xueming and C.B. Bhattacharya (2006), "Corporate Social Responsibility, Customer Satisfaction, and Market Value," *Journal of Marketing*, 70 (October), pp. 1–18; Luo, Xueming and C.B. Bhattacharya (2009), "The Debate over Doing Good: Corporate Social Performance, Strategic Marketing Levers, and Firm-Idiosyncratic Risk," *Journal of Marketing*, 73 (November), pp. 198–213.

[27] Janssen, Catherine, Sankar Sen, and C.B. Bhattacharya (2015), "Corporate Crises in the Age of Corporate Social Responsibility," *Business Horizons*, 58, pp. 183–192; Sun, Wenbin and Kexiu Cui (2014), "Linking Corporate Social Responsibility to Firm Default Risk," *European Management Journal*, 32, pp. 275–287.

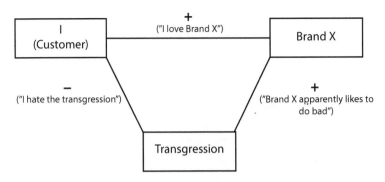

Fig. 8.2 Cognitive consistency and brand transgressions

tomer. Inconsistency occurs if the product of the signs of the three relations is negative. For example, "I love Nike" (+), "I hate child labor" (−), and "Nike apparently is okay with child labor" (+) gives: (+) x (−) x (+) = (−). As people dislike cognitive inconsistency, they are strongly motivated to change something in their mental triad. The customer has three response options:

(1) *Change my opinion about the brand* ("I have been deceived. Nike is bad news after all."). This changes the customer-brand connection from (+) to (−) and cognitive consistency is restored: "I dislike the brand that apparently is okay with doing bad," (−) x (−) x (+) = (+). This response is what the brand obviously will want to avoid.
(2) *Change my opinion about the transgression* ("Child labor is deplorable but perhaps necessary in that country to put food on the table. The alternative is starvation, not education."). This changes the customer-transgression connection from (−) to (0/+).
(3) *Break the association between the brand and the transgression* ("Child labor is deplorable but I cannot imagine Nike was aware of this happening."). This breaks up the triad.

The customer's response is contingent upon the characteristics of the brand transgression. Depending on those characteristics, CSR will or will not be an effective insurance policy. CSR activities are more likely to mitigate the fallout under the following conditions:

- *The CSR activities have built significant reputational brand capital.* Reputational capital acts as buffering goodwill making it easier for customers to attribute the negative event to managerial maladroitness (response (3)) rather than malevolence (response (1)), and temper their reactions accordingly. As we have seen, altruistic CSR builds more reputational brand capital than self-interested CSR activities.
- *The transgression is a product-harm crisis.* The sense of betrayal is greater when the transgression is in the domain in which the reputational capital is built. A product-harm crisis (e.g., faulty or defective product) rather than a CSR crisis (e.g., pollution, child labor, tax dodging) makes it psychologically easier for the customer to hold on to the love for the brand and separate it from what went wrong, favoring response (3).
- *Crisis severity is low.* The customer can then downplay what is happening (response (2)).
- *Company responsibility is low.* The customer can attribute the transgression to bad luck. Again, this weakens the association between the brand and the transgression (response (3)).
- *The company's response is quick, decisive, transparent, and contrite.* The customer does essentially nothing. The cognitive inconsistency is fleeting as the company's actions restore the "natural order" ("The brand I love is doing good things, rather than bad things.").

The Volkswagen Emission Scandal

If we apply these conditions to Volkswagen, the outcome is worrisome. On the positive side, Volkswagen had built considerable reputational capital. According to research by the Reputation Institute, in early 2015 consumers placed Volkswagen among the world's most socially responsible firms. But when news broke of its cheating on diesel emissions tests in September 2015, VW had a scandal of the first order on its hands. In contrast to product-harm crises that hit Toyota and Honda in recent years, this was clearly a CSR crisis.

The sense of betrayal was palpable. For many years, VW had touted the environmental credentials of its diesel cars with advertisements using such taglines as "Diesel. It's no longer a dirty word" and "Green has never felt so right," claiming that the cars were "clean as a whistle." In one advertisement, testers placed white coffee filters on the tailpipes of a Volkswagen Touareg and a traditional diesel vehicle. After the "test," the Touareg filter was still sparkly white, while the other had a black stain.[28] Other ads claimed the diesel cars reduced nitrogen oxide emissions, a harmful pollutant, by 90%. In reality, according to the US Federal Trade Commission, the cars emitted up to 4000% more than the legal limit of nitrogen oxide.

The crisis was severe, affecting over ten million cars around the globe across multiple of its brands including its namesake Volkswagen brand, Audi, and Porsche. The company attempted to blame a few rogue engineers. That spin gained no traction. The company's response was anything but quick, decisive, transparent, and contrite.

So, the negatives outweighed the positives. Its full-year 2015 sales declined 2%, the first year-on-year decline since 2002, and US sales in the first half of 2016 were 13% lower than sales in the same period in 2015. However, Volkswagen CEO Matthias Müller felt the results could have been a lot worse. Volkswagen's large stock of reputational capital helped it buffer some of the negative consequences, although there is no doubt that the company aggravated an already difficult situation by its slow and reluctant response. It remains to be seen how quickly Volkswagen can restore its previously stellar reputation.

Forevermark: CSR in Love

Diamonds are an ultimate gift of love. Arguments that they are just highly organized carbon sold for an outrageous price cut no ice if the marriage proposal is to go well. Giving a "rock" is not a Dutch tradition but I had already gotten the message that "size matters" in the United States and acted accordingly. It worked. My (American) girlfriend said "Yes" and proudly, she showed off her engagement ring to her friends, notwithstanding that she could easily afford to buy such a ring herself.

---

[28] For examples, see: https://www.youtube.com/watch?v=fH834IFpGTQ and https://www.youtube.com/watch?v=WNS2nvkjARk; accessed September 27, 2016.

The jewelry industry rates the quality of diamonds according to the four Cs—carat (weight), cut, clarity, and color. People did not think about where they came from and under what conditions. This changed in the 1990s when journalists began to report on terrible labor conditions, oppression, pillage, and murder in the diamond-mining operations of such African countries as Angola, Liberia, and Sierra Leone, where warlords and insurgents were mining and selling diamonds to finance their bloody activities. These stones became known as "blood diamonds" or "conflict diamonds." The 2006 political thriller *Blood Diamond* starring Leonardo DiCaprio raised Western awareness of the tragedy associated with the production of diamonds. This awareness threatened the diamond industry and its main purveyor, South Africa's De Beers.

In response, in 2008, De Beers introduced the brand Forevermark. Each Forevermark diamond has to meet very high standards of quality for clarity, color, carat, and cut as well as high business, social, and environmental standards at every step of its journey. De Beers selects Forevermark diamonds only from sources that adhere to the UN mandated Kimberley Process. This adherence exemplified De Beers' commitment to CSR.

Forevermark's proposition combines traditional benefits (superior quality on the four Cs) with environment, community, and workplace benefits that it summarizes under "responsibly sourced." De Beers highlights these benefits in its brand proposition on its own brand websites, websites of jewelers that sell the brand, and their sales pitch to customers. The chosen CSR associations are broad but interrelated: they concern diamond mining communities (political climate, human rights record, healthcare, education), mining operations (welfare and security of employees), and impact on the local environment (conservation, water usage).

These CSR associations fulfill the three key selection criteria set out above: they are relevant to the global target segment, they fit with the product category, and they differ from competition. The good fit with the brand meant that the target segment viewed the activities as not just self-interested but also—possibly predominantly—altruistic. However, their relevance is subjective and differs between countries. According to Stephen Lussier, CEO of Forevermark, CSR is very important to

American and Japanese consumers but Chinese consumers tend to focus more on quality of the stone.

The Forevermark brand promise of being beautiful, rare and responsibly sourced worked well. Strong reputation allowed it to sell its products at a price 15% higher than those offered on the generic market, and the retail value of sales exceeded $750 million in 2014. While rough diamond sales fell by 36% in 2015, Forevermark recorded double-digit sales growth and is now available in 1760 outlets worldwide, a 14% increase over 2014.

The Second Wave of CSR

In the past, CSR investments often improved firm profitability and shareholder value. CSR rewards itself, right? What is not to love about that? Yet, many of these so-called first wave of CSR policies focused on saving energy, cutting waste, and streamlining logistics. According to *The Economist*, we could just have easily called these efforts efficiency policies. Cutting waste in your business processes and facilities is good economics, regardless of the impact on the environment.[29]

It is hard to say whether CSR activities pay for themselves going forward. This so-called second wave of CSR could easily raise costs, not cut them. Higher wages, shorter work weeks, community efforts to train and develop local talent and manufacture environmentally friendly goods often make the products more expensive or the firm less profitable. For example, in 2015, Walmart gave in to long-standing societal pressure and decided to increase the minimum starting pay to at least $9 an hour in 2015, increasing to at least $10 an hour in February 2016. It also committed to investing more money in training employees. There are commendable CSR policies but when Walmart announced in October 2015 that its earnings would decrease 6% to 12% in 2016, its share price fell 10%, the biggest drop in 27 years.

Yet, according to Paul Polman, Unilever CEO, good CSR policies still improve the fundamentals of businesses, albeit in the long run. He believes that these policies change customers' behavior in beneficial ways

---

[29] *The Economist* (2014).

and also please investors concerned about environmental threats. The trouble is that customer behavior is often slow to change and, if CSR products are too expensive the firm risks losing market share. CSR investors are still a minority among shareholders, most of whom continue to focus on quarterly earnings. Polman fully understands the risk, "The moment Unilever underperforms, the guns will come out."

While the first wave of CSR aligned "doing good" with "doing well," the new wave might not. More likely, it will boost adopters' long-term competitive position rather than their short-term profits. Unlike the rewards of the first wave, those of the second wave could take years to materialize. Consider Danish toy maker Lego. In 2015, Lego embarked on a 15-year process to find a bio-based alternative to the petroleum-based plastic that it had used to make its bricks for decades. The popular building blocks are a significant contributor to the company's carbon footprint: Lego uses 77,000 tons of petroleum annually to manufacture over 60 billion bricks. There is no expectation that these investments in R&D will pay off, unless oil prices explode. Yet, Lego believes this is what customers demand.

Lego is a harbinger of the second wave of CSR. To remain respected and valuable members of the global society, MNCs will want to increase their CSR efforts, investing now to operate tomorrow, when consumers, lobbyists, and regulators will have greater expectations of MNCs' behavior.

Managerial Takeaways

Basically, you have two routes to brand profitability—cutting costs or increasing revenues. The first wave of CSR traveled largely the first route by cutting waste from the production process. We are now entering the second wave, which is likely to increase, not reduce costs. To maintain profitability, MNCs therefore have to increase brand revenues. Hence, imbuing the global brand with CSR associations and leveraging these associations in the marketplace will be more important than ever before. A hands-off approach, the hope for CSR trickle down, will not suffice. Your firm needs to actively integrate social responsibility in the global brand's proposition and strategy execution. Here is a summary of the process for executives.

1. *Ensure that your brand can deliver on its promises.* Establish that your social goal is truly an integrative element of your corporate strategy, even when its returns are uncertain and remote. Do you have the organizational structure and global brand management processes in place to fulfill the CSR promise around the world? Can you leave leeway for local managers in CSR execution?

2. *Select the social, environmental, or economic component to integrate into your brand's proposition.* Executives should choose one or two CSR aspects that are relevant to the global target segment, fit with the product category, and differentiate the brand from other brands.

3. *Communicate the brand's efforts.* Build awareness through advertising, on-pack label and design, social media, and your own workforce as brand advocates. Manage customer attributions why your brand engages in CSR. Customers understand that CSR is not necessarily completely altruistic but if they suspect it is done for self-interested motives, the effect on customer behavior will be minor. Brand reputation might even suffer if people regard the brand as being dishonest and manipulative.

4. *Monitor your progress.* Do members of the target segment in key countries see your brand as socially responsible? What motives do customers attribute to your CSR efforts? Are perceptions improving over time?

If you follow these steps, you will more likely imbue your global brand with CSR associations and generate favorable customer outcomes. Some benefits will materialize in the short run (revenues). The short-term transactional outcomes will be greatest if you maintain rather than compromise the quality of the product, your efforts fit the criteria for including in the brand's customer proposition, you charge a small rather than large price premium, and your primary target segment is millennials.

However, expect that brand outcomes of CSR activities largely emerge in the longer run (relational outcomes), in the form of more favorable brand attitudes, higher brand trust, emotional attachment, advocacy, and higher brand loyalty. Last but not least, if you follow these recommendations, your commitment to socially responsible behavior acts as a long-term insurance policy when bad things happen to your brand. Just as neighbors help neighbors in troubled times, your neighborly goodwill will help you pull through.

Part III

Global Brand Performance

If you properly align brand-building activities (Part I) and organizational structures and processes (Part II), the outcome should be a strong global brand that creates value for its customers and the firm's shareholders. But how do we define a strong brand? Some executives focus on what customers think, on the brand's esteem and relevance in the minds of its target segment. Others point to revenues and pricing power. Again others, especially the CFO, think about profitability.

All these executives are right. Strong global brands score well on customer outcomes, market outcomes, and financial outcomes. They all contribute to global brand equity—which is succinctly and powerfully expressed by the dollar value of the brand (Chapter, "Global Brand Equity"). As Table III.1 shows, global brands can be enormously valuable.

The message is clear: if managed and nurtured well, global brands generate tremendous value. On the other hand, if the global brand is mismanaged and loses its relevance in the marketplace, its performance will decline. While brand strength is a kind of insurance for brand missteps, it does not protect the brand against series of mistakes. In 2008, Millward Brown ranked Nokia the ninth most valuable brand in the world, Tesco 25th, Dell 41st and Yahoo! 62nd. None of these brands made Millward Brown's top-100 list in 2016. For example, UK-based retailer Tesco, because of a series of mistakes ranging from its ill-fated attempt to enter the United

States to ignoring the threat posed by hard discounters Aldi and Lidl in its home market, saw its brand value decline by 62 % in this period.

At the end of the day, strong global brands are only a means to the metric that matters the most in the C-suite: the creation of shareholder value. In an era of ever greater financial accountability senior marketing executives must be able to show how strong global brands create shareholder value. Table III.1 shows the percentage of the firm's market capitalization that the CMO can trace back to brand equity. However, as we will see in Chapter, "Global Brands and Shareholder Value,, the picture is more nuanced. Financial markets discount brand value in their assessment of a firm's market value, due to uncertainty surrounding brand equity estimates. We also need to consider other metrics, most importantly the effect of global brands on shareholder return, shareholder risk, and on firm value in mergers and acquisitions. Taken all together, the news is resoundingly positive. Global brands create shareholder value in multiple, mutually supporting ways. The CMO can take his or her seat in the C-suite with head held high.

Table III. 1 Equity of the most valuable global brand in selected industries

B2B/B2C	Global brand	Industry	Brand equity 2016 ($ bn.)	Change 2016 vs. 2015 (%)	Brand equity as % of market cap
B2B	IBM	IT services	86.2	−8 %	58 %
	General Electric	Conglomerate	54.1	−9 %	19 %
	SAP	Enterprise software	39.0	2 %	39 %
	Accenture	Professional services	22.8	13 %	31 %
	Huawei	Telecom infrastructure	18.7	22 %	–
	Boeing	Aerospace & defense	14.0	−8 %	17 %
	Goldman Sachs	Investment banking	7.5	−10 %	12 %
	BASF	Chemicals	6.3	−2 %	9 %
	Caterpillar	Heavy machinery	7.9	1 %	17 %
	John Deere	Agricultural equipment	3.8	−14 %	14 %

(continued)

Table III. 1 (continued)

B2B/B2C	Global brand	Industry	Brand equity 2016 ($ bn.)	Change 2016 vs. 2015 (%)	Brand equity as % of market cap
B2C	Google	Technology	229.2	32 %	45 %
	Visa	Payments	100.8	10 %	58 %
	Coca Cola	Soft drinks	80.3	−4 %	41 %
	McDonald's	Restaurants	88.7	9 %	83 %
	Marlboro	Tobacco	84.1	5 %	30 %
	Amazon	Retail	99.0	59 %	29 %
	UPS	Logistics	49.8	−4 %	54 %
	Disney	Entertainment	49.2	15 %	31 %
	T-Mobile	Telecom	37.7	12 %	–
	Nike	Apparel	37.5	26 %	42 %
	Toyota	Automotive	29.5	2 %	18 %
	Louis Vuitton	Luxury	28.5	4 %	33 %
	Budweiser	Beer	27.9	5 %	15 %
	HSBC	Retail banking	20.3	−16 %	15 %
	Pampers	Baby care	22.9	−4 %	10 %
	L'Oréal Paris	Personal care	23.5	1 %	25 %
	Emirates	Airlines	7.7	17 %	–
	Manchester United	Soccer	1.2	−3 %	43 %

Note: Indicated is whether the primary market is B2B or B2C. Brand equity data come from Millward Brown (2016) except for Boeing, BASF, Caterpillar, John Deere, Emirates, and Manchester United, which are taken from Brand Finance (2016). Market capitalization refers to June 8, 2016 (i.e., the day Millward Brown released its 2016 brand equity data)

9

Global Brand Equity

What is the payoff of successful global brand building and management activities? Higher brand equity. In accounting terms, brand equity is the goodwill adhering to the brand—the positive (or negative!) outcomes that a company realizes from a product with its name on it. Say you wanted to offer a new brown, carbonated soft drink, "You Cola." Customers could prefer the taste of your brand, recommend You Cola to others, support your global water replenishment initiative, put your visitor center on their vacation itinerary, buy You Cola merchandise, become willing to pay you a price premium, name you their exclusive vendor, and strike other long-term deals for such rights as licensing, production, and distribution of You Cola, all resulting in greater or more stable profits. Coca-Cola realizes all of the above outcomes.

When I work with executives, I talk about these outcomes in three categories of equity: customer-based brand equity, sales-based brand equity, and profit-based brand equity (Fig. 9.1). These components are critical for global leaders to understand as they analyze the economics of their brand.

© The Author(s) 2017
J.-B. Steenkamp, *Global Brand Strategy*,
DOI 10.1057/978-1-349-94994-6_9

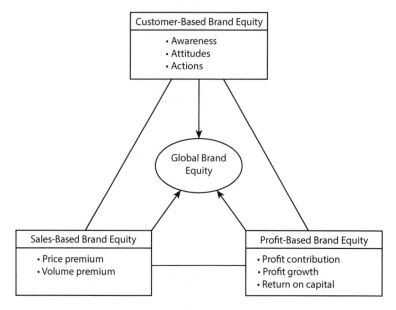

Fig. 9.1   Global brand equity triangle

Customer-Based Brand Equity

The heart of any strong global brand is the difference it makes in the hearts and minds of customers. Do customers think differently about the beer when they learn that it is Stella Artois and not Budweiser or Tesco private label? Or that you work for McKinsey and not the Boston Consulting Group? Or that you went to INSEAD and not to the London Business School? This is called customer-based brand equity (customer equity for short). Yes, cutting waste and achieving economies of scale are important; but the ultimate power of a global brand resides in what customers do and how they feel when they see or think of your brand. A Coca-Cola executive once said that, if the brand were to lose all its production-related assets in a disaster, the company would have little difficulty in raising enough capital to rebuild its factories. By contrast, if consumers around the world were to lose their memories and forget everything related to Coca-Cola, the company would go out of busi-

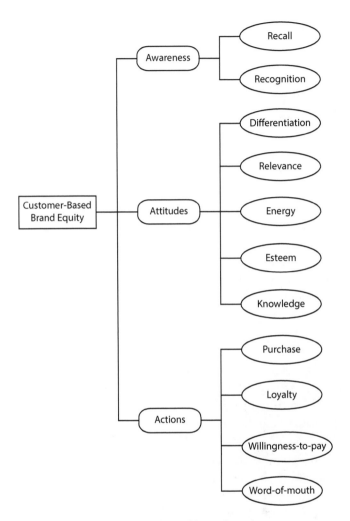

Fig. 9.2 Components of customer-based brand equity

ness. It is precisely the indelible representation of Coca-Cola—branded in the minds and ingrained in the habits of consumers—that provides equity for the brand name Coke. In my work, I talk about three aspects of customer-based brand equity, the 3A's: Awareness, Attitudes, and Actions. Figure 9.2 presents specific metrics for each.

Awareness

By *brand awareness*, I mean whether a customer recognizes and even recalls a particular brand of goods or services. Let's say I offered you a spoonful of Calvé or Helaes pindakaas. Which would you choose? What if I expanded your options to include Skippy and Jif? You would probably deduce that *pindakaas* is the Dutch word for peanut butter. But, peanut allergies aside, which would you choose? If you are a Dutchman, you would go for Calvé as everybody has heard of the brand, but if you are an American, Skippy or Jif will be your choice. In one study, researchers asked participants to taste two samples of peanut butter. One of these samples was a superior peanut butter (preferred in blind taste tests 70% of the time) in an unlabeled container. Another was an inferior peanut butter (not preferred in taste tests) in a container labeled with a brand known to but never purchased nor used by the respondents. Over 70% of the respondents selected the inferior, named-brand option as the better tasting peanut butter.[1] The lesson is clear; you can't love what you don't know, and better the devil you know. Brands known round the world dominate all rankings of the strongest global brands. Who doesn't know names like Coca-Cola, Samsung, and Nike? The McDonald's logo is even claimed to be the most recognized symbol in the world.[2]

We should distinguish between *brand recognition* (aided awareness) and *brand recall* (unaided awareness). Brand recognition sounds trivial: you merely have to identify which brands you have heard of on a list. Quite the contrary, brand recognition correlates strongly with consumer attitudes toward the brand, its market share by volume and value, and the price premium it can charge in the marketplace.[3]

Brand recall requires work: you ask a person which brands of smartphones or mobile service providers they can recall. Consumers often name really strong brands first in such a task. We call these "top of mind"

---

[1] Hoyer, Wayne and Steven P. Brown (1990), "Effects of Brand Awareness on Choice for a Common, Repeat-Purchase Product," *Journal of Consumer Research*, 17 (September), pp. 141–148.

[2] http://www.businessinsider.com/amazing-facts-mcdonalds-2010-12; accessed May 2, 2015.

[3] Huang, Rong and Emine Sarigöllü (2012), "How Brand Awareness Relates to Market Outcome, Brand Equity, and the Marketing Mix," *Journal of Business Research*, 65 (1), pp. 92–99. Correlations were in the range 0.5–0.6.

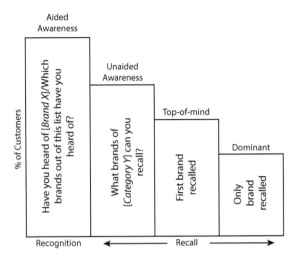

Fig. 9.3 Brand awareness waterfall

brands. When a person can recall only a single brand, we call it the dominant brand. By definition, there is a drop-off from the percentage of consumers that recognize a brand to the percentage for whom your brand is
the dominant brand (Fig. 9.3).

Attitude

While customer awareness is necessary for customer equity, it is not sufficient. How does a person feel toward the brand? Marketing practitioners
have developed several measures of consumer attitudes, such as Young &
Rubicam's Brand Asset Valuator (BAV). BAV consists of five pillars: differentiation, relevance, energy, esteem, and knowledge.

Differentiation

Differentiation is the extent to which customer see the brand as unique. It
is the starting point of global brand building in any category. For example,
beer brands that have ranked among the top ten most valuable over a ten-

year period (2006–2015) —such as Budweiser, Heineken, and Corona—have an average differentiation score 26% higher than brands that dropped from the top ten during that period (e.g., Amstel, Miller Lite).[4]

All five types of global brands—value, mass, premium, prestige, and fun brands—need differentiation to create global brand equity, albeit the basis for distinction differs from type to type. For example, value brands need to differentiate themselves on their price/value ratio, while fun brands need to set themselves apart by continually redefining *hip* and spotting distinct trends.

How do brand managers increase their brand's performance on differentiation? Differentiation starts with a strong and distinctive customer proposition. Brands need to be different with a purpose that's inspiring and relevant to consumers. Which marketing mix instruments can be used to create differentiation in the minds of customers? While all marketing activities potentially help, advertising and price are particularly powerful instruments. On the other hand, widespread distribution tends to reduce brand differentiation. It is challenging to be both unique and ubiquitous.[5]

Relevance

Relevance is the extent to which customers consider the brand applicable to their needs. It measures the connection that people have to brands—how much significance, impact, and purpose a product or service has in their lives. If a brand lacks relevance to a significant global segment, it will not attract and keep customers, certainly not in any great numbers. For example, with prices starting north of $120,000, Aston Martin is very high on differentiation but low on relevance because the cars (and the required auto insurance and road taxes) are impractical, even if you love James Bond.

---

[4] Millward Brown (2015), BrandZ Top 100 Most Valuable Global Brands 2015.

[5] Information on the effect of various marketing mix instruments on the BAV factors is partially based on Stahl, Florian, Mark Heitmann, Donald R. Lehmann, and Scott A. Neslin (2012), "The Impact of Brand Equity on Customer Acquisition, Retention, and Profit Margin," *Journal of Marketing*, 76 (July), pp. 44–63.

Relevance correlates with household penetration. Relevance is especially important for value and mass brands, the business models of which need large sales volumes to work. Managers can increase brand relevance by advertising and increasing distribution for the brand, and by charging a price that makes the brand accessible to more customers, or alternatively, by running price promotions—in moderation; overpromoting hurts customer equity. Moreover, to remain relevant, a continuous stream of new products launches, even if they are relatively minor product improvements and adaptations, keep the brand relevant in an ever changing environment.

Most smartphones now come in two sizes—big and huge. Apple saw an opportunity to reach out to consumers with smaller hands or who just prefer a smaller phone—about 20–25% in countries like China and the United States. In March 2016, it introduced the 4-inch iPhone SE. It looks like a throwback to an earlier version, the iPhone 5S, but has much better performance, using the same processor as used in the larger iPhone 6S. The iPhone SE increases the brand's relevance in two ways. First, it targets a segment no longer served by premium smartphone brands. Second, at a starting price of $399—Apple's lowest ever—the brand is more accessible to lower income customers. The danger is that consumers relegate the iPhone SE to "cheap iPhone" status—the image that sank Apple's previous low-cost handset, the iPhone 5C.

Energy

Energy is the extent to which the brand is seen as innovative, dynamic, and responsive to changing customer tastes and needs. Apple comes to mind: it created entirely new product categories from mp3 players to tablets. Brands that score high on energy include many technology brands, but not exclusively. Nike, UPS, and PayPal score high on energy too, for example. In the period 2006–2015, brands that scored in the top third on energy increased on average 161% in brand value. The value of brands that scored in the bottom tertile increased only 13%.[6]

---

[6] Millward Brown (2015). Millward Brown uses the term trend-setting.

Small brands and start-ups often score higher on energy than established brands, encumbered by bureaucracy. Take Tory Burch, a fashion brand hailed for "weaving sensibility into style, and never letting growth compromise authenticity."[7] She built a tech-forward, bohemian (boho) chic empire of versatile women's accessories and apparel with high-profile clientele. From its single store in Manhattan's Nolita neighborhood, Tory Burch has more than 120 freestanding boutiques and is sold in more than 3000 department and specialty stores globally.

Innovation is the key to create energy for your brand. As categories become more competitive, being a high-energy brand means being seen as trendsetting, leading, shaping the marketplace. Brands need to be forward looking and deliver innovative brand experiences beyond customers' expectations. Even without breakthrough products, brands still need to make sure their communications look and feel innovative. Active presence in social media is indispensable.

Energy is a make-or-break issue for premium brands in order to maintain a technological edge over mass brands, for fun brands that serve a fickle target segment, and for those mass brands that primarily target millennials.

Esteem

Esteem is the extent to which consumers admire a brand and hold it in high regard. It relates closely to perceived quality, reliability, and category leadership. Brands such as Toyota, Caterpillar, and IBM have established reputations for consistently delivering high quality, whereas Chinese brands have historically suffered from an esteem deficit. Western consumers do not always recognize their good quality by objective standards because building esteem takes time and effort. You must relentlessly improve actual quality before your esteem improves in the market. The market esteem for Samsung, Toyota, and Honda lagged these brands' actual quality for many years.

---

[7] http://www.entrepreneur.com/article/235945; accessed June 14, 2015.

The increased globalization of world markets, spread of manufacturing technology, and increased connectivity in the digital world have reduced the time it takes to build brand esteem. Facebook has gained esteem around the world in less than a decade, and also Chinese brands like Alibaba, Lenovo, and Huawei have reached respectable levels of esteem considerably faster than Toyota or Samsung in the past.

Mass, premium, and prestige brands sold on a promise of quality—especially for a premium price—need to earn and sustain customer esteem. A brand can improve its performance on esteem by stimulating electronic word of mouth and by employing marketing activities that customers use as a signal of quality—price, advertising, and distribution. Customers infer that heavily advertised brands have to be of high quality because such investments would be lost if the brand does not live up to its expectations, and in every culture, higher price sends a signal of quality. For mass brands, wide distribution is a signal of quality because it shows broad market acceptance. Conversely, premium and especially prestige brands should use selective distribution using upscale outlets as it suggests exclusivity, and in case of prestige brands, scarcity.

Knowledge

Finally, *knowledge* is the extent to which customers understand the brand's identity and behavior. Knowledge is the culmination of brand building efforts. Customers learn about your brand not simply by exposures to it but by first-hand experience with it or by hearing about first-hand experiences from friends. The strength of global mass brands like Coca-Cola, premium brands like Jaguar, and prestige brands like Gucci depends on brand knowledge. Prestige brands especially derive much of their value from their mystery. If you do not know the essence of Loro Piana apparel or have not touched the brand in one of its exclusive stores, then you will not likely pay $1400 for a Loro Piana sweater. Advertising, social media, and distribution are a key instrument to build brand knowledge.

Customer Equity Power Grid

To help executives visualize their customers' attitudes toward their brand, you can use the Customer Equity Power Grid (Fig. 9.4). It maps *brand vitality*—the combined strengths of differentiation, relevance, and energy—against *brand stature*, the combined strengths of esteem and knowledge. What brand vitality is to growth, brand stature is to longevity. The figure shows two common trajectories, one going from new brands via emerging brands to dominant brands, and a second, more troubling one going from dominant brands via receding brands to weak brands.

Dominant brands—Amazon, Apple, BMW, Caterpillar, Disney, Facebook, GE, Gillette, Google, IBM, McDonald's, and Toyota—combine high stature with high vitality. Their dominant position makes them targets, but not necessarily easy ones: their strength enables them to handle challengers and address societal discontent. For example, McDonald's developed the McCafé concept as a lower-priced alternative to Starbucks. To remain among the world's most valuable brands, McDonald's must continue to act quickly and decisively to address public concern for healthy meal options, ethical supply chains, and environ-

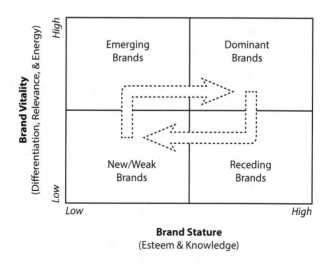

Fig. 9.4   Customer equity power grid

mental sustainability. In all fairness, other fast food chains should address these concerns as well, but high winds blow on high hills.

Receding brands are those that can draw upon a reservoir of customer esteem and knowledge but are losing their vitality. Brands in this quadrant have often dominated their segments—think of Dell, Sony, Fiat, Barclays, Chevrolet, Abercrombie & Fitch, and Gap—and people still respect them, but more nostalgically than expectantly. They struggle to maintain their relevance, energy, even differentiation in a changed marketplace.

Emerging brands such as Alibaba, Huawei, Sany, Airbnb, Tesla, or Uber have significant growth potential but are relatively low on stature because they are relatively new to the global party. Their brand managers are working to develop emotional capital so that they might dominate their categories because they have come to understand that strong brands overlay functional logic with emotional magic. Feelings follow functionality.

Finally, brands that are low on all customer equity dimensions are either *new brands* or *weak brands*. Weak brands may be former power brands whose brand vitality dropped and then its brand stature declined. To arrest their downward slide is difficult—Apple accomplished that albeit the genius of Steve Jobs was required to pull this off. In 2008, BlackBerry was the dominant smartphone brand. But even President Barack Obama's well-publicized attachment to the brand could not save it from Apple and Samsung. BlackBerry was blindsided by the emergence of the "app economy," which drove massive adoption of iPhone and Android-based devices and insisted on producing phones with full keyboards, even after it became clear that users preferred touchscreens. When BlackBerry finally did launch a touchscreen device, it was seen as a poor imitation of the iPhone. Its global market share fell from 44% in 2008 to less than 1% in 2015 and in September 2016 it abandoned smartphone making altogether and pulled out of the devices business.

Another example is Alfa Romeo, owned by Fiat Chrysler Automobiles (FCA). In my youth, it was a leading performance brand. One company tried to persuade me to join them by promising I could have an Alfa as a lease car. These days are far behind us. Over time, mismanagement, lack of innovation, and indistinctive new models sapped the brand's vitality, and with rapidly declining sales went its brand stature. In 2015, FCA's

CEO Sergio Marchionne launched the marque's biggest product offensive since 1985. Analysts and industry insiders are skeptical: Alfa's sales have fallen successively for 15 years, and its brand value in 2016 stood at a mere $467 million, 12% lower than in 2015.[8]

Action

The third contributor to customer equity is customer action—purchasing, purchasing again, paying more per unit, and promoting to others.[9] Loyal customers are those who rebuy or even subscribe to a brand, consider only that brand, and search little for information on other brands. Thus, customers who are loyal to a particular brand are less open to the marketing efforts of competitors, reducing churn among the brand's customer base. In general, customers are more loyal to dominant brands than to weak brands.

Customers, loyal or not, can and generally do pay more for dominant brands than for weak brands. A global study found that the larger the difference in esteem between brands and private labels, the higher the price premium individuals will pay for brands.

Loyal customers will talk about the brand by word of mouth or mobile. Remember, in today's digital world, social media platforms can multiply the effect of one person's brand experience and influence the behavior of a multifold of consumers. They may be speaking positively about your brand—not just their use of the product itself, but of customer service, after care, and your protection of their privacy and identity (i.e., you don't sell their data to other vendors and you do secure your servers from hackers).

---

[8] Sharman, Andy (2015), "Alfa Romeo Gears Up to Inject a Dash of Ferrari," *Financial Times*, June 25, p. 18; Sylvers, Eric (2015), "Alfa Romeo Plots Revival with Luxury Sedan," *Wall Street Journal*, June 25, p. B6. Brand value taken from Brand Finance.

[9] Chaudhuri, Arjun and Morris B. Holbrook (2001), "The Chain of Effects from Brand Trust and Brand Affect to Brand Performance: The Role of Brand Loyalty," *Journal of Marketing*, 65 (April), pp. 81–93; Steenkamp, Jan-Benedict E.M., Harald van Heerde, and Inge Geyskens (2010), "What Makes Consumers Willing to Pay a Price Premium for National Brands over Private Labels?" *Journal of Marketing Research*, 47 (December), pp. 1011–1024; Swait, Joffre, Tülin Erdem, Jordan Louviere, and Chris Dubelaar (1993), "The Equalization Price: A Consumer-Perceived Measure of Brand Equity," *International Journal of Research in Marketing*, 10 (1), pp. 23–45.

Customer Equity Tracking Instrument

Clearly, customer equity is the bedrock of any strong brand, and so you should track it over time. If your global brand building and managing efforts succeed consistently, then you should see a steady increase in customer equity *before* you register increases in sales and profitability; if your activities fail, then customer equity should decrease. Therefore, changes in customer equity serve as an early signal, either to develop remedial actions or to adjust inventory and production levels.

Tool 9.1 is a tracking instrument for customer equity. I recommend that at a minimum, you administer it at least once a year to 500 customers in all countries that account for 10% or more of the brand's sales in the local language.[10] You can derive a global score by averaging the country means, weighted by the country's share of total sales in the industry in which your brand operates. Data collection costs should be low for so short an instrument. It can be part of an omnibus survey regularly conducted by market research agencies, which further reduces costs.

You will find that customer equity often will differ between countries. For example, Aldi's customer equity in Germany is high, but much less so in the States. Coca-Cola and Colgate score equally high on various customer equity components in America and China; but, on most aspects, their main competitors (Pepsi and Crest, respectively), score considerably lower in China.

Sales-Based Brand Equity

Strong global brands should possess customer equity but also exhibit the ability to transform this positive customer mindset into a sales premium in the marketplace—sales-based brand equity. Sales-based brand equity

---

[10] The precision of the mean score on an item increases with the square root of the sample size, which means that sample size increases have progressively less effect on precision. In my experience, increasing the sample size above 500 is not worth the additional costs. For B2B firms will need to lower the sample size, which means that sample size increases have progressively less effect on precision as it is often not feasible or too costly to survey 500 customers. Even with a sample size of 100, you can get reasonably accurate estimates of item means.

Question	Response
1. Which brands of [*Category X*] do you recall?	....
2. Present a list of [*Category X*] brands. Ask the respondent, "Which brands on this list have you heard of or seen?"	....

Statement (1 = strongly disagree; 7 = strongly agree)	Score (1-7)
3. [*Brand Y*] stands out from its competitors	☐
4. [*Brand Y*] is relevant to me	☐
5. [*Brand Y*] is an innovative brand	☐
6. [*Brand Y*] stands for high quality	☐
7. I have a detailed understanding of what [*Brand Y*] stands for	☐
8. [*Brand Y*] stands for something unique	☐
9. [*Brand Y*] fits my lifestyle	☐
10. [*Brand Y*] is a dynamic brand	☐
11. I hold [*Brand Y*] in high regard	☐
12. I know a lot about [*Brand Y*]	☐
13. Next time I buy [*Category X*], I am likely to buy [*Brand Y*]	☐
14. I feel loyal to [*Brand Y*]	☐
15. I talk about [*Brand Y*] with my friends or share my thoughts and experiences about [*Brand Y*] on social media	☐
16. I would pay extra to buy [*Brand Y*]	☐

Interpretation:
• Items 1-2 measure brand awareness, items 3-12 attitudes, and items 13-16 actions.
• Item 1: The percentage of respondents that mention [*Brand Y*] is the measure of brand recall. The percentage of respondents that mention [*Brand Y*] first is the brand's top-of-mind score, and the percentage of respondents that can only mention [*Brand Y*] is the measure of brand dominance.
• Item 2: Brand recognition is the percentage of respondents who checked "yes" for [*Brand Y*]. By combining the results for items 1 and 2, you can construct the brand awareness waterfall.
• The brand's score on differentiation is obtained by averaging the scores on items 3 and 8, on relevance by averaging the scores on items 4 and 9, energy 5 and 10, esteem 6 and 11, and knowledge 7 and 12.
• Item 13 measures purchase intention, item 14 brand loyalty, item 15 word-of-mouth, and item 16 willingness to pay.
• If resource constraints prohibit administration of all 16 items, drop items 8-12.

Tool 9.1   Tracking instrument for customer equity

(sales equity for short) is the difference in sales revenue (net price multiplied by global sales volume) between the global brand and an unbranded benchmark product, such as the corresponding private label. If no private label, then a weak brand. Sales equity thus has two components: any extra price premium and volume premium delivered by these brand associations.

The most commonly considered metric for sales equity is the price premium of a brand over the unbranded alternative. Strong and differentiated brands enjoy monopolistic power that enables them to command a price premium. For example, the Porsche Cayenne and the VW Touareg result from a joint development initiative and are built on the same platform. Manufacturing costs are broadly comparable, but Porsche is able to charge a much higher price (starting at $58,300) than Volkswagen (starting at $24,890) largely because of the strength of its brand. For around $40,000 you can either buy a three-year old John Deere 4320 tractor or a broadly comparable brand-new Mahindra 3550 PST.

In CPG industry, marketers commonly use private label as proxy for the unbranded product. Table 9.1 shows the average global price premium of manufacturer brands over private labels for as number of product categories.[11] Led by such brands as P&G's Pantene and L'Oréal's Garnier, brands in the shampoo category have succeed in commanding a larger price premium than in categories like frozen meals or toilet tissue, which are dominated by local brands.

Let's look at the sales equity in the highly regulated accounting industry. By law in New Zealand, local subsidiaries of global accounting firms (with the exception of then Price Waterhouse) had to use their local name before 1983. For example, Deloitte's subsidiary went by Hutchinson Hull & Co. and Coopers & Lybrand went by Barr Burgess & Stewart. Global-named Price Waterhouse commanded an audit fee premium of around 4% over the others. Within one year of the rule change, all subsidiaries took on their global parent's brand. Nothing else major changed: not structure, not operations, not even management. Within one year, all renamed accounting firms were commanding an audit fee of around 4% higher than local firms' fees. In addition, their market share grew as well,

---

[11] AC Nielsen, "The Power of Private Label: A Review of Growth Trends Around the World."

Table 9.1 Global price premium of brands over private labels

Category	Price premium of brands (%)	Examples of global brands
Shampoo	104	Pantene, Garnier
Disposable razors	96	Gillette, Schick
Dog food	75	Pedigree, Purina
Feminine hygiene	72	Always, Kotex
Deodorants	69	Axe, Nivea
Breakfast cereals	67	Kellogg's
Water	52	Evian, Aquafina
Laundry detergent	52	Ariel, Persil
Potato chips	49	Lay's, Pringles
Facial tissue	45	Kleenex
Toothpaste	43	Colgate, Crest
Tomato ketchup	43	Heinz
Beer	39	Corona, Budweiser
Dry pasta	37	Barilla, Buitoni
Coffee	37	Nescafé, Jacobs
Diapers	33	Pampers, Huggies
Yogurt	20	Danone, Yoplait
Toilet tissue	15	–
Frozen meals	5	–

Source: Based on 38 countries around the world; adapted from Nielsen (2005)

although analysts could not determine a precise percentage because of no disclosure requirements on number of clients and total fees.[12]

If anything, global value brands like Aldi, IKEA, or Costco or fun brands like Swatch or H&M sell at a price *discount* rather than a *premium* compared to mass brand competitors. Yet, these brands still have considerable sales equity because of large volume. Truly strong brands such as Coca-Cola and Pepsi Cola command both a volume and price premium over their generic alternative (see Table 9.2).[13]

Millward Brown provides estimates of sales equity, which it calls *brand contribution*. It estimates the purchase volume and any extra price premium delivered by the brand's customer equity across many

---

[12] Firth, Martin (1993), "Price Setting and the Value of a Strong Brand Name," *International Journal of Research in Marketing*, 10 (4), pp. 381–386.

[13] Passport GMID does not provide separate data for carbonated cola.

Table 9.2 Sales equity of Coca-Cola and Pepsi Cola

	Coca-Cola		Pepsi Cola	
Year	Volume premium (%)	Price premium (%)	Volume premium (%)	Price premium (%)
2007	479	57	168	31
2008	482	62	165	38
2009	478	61	165	37
2010	488	72	157	48
2011	493	76	149	50
2012	509	78	150	54
2013	536	81	160	55
2014	563	80	170	56
2015	565	77	171	54

Source: Author's calculations based on Passport GMID
Note: Percentages are relative to private label. For example, the Coca-Cola volume premium of 479% and price premium of 57% in 2007 means that the volume (in liters) of Coca-Cola sold in 2007 is 479% higher than the private label volume of carbonated soft drinks globally, for a price that is, on average, 57% higher than the price of private label carbonated soft drinks per liter.

industries. The agency summarizes these analyses in an overall score ranging from one to five where five is highest. Table 9.3 shows that sales equity is generally higher in B2C industries than in B2B industries. However, sales equity can be significant in B2B, too. Consider IBM, Accenture, Huawei, or Goldman Sachs. Only in commodities (mining, oil & gas) does the brand per se add very little to volume and price premium. This makes sense. Would you go the extra mile to get BP gas rather than Exxon gas?

Profit-Based Brand Equity

While a global brand's customer and sales equity scores might impress the firm's chief financial officer (CFO), the CFO cares most about the brand's contribution to firm profitability. More than anything else, profits (or earnings) are a proxy of share price. Global brand managers need a firm grasp on brand profitability as a metric.

Table 9.3 Sales equity for selected global brands

B2B/B2C[a]	Industry group	Brand	Home country	Sales equity (rating)[b]
B2B	Building materials	Cemex	Mexico	2
	Engineering	Siemens	Germany	2
	Enterprise software	SAP	Germany	3
	Investment banking	Goldman Sachs	USA	3
	IT services	IBM	USA	4
	Mining	Vale	Brazil	1
	Oil & gas	Shell	Netherlands/UK	1
	Professional services	Accenture	USA	3
	Telecom infrastructure	Huawei	China	3
B2C	Apparel	Nike	USA	4
	Automotive	Toyota	Japan	3
	Beer	Heineken	Netherlands	4
	Entertainment	Walt Disney	USA	4
	Footwear	Havaianas	Brazil	4
	Insurance	AXA	France	2
	Jewelry	Tanishq	India	3
	Logistics	UPS	USA	4
	Luxury	Gucci	Italy	5
	Payments	Visa	USA	4
	Personal care	Gillette	USA	4
	Restaurants	McDonald's	USA	4
	Retail	Ikea	Sweden	3
	Retail banking	Santander	Spain	3
	Soft drinks	Coca-Cola	USA	5
	Technology	Apple	USA	4
	Telecom	Vodafone	UK	3

Source: Adapted from Millward Brown (2016)
[a]Indicated is whether the primary market is B2B or B2C
[b]Sales equity is measured on a scale from 1 to 5, with 5 being the highest, and refers to 2016

Profit Contribution

Customer and sales equity contribute to brand profitability primarily through their effect on the timing and magnitude of revenues, while other potential sources of global brand value—economies of scale and scope, transnational innovation, and organizational benefits—contribute by reducing costs. Profit is a function of the number of units sold, the average selling price, cost of goods sold (i.e., materials and direct labor used to produce the good), and operating expenses (marketing, R&D, general & administrative expenses). Figure 9.5 shows multiple paths to profitability. However, the key drivers of profitability differ among the five types of brands (Table 9.4).

Value Brands

The very low price of value brands requires a firm to tightly control cost of goods sold (COGS) (e.g., cheap materials) and operations (e.g., austere offices and low R&D, perhaps copying mass brand innovations) to attain profitability. If the value brand manages these costs effectively, then its operating margin can be substantial). For example, Dacia's average

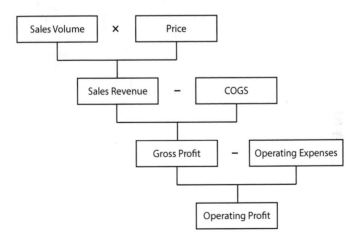

Fig. 9.5 Drivers of global brand profitability (*Note:* COGS = cost of goods sold)

Table 9.4 Typical performance of global brand types on drivers of profitability

| Global brand | Revenues | | | Costs | | |
	Sales volume	Price	COGS	R&D	Marketing	G&A
Value brand	High	Very low	Very low	Very low	Low	Very low
Mass brand	Very high	(Slightly) above average	Average	High	Very high	High
Premium brand	Average/ low	(Very) high	High	Very high	High	Above average
Prestige brand	Very low	Extremely high	Very high	Below average	Above average	Average
Fun brand	Above average	Low	Low	Very low	Average/ high	Low

Note: COGS cost of goods sold, *G&A* general and administrative expenses

operating profit margin of 8–9% is considerably better than the 3–4% Renault earns on its namesake brand.[14] Value brands can command good operating margins in other industries as well; think about Aldi and Lidl (groceries), IKEA (home furnishings), and Ryanair (airlines).

Mass Brands

What extremely low cost is to value brand profitability, extremely high revenues are to mass brands. Everybody values high quality. Quality plus a higher price makes for high gross profits for mass brands. But their operating expenses are much higher than value brands because brand managers spend more on marketing to generate large sales volume and more on R&D to stay ahead of value copy-cats.

---

[14] Bryant, Chris (2015), "VW Turns to Diess's 'Kostenkiller' Instinct," *Financial Times*, August 21, p. 15; Rosemain, Mathieu and Andra Timu (2014), "Can Renault Keep Dacia Cheap?" *Bloomberg Businessweek*, October 2, p. 27.

Premium Brands

High gross margin on a (very) high price makes for high gross profit per unit sold. With a substantial sales volume, premium brands generate disproportionately high gross profits. Of course, the brand incurs high costs to manufacture and market such a premium product. Premium brands are the first movers in new technologies, and so R&D costs are high. For example, Mercedes Benz and BMW spend between $2500 and $3000 on R&D per vehicle sold, while Toyota, Peugeot, or Nissan spend less than $1000 per vehicle.[15]

Notwithstanding the high costs, premium brands occupy the sweet spot in many industries. Luxury cars account for about 10% of the global sales volume but about a third of global car industry profits.[16] In smartphone industry, the Apple iPhone captured on average around 70% of total operating profits over the period 2010–2015, although it accounted for less than 20% of the global unit sales in the same period. The drivers are a high operating margin (35–40%) on the high average price, which in 2015 was $670. In contrast, the average selling price of mass brand Samsung's smartphones was just $343, and its operating margin was less than 10%.[17]

Prestige Brands

These brands achieve a very high profit per unit sold by limiting quantity and charging an extraordinarily high price. Customers expect sumptuous counters or boutiques in high-rent locations, and so these brands rack up very high distribution costs. However, brand managers can more easily identify and reach the narrow target segment with high precision, and the brand benefits from display value and free publicity. Prestige brands— often heirlooms with longer lifecyles than premium brands—rarely com-

---

[15] *Financial Times* (2015), "Under the Hood," March 19, p. 12.

[16] Wright, Robert (2015), "Cadillac in Race to Catch Its Rivals," *Financial Times*, January 14, p. 17.

[17] Cheng, Jonathan (2016), "Samsung Bets on Lower Price," *Wall Street Journal*, April 8, p. B4; http://appleinsider.com/articles/15/11/16/apple-inc-now-inhaling-94-percent-of-global-smart-phone-profits-selling-just-145-percent-of-total-volumes; accessed April 18, 2016.

pete at the cutting edge of technology, and so firms can amortize R&D over the longer time period. Actually, rapid turnover of the assortment can undermine brand equity since the value of a prestige brand is its timelessness, heritage, and authenticity. Consider Patek Philippe's slogan, "You never actually own a Patek Philippe. You merely look after it for the next generation."

Fun Brands

These generate their profits by selling a substantial volume to a global segment, earning a modest profit per item sold. Inventory turnover is fast, which reduces operating expenses. For example, the fast-fashion chain Primark replenishes store inventory daily and brings hundreds of new lines into stores each month so that shoppers visit frequently to discover what's new. If a product does not sell well, the company marks it down to get rid of it quickly and make room for new items. Consequently, Primark's global net sales per square foot of selling space stand at $747, compared with $459 for H&M and $174 for Macy's. According to Primark's CFO John Bason, his company's unrelenting focus on volume allows it to operate on far thinner margins than those of rivals.[18]

Brand Profitability at the Volkswagen Group

Volkswagen A.G. is one of the few companies in the world that has each type of brand in its portfolio. This allows for a nice comparison of brand economics (Table 9.5).[19] As one would expect, the average price is lowest for Skoda and highest for Bentley. Its eponymous mass brand has by far the highest sales volume while Bentley's is tiny. Audi's high sales volume is

[18] Chaudhuri, Saabira (2015), "Primark's Enters Fast-Fashion Fray in U.S.," *Wall Street Journal*, September 9, p. B6.
[19] Volkswagen Group China is a separate entity—as a joint venture with First Automotive Works (FAW). Through this JV, Volkswagen sold 3.4 million cars in China in 2015. Source: Volkswagen AG Annual Report 2015.

Table 9.5 Brand profitability at the Volkswagen Group

Brand	Global brand type	Units sold ('000)	Revenues (€ mn)	Net price (€)	Operating profit (€ mn)	Operating margin (%)
Skoda	Value	800	12,486	15,608	915	7.3%
Volkswagen	Mass	4424	106,240	24,014	2102	2.0%
Audi	Premium	1803	58,420	32,402	5134	8.8%
Porsche	Premium	219	21,533	98,324	3404	15.8%
Bentley	Prestige	10.6	1936	182,642	110	5.7%
SEAT	Fun	544	8572	15,757	−10	−0.1%

Source: Author's calculations based on Volkswagen A.G. Annual Report 2015. Operating profit is before special reservations to cover the costs of the emission scandal

somewhat of an anomaly, fueled by downward stretching, which accounts for the relatively small price gap between Audi and Volkswagen. The A1, A3, and Q3 account for one-third of Audi's sales volume but retail below $35,000 while the flagship A8—which retails north of $80,000—sells fewer than 30,000 units. In Chapter, "Customer Propositions for Global Brands," we have seen the dangers of downward stretching for the pricing power of premium brands.

Skoda shows that value brands can generate good operating margins. But it is a high operating margin on a low price, so operating profits are modest. The high operating margin for the premium brands is what one would expect but the operating margins for Bentley and Volkswagen's namesake brand are too low. These brands are underperforming on brand economics. Taken together, the less-than-stellar brand economics of the Volkswagen Group show up in the value of its brands. The total value of its entire portfolio of brands in 2016 was $37.8 billion, roughly the same as the brand value of much smaller BMW ($35 billion), according to Brand Finance.

Profit Growth

Global brands that command high customer equity offer a higher potential to extend existing product lines, expand into related and new product categories, enter new markets, and increase revenues by licensing brand names to be used in other categories. Luxury fashion brands such as Hugo Boss demonstrate how the brand name helped expand the business into new categories (e.g., women's wear), open new stores across the world, and license the brand for sunglasses, cosmetics, etc. As a result, revenues of the company rose considerably over the last 20 years and the brand possesses high sales equity—Millward Brown gave Hugo Boss a brand contribution score of 4 in 2015. It is the greater awareness and positive associations potential customers hold with respect to a strong brand that reduce entry barriers and result into faster trial, referrals, and adoption and stronger preferences for the new product.

A study by Marc Fischer and colleagues from the University of Cologne (Germany), covering 614 companies from a range of B2C industries uses five-year consensus forecasts of financial analysts as proxy for profit growth—note that what analysts think about your company is of great importance to the C-suite in its own right. The study finds that the expected profit growth for companies whose brands score in the highest 25% on customer equity is three percentage points per year higher than that for companies in the lowest quartile (14% versus 11%).[20]

Return on Capital

Strong brands should be able to make more efficient use of invested capital. Demand fluctuations are dampened by customer loyalty. The market potential for line extensions is higher because they can draw upon existing high awareness and positive attitudes. This allows a larger volume to be produced with the same installed capital base. The aforementioned study by Fischer and colleagues found that the return on capital (net profit divided by invested capital) was nine percentage points higher for companies in the highest quartile on customer equity than for companies in the lowest quartile (30% versus 21%).

---

[20] Fischer, Marc, Max Backhaus, and Tobias Hornig (2016), "How Do Brands Generate Value for Investors? It's from New Business and Competitive Distinctiveness," Working Paper, University of Cologne.

Calculating Global Brand Equity

Customer, sales, and profit equity all contribute to the dollar value of the brand. But how do we actually calculate it? We use a multistep valuation process:

1. Conduct a financial analysis to determine the amount of corporate earnings attributed to a particular brand. If the firm adopts a branded house strategy (possibly with sub brands), this determination is straightforward. Otherwise, you need to allocate the earnings of the firm across brands. To avoid a possibly atypical year, you could consider using the average earnings over the last three years.
2. Assess the brand's strength. The brand strength score derives from customer equity, and is routinely calculated by various brand valuation consultancies. For example, Brand Finance rates brand strength on a scale from 0 to 100. In 2015, Lego received a score of 93.4—the highest score of all brands—McKinsey received a score of 90.1, Coca-Cola 89.6, and Disney 89.5.
3. Estimate the brand multiple, M, which is an indicator of confidence about the brand's future earnings prospect. Brands with a higher brand strength score receive a higher brand multiple than brands with a low score. Here are two ways how can you arrive at the multiple for your brand:

   - External approach: Look at the multiples in your industry used in acquisitions in recent years, and adjust the multiple for your brand strength versus that of the acquired brands. If your brand has a higher score, adjust upward; if your brand's score is lower, adjust downward.
   - Internal approach: Determine the brand multiple on internal financial estimates:
     - Determine the discount rate i for your brand, which is the sum of the cost of capital and a risk premium applied because the future is uncertain. Adjust the risk premium based on the brand

strength score. Stronger brands carry a smaller risk premium because future earnings are more stable.
- Next, estimate the long-term ("perpetuity") growth rate of the brand's earnings, g.
- The brand multiple $M = 1/[i-g]$. This only works if $i > g$, so it is not useful for valuing extremely fast growing brands.

4. Calculate brand value by multiplying current earnings by the brand multiple.

The multiplier analysis is similar to the calculation that financial analysts use to determine the market value of stocks (e.g., 6× earnings or 12× earnings). A global CPG company used the external multiplier method to value its brands in three categories—household and hygienic products, food products, and pharmaceutical products.[21] The company estimated that 5% of its earnings came from sales under private labels. It allocated the remaining 95% of its earnings to its three divisions: household and hygienic brands ($99.5 million), food brands ($45.7 million), and pharmaceutical brands ($31.6 million). For household and hygienic brands, it used a brand multiple of 20, which was the multiple it applied when it acquired a global brand from another company three years before. For food brands, the brand multiple of 17 was based on recent acquisitions by other companies. Finally, a multiple of 20 was used for its pharmaceutical brands. This was lower than the multiple of around 30 that was used in recent acquisitions in the pharmaceutical industry because the strength of its own brands was lower than that of the brands involved in these transactions. This led to the following brand valuation:

- household and hygienic brands: 99.5 × 20 = $1990 million;
- food brands = 45.7 × 17 = $776.9 million;
- pharmaceutical brands: 31.6 × 20 = $632 million.

When Procter & Gamble acquired Gillette Co. in 2005, Merrill Lynch was hired to determine the value of Gillette's business. As part of the anal-

---

[21] Example taken from Kapferer, Jean-Noel (2012), The *New Strategic Brand Management*, London: Kogan Page, 5 ed.

ysis, Merrill Lynch estimated the discount rate and the perpetuity growth for different business segments, including consumer batteries brand Duracell. Duracell's earnings before interest and taxes (EBIT) in 2004 were $398 million. Merrill Lynch used a discount rate i of 9.5% and an estimated perpetuity growth rate g of 0.9%. This gives a brand multiple of 11.6 (1/(0.095–0.009), and values Duracell at 398 × 11.6 = $4617 million.[22]

Global Brand Equity Valuations

Companies do these calculations themselves or turn to a global brand consultancy such as Brand Finance, Interbrand, or Millward Brown. Each has developed its own proprietary methodology to isolate earnings attributable to the brand, forecasting earnings growth and discounting them. Sometimes, the results are quite similar. For example, in 2015, all three agencies pegged the global brand equity of eBay between $14.0 and $14.4 billion and the equity of Audi between $9.6 and $10.3 billion.

In many cases though, brand equity estimates differ markedly. Table 9.6 compares three estimates for ten of the world's most valuable global brands.[23] Look at the range of estimates for Apple (from $128.3 billion to $247.0 billion) and Google (from $76.7 billion to $173.7 billion). You might argue that estimating brand equity for high tech firms is tricky because of rapid and sometimes difficult-to-understand innovations and very high growth rates. However, Table 9.6 shows that estimates can even differ dramatically in mature and low tech industries: Coca-Cola's valu-

---

[22] http://www.sec.gov/Archives/edgar/data/80424/000095012305006039/y06542a2sv4za. htm; and http://sec.edgar-online.com/gillette-co/10-k-annual-report/2005/03/14/section25. aspx; accessed March 23, 2016. The calculations are mine. My calculations assume that all earnings of the Duracell division are attributable to the namesake brand. If the division has non-brand related sources of income (e.g., private label sales), these should be subtracted from EBIT and the estimate of Duracell's global brand equity would be commensurately lower. Disclaimer: I do not imply that Merrill Lynch necessarily agrees with my calculations. Merrill Lynch used multiple estimates for perpetuity growth rate and discount rate, and complemented this analysis with a multiple analysis based on recent acquisitions in the industry.

[23] I use 2015 for this comparison as the Interbrand estimates for 2016 were not available yet at the time of writing.

Table 9.6 Global brand equity estimates by brand valuation agency

| Global brand | Global brand equity estimates ($ billion) | | |
	Interbrand	Millward Brown	Brand Finance
Apple	170.3	247.0	128.3
Google	120.3	173.7	76.7
Coca-Cola	78.4	83.8	35.8
Microsoft	67.7	115.5	67.1
IBM	65.1	94.0	35.4
Toyota	49.0	28.9	35.0
Samsung	45.3	21.6	81.8
General Electric	42.3	59.3	48.0
McDonald's	39.8	81.2	22.0
Amazon	37.9	62.3	56.1

Source: Websites of the brand valuation agencies
Note: Figures refer to 2015; reported are the brand equity estimates of the ten
most valuable brands according to Interbrand

ation varies between $35.8 billion and $83.8 billion and McDonald's between $22.0 billion and $81.2 billion.

I analyzed the convergence in global brand equity estimates statistically by correlating the 2015 dollar value estimates of 100 of the world's largest global brands by each consultancy.[24] A correlation of 1 indicates perfect convergence while a correlation of 0 means no convergence whatsoever. As rule of thumb, correlations above 0.7 indicate strong convergence. The correlation between Millward Brown and Interbrand is 0.28, between Millward Brown and Brand Finance is 0.56, and between Interbrand and Brand Finance is 0.48. We cannot consider this level of convergence satisfactory, especially not in discussions with accounting and finance colleagues who are used to a high level of precision. Why is the convergence between estimates unsatisfactory? Reasonable people can choose quite different assumptions—about market conditions, timing of events, consumer behavior, cost of capital, and so forth—that result in different conclusions. There can also

[24] I used the Interbrand Top 100 to select the top 10 brands because Interbrand provides the fewest publicly available global brand equity estimates. I used pairwise deletion, that is, the correlation between each pair of brand consultancies uses all the brands for which both consultancies provided a dollar figure.

be information asymmetries, where one firm has inside knowledge or unique market intelligence.

The absence of strong convergence between the different brand equity estimates has two implications. First, the C-Suite should consider the three components of global brand equity, customer, sales, and profit equity as brand performance metrics in their own right. Second, any specific dollar estimate for a particular year is less informative than the evolution in brand equity over time. The MNC should track global brand equity over time using one particular methodology. For example, the Indian conglomerate Tata & Sons uses Brand Finance's services and compares results year over year. It has set the goal that the Tata brand should be among the top 25 most valuable brands of the world in 2025.

Stability in Global Brand Equity Rank Over Time

If you are one of the most valuable brands today, then how likely will you rank among the most valuable in ten years? To answer this question, I compared global brand value between 2006 and 2015 and identified the brands that belonged to the top 50 in either or both years.[25] Although their relative rank and change in dollar value could—and often did—differ between top brands, if your brand belonged to the top 50 in 2006, you had a 72% chance of being among the top 50 in 2015.

Extrapolating these results, today's top 50 brands have a 72% chance of making the 2025 list. That's how stable strong global brands are across industries: technology (e.g., Google, Apple, Microsoft, Cisco), automobiles (Toyota, Mercedes, BMW), telecoms (Vodafone), payments (American Express), media (Disney), apparel (Nike), retail (Walmart), logistics (UPS), and consumables (Coca-Cola, Marlboro, McDonald's). Of the 14 global brands that dropped out of the top 50 by 2015, three are—no surprise—banks (Santander, Morgan Stanley, and Deutsche) and four are automotive (Chevrolet, Ford, Nissan, and Harley-Davidson).

---

[25] I use Millward Brown for this analysis. Some of the brands in the top-50 are not really global (e.g., China Construction Bank, Royal Bank of Canada). I focused on what I consider the 50 most valuable *global* brands.

Which brands are in the top 50 in 2015 that were not there in 2007? Such technology brands as Alibaba, Amazon, Baidu, Oracle, SAP, Tencent, and the youngest of the lot, Facebook (founded in 2004).

Managerial Takeaways

Gear all your global branding efforts toward increasing brand equity. In formal terms, global brand equity is the goodwill adhering to the brand. Any accountant will tell you that goodwill is intangible, and so you need partial measures that you can easily track over time. Here are crucial metrics.

- Customer-based brand equity is the bedrock of strong brands. Absent customer equity, even satisfactory sales-based and profit-based equity are subject to a rapid decline if a competitor launches a better product into the global marketplace, a new player enters the market, your brand faces a crisis, or the global economy nosedives.
- To measure customer equity, you can administer Tool 9.1 annually to customers in your major countries and track your scores over time. No brand can be strong without high awareness. The attitude metrics allow you to dig below the surface. How about brand stature and brand vitality? What about weak spots? What are customers likely to do in the future? Do customers practice what they preach (actions)?
- In various industries, ranging from CPG to cars, brand managers tend to run ever deeper price promotions to keep volume high. This practice is more a bad habit than a strategy. Strong brands should translate their customer equity into a price premium, a volume premium, preferably both. Sales equity provides the funds to invest continually in the brand. You can track and evaluate both price and volume premium closely in unison. You can get historical data from your company records and benchmark data from the outside.
- I have worked with marketing executives who lacked deep knowledge of the cost structure of their brands. Yet their CFOs are more interested in earnings than in sales revenues. How does your brand perform on each element of Fig. 9.5? Compare your brand's performance with

the benchmark for a typical brand in Table 9.4. If there are discrepancies, devise a plan. Engage your CFO on brand economics.
- Track overall global brand equity over time, using one of the brand consultancies. Each consultancy has its own methodology, touted as superior to the others. Which consultancy matters less than sticking with the same consultancy over time.

10

Global Brands and Shareholder Value

Chief marketing officers and brand managers traditionally formulate the goals of global branding from a customer perspective, not a shareholder perspective. While little value creation takes place if the brand does not resonate with customers, marketing executives can no longer base their decisions solely on sales or market share response. Even though many companies are working to contribute to their communities, design work to intrinsically motivate employees, and are cognizant of the wage gap between front line workers and senior management, the C-suite of most publicly-traded companies still puts shareholders first. If you happen to be an employee who also owns company stock—and most top executives do—then you are a member of the company's ultimate target audience. You probably watch your company's stock price. If you don't, then maybe you should. Senior marketing executives must be able to show how their global brand building efforts contribute to shareholder value. Much can still be gained here. Less than 5% of the marketing-mix decisions made by US (senior) vice presidents of marketing or sales or CMOs consider the effect on stock prices, stock returns, or Tobin's q. A follow-up study found that this applies to senior marketing executives in other major economies as well.[1]

Toyota's marketers spend $3.2 billion dollars per year on advertising alone. Add promotions, channel development, and sales expenses, and you are talking over five billion dollars in brand investments per year. Toyota is not even the biggest spender. Procter & Gamble's (P&G's) advertising investments exceed $10 billion per year, and its trade and consumer promotions are in the same order of magnitude. The C-suite wants proof that these marketing expenditures are building shareholder value rather than wasting profits.

So how do you make the case? By taking a closer look at how your brand creates shareholder value. I will do this from four different angles through the eyes of your finance and accounting colleagues (Fig. 10.1).[2] These insights will help CMOs to keep their seats at the executive table.

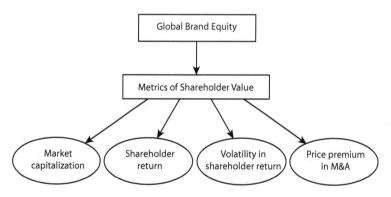

Fig. 10.1 Global brand equity and shareholder value

---

[1] Mintz, Ofer, Jan-Benedict E.M. Steenkamp, and Imran S. Currim (2016), "Marketing Metric Use around the World," working paper, University of North Carolina.

[2] The empirical evidence introduced in this chapter does not always focus on global brands per se. However, given the size of the firms and the examples provided in the articles, it is clear that the results are heavily dominated by global brands.

Table 10.1 Global brand equity as percentage of firm market capitalization by brand valuation agency

Global brand	Global brand equity as% of market capitalization	
	Lower bound	Upper bound
Apple	22	42
Google	15	33
Coca-Cola	19	45
Microsoft	15	26
IBM	27	70
Toyota	14	23
Samsung	16	61
General Electric	13	19
McDonald's	20	75
Amazon	12	20

Note: I included the top brands from Interbrand's annual ranking. I based my calculations on 2015 brand equity estimates from the three paramount rating agencies, Interbrand, Millward Brown, and Brand Finance. I calculated the lower bound percentage by dividing the lowest of the three brand equity estimates by the market cap as of December 31, 2015. I did the same for the upper bound. I divided the highest of the three brand equity estimates by the market cap.

Market Capitalization of the Firm

How do global brands affect the market value of a firm? That might strike you as an obvious question, since we just studied how to calculate the dollar value of a brand. One dollar extra in global brand equity should translate directly into one dollar extra in the market capitalization of the firm, right? Unfortunately, life is not that so simple. This ignores considerable uncertainty in brand equity estimates. Table 10.1 shows the lower and upper bound of the percentage of a firm's market capitalization that we can attribute to brand value for the world's top-ten brands according to Interbrand. The good news is that global brands do account for a significant portion of the firm's market capitalization. The bad news is that investors discount brand equity when valuing a company.

So, what do we know about the effect of brand equity on firm value? Actually quite a lot. One study found that one dollar increase in brand equity increases firm value by 25–30 cents.[3] The pass-through rate is not 100% because of the fickleness of brand equity estimates. Another study analyzed and integrated the findings across 32 studies.[4] Such a "study of studies" is called meta-analysis. The study finds that 1% increase in brand equity translates into 0.22% increase in market capitalization of the firm. A third study focused on the market capitalization of the firm relative to its book value, the total value of a firm's assets on its balance sheet (market-to-book ratio). A 1% increase in global brand equity translates into 0.25–0.30% increase in the market-to-book ratio.[5]

The positive effect of brand equity on firm value found in these studies means that investments in global brands create firm value, because market capitalization only increases if the value-creating effects of investments exceed the costs incurred.

There is also evidence for the effect of customer equity on firm value. The five attitudinal brand asset valuator (BAV) factors (differentiation, relevance, energy, esteem, and knowledge) affect firm value in a range of industries, albeit different factors matter more in different industries. A brand's score on energy and knowledge factors more into company valuation for industrial firms and nondurable goods firms while differentiation and relevance are primary drivers of the value of financial, high-tech, and durable goods firms.[6]

Two studies looked at customer satisfaction with the brand, a proxy for a customer's intended action, as it is strongly related to purchase, loyalty, and word of mouth. One study found that 1% change in customer satisfaction is associated with a 4.6% change in the market capitalization

[3] Barth, Mary E. et al. (1998), "Brand Value and Capital Market Valuation," *Review of Accounting Studies*, 3 (1–2), pp. 41–68.

[4] Edeling, Alexander and Marc Fischer (2016), "Marketing's Impact on Firm Value – Generalizations from a Meta-Analysis," *Journal of Marketing Research*, 53 (August), pp. 515–534.

[5] Kerin, Roger A. and Raj Sethuraman (1998), "Exploring the Brand Value-Shareholder Value Nexus for Consumer Goods Companies," *Journal of the Academy of Marketing Science*, 26 (4), pp. 260–273.

[6] Mizik, Natalie and Robert Jacobson (2008), "Valuing Branded Businesses," *Journal of Marketing*, 73 (November), pp. 137–153.

of the firm.[7] A second study examined the effect of customer satisfaction on Tobin's q ratio, a measure proposed by Nobel laureate James Tobin. To calculate your company's Tobin q, you divide the market value of equity plus the book value of debt by the replacement cost of its assets. The intuition is that replacement cost (the denominator of q) is a logical measure of alternative uses of a firm's assets. A firm that creates a market value that is greater than the replacement cost of its assets is perceived as using its resources more effectively and thus as creating shareholder value. A firm that does not create incremental value has a Tobin's q equal to 1. The study found that 1% increase in consumer satisfaction is associated with 1.6% increase in Tobin's q.[8]

Shareholder Return

Strong global brands command more loyalty from customers and are less vulnerable to competitive actions. This loyalty gives brand managers a degree of freedom to set higher prices without adversely affecting brand sales volume resulting in a higher level of operating earnings. The presence of global brands also increases the likelihood that investors will consider the firm for inclusion in their portfolio. Why is that the case? Stock markets reflect information asymmetry between firms and investors. Management conveys economic information that only insiders know (e.g., competitive viability, R&D pipeline) through various signals, one of which is the brand. Strong, globally recognized brands are indicators of financial well-being.[9] No surprise investors prefer to seek and hold the stocks of firms with well-known brands because they lack expertise across the entire universe of stocks, and stocks with a larger investor base

[7] Fornell, Claes et al. (2006), "Customer Satisfaction and Stock Prices: High Returns, Low Risk," *Journal of Marketing*, 70 (January), pp. 3–14.

[8] Anderson, Eugene W., Claes Fornell, and Sanal K. Mazvancheryl (2004), "Customer Satisfaction and Shareholder Value," *Journal of Marketing*, 68 (October), pp. 172–185.

[9] Hsu, Liwu, Susan Fournier, and Shuba Srinivasan (2012), "Branding and Firm Value," in *Handbook of Marketing and Finance*, Sundar Bharadwaj and Shankar Ganesan (eds.), Northampton (MA): Edward Elgar, pp. 155–203.

generate higher returns.[10] This effect becomes even more pronounced if we take into account that investors are turning to global stock markets to diversify their portfolios and discover the best opportunities. There are simply too many foreign companies to investigate in detail, and so the stock of those companies with recognizable brands will benefit from a larger investor base.

Empirical evidence strongly supports the positive effect of global brand equity on shareholder return. The aforementioned meta-analysis found that 1% increase in brand equity translates on average into 0.43% increase in shareholder return. Another study examined the stock price performance of a portfolio of over 100 US firms with strong global brands over seven years. The average monthly return to shareholders was 1.15 percentage points higher than the overall market.[11]

Millward Brown reports that, in the period April 2007–April 2016, the stock market value of the BrandZ Strong Brands Portfolio, a subset of the Global Top 100, appreciated 105.9%, significantly outperforming the 60.7% rise in the S&P 500 over the same period and the 20.1% gain of the MSCI World Index, a weighted index of global stocks. According to Millward Brown, this "affirms that valuable brands deliver superior returns over time and regardless of market disruptions. It also demonstrates the positive return on money invested to build meaningfully different and salient brands [brands with high customer equity]."[12]

The effect of customer equity on shareholder return has also received significant attention. The meta-analysis found that 1% increase in brand equity translates on average into 0.75% increase in shareholder return. In another study, the cumulative capital gains of a diversified portfolio of firms that are in the top 20% in brand satisfaction in their industry is nearly twice that of the Dow Jones Industrial Average and three times that of the S&P 500 over a six-year period.[13]

---

[10] Shiller, Robert J. (2002), "Bubbles, Human Judgment, and Expert Opinion," *Financial Analysts Journal*, 58 (3), pp. 18–26; Merton, Robert C. (1987), "A Simple Model of Capital Market Equilibrium with Incomplete Information," *Journal of Finance*, 42(3), pp. 483–510.

[11] Madden, Thomas J., Frank Fehle, and Susan Fournier (2006), "Brands Matter: An Empirical Demonstration of the Creation of Shareholder Value through Branding," *Journal of the Academy of Marketing Science*, 34 (2), pp. 224–235.

[12] Millward Brown (2016), *Brand Z Top 100 Most Valuable Global Brands*, p. 15.

[13] Fornell et al. (2006).

Volatility in Shareholder Return

Most shareholders are risk averse and will trade higher returns for lower volatility. We have seen that high global brand equity translates into higher shareholder returns. But do these returns come with higher volatility? Many investors will prefer a stock that has an expected return of 8% ± 1% than a stock with an expected return of 9% ± 4%.

On the one hand, we might think that global brands add more risk to the company since any crisis anywhere in the world could hit sales and profitability elsewhere. For example, the Deepwater Horizon disaster hurt BP's global image and its stock price. In one month, its share price fell by 55%.[14] At one point, BP's loss in market capitalization stood at a staggering $104.4 billion, considerably more than what it ultimately had to pay in damages.

Honda is one of the world's most valuable car brands, but a half-dozen recalls over one year dented its global reputation. In the period November 22, 2013, to January 6, 2015, its share price fell by 33%. Honda attributed its quality problems to its policy of aggressive volume growth and its opening its supply chain to a diverse group of international suppliers. Then came the recall of millions of cars fitted with Japanese supplier Takata's potentially faulty airbags.

So highly valuable global brands in your stock portfolio might increase portfolio risk because in today's connected world, they have more to lose. Big global brands are also more likely to attract class-action lawsuits (founded or not), antitrust actions, IP infringements, and interference by foreign governments who might be less likely to go after local brands.

On the other hand, customer equity sustains high brand equity. Customers feel strongly connected to the brand. Loyal customers are less susceptible to the marketing efforts of rivals, reducing churn among the brand's customer base. Consequently, the demand for strong brands should be less sensitive to price (exhibit smaller price elasticity), and firms

---

[14] From April 20, 2010, to June 25, 2010, BP's share price fell from $60.48 a share to $27.02 a share.

with brands that have a smaller price elasticity of demand exhibit lower volatility in shareholder return.[15]

Firms with strong global brands are generally better known among investors, and therefore generally should be included in the portfolio of more investors around the globe. This makes them less vulnerable to the volatile actions of a small number of shareholders. In addition, what investors know about firms with strong global brands should be more positive (given their high brand equity and related associations) than firms with weak brands. In other words, the deep roots of strong brands in the hearts and minds of customers and investors dampens the effect of overall market skittishness.

So, which is it? Are the stock returns for firms with strong global brands more or less variable than the stock returns for the market in general? The evidence indicates that global brands help to stabilize stock returns. The aforementioned study of the 100 or so US firms with the strongest global brands also compared their market volatility as a portfolio with the market volatility of the benchmark portfolio.[16] Financial analysts and CFOs calculate market volatility as beta coefficient which indicates the extent to which the return of a given stock or portfolio of stocks move up and down with the overall stock market. The overall market has a beta of one; a value below one means that the stock (portfolio) is less volatile than the market, while a value above one means more volatile. The beta of the portfolio with valuable global brands was 0.84, that is, 16% less volatile than the market.

Other work focused on customer equity. One study found that firms that command high customer equity have less risk associated with share price.[17] This study also examined the asymmetry in the dampening effect of strong brands. When the stock market increases, would the increase in stock price of firms with strong global brands exceed or be less than the market? That's called *upside risk*, and any dampening would prevent an excessive price increase. When the market decreases,

---

[15] Subrahmanyan, Marti G. and Stavros B. Thomadakis (1980), "Systematic Risk and the Theory of the Firm," *Quarterly Journal of Economics*, 94 (3), pp. 437–451.

[16] Madden et al. (2006).

[17] Rego, Lopo L., Matthew T. Billett, and Neil A. Morgan (2009), "Consumer-Based Brand Equity and Firm Risk," *Journal of Marketing*, 73(November), pp. 47–60.

would the stock price fall more or less than the market? That's *downside risk*, and dampening would limit the stock price's tumble. In the study, the dampening effect of strong brands is three times larger for downside risk (when stock prices are falling) than for upside risk (when stock prices are rising). Though customer equity always reduces stock return volatility, it is especially powerful in protecting the firm's returns during market downturns because of the stronger loyalty and commitment of customers. That is of course what investors like.[18]

A second study showed that strong global brands reduced the downside risk during the collapse of the stock market precipitated by the bankruptcy of Lehmann Brothers in fall 2008. The drop in share price of firms with global brands that command high customer equity was 29.5%, five percentage points less than the S&P 500 drop of 34.7%.[19] In another study, a portfolio of firms that are in the top 20% in brand satisfaction in their industry had a beta coefficient of 0.78, indicating that volatility was 22% less than the market.[20]

Global Brand Value in Mergers and Acquisitions

A brand's contribution to shareholder value becomes quite apparent when one company acquires another. To complete the acquisition, the acquirer usually must pay a premium over the market price of the target to the target's shareholders. An analysis conducted by the Boston Consulting covering 40,000 M&A transactions over 25 years shows that the average M&A premium is 32% above a target's pre-acquisition share

---

[18] At first sight, investors should gladly accept upward risk. Who doesn't want to benefit from a stronger than expected stock price increase? However, this depends on your investment strategy. If you go short, you anticipate a decrease in share price and high upward volatility makes the stock more risky for you. Sudden price increases can also trigger the execution of various agreements such as forward contracts at a moment you do not expect it.

[19] Johansson, Johny K., Claudiu V. Dimofte, and Sanal K. Mazvancheryl (2012), "The Performance of Global Brands in the 2008 Financial Crisis: A Test of Two Brand Value Measures," *International Journal of Research in Marketing*, 29(3), pp. 235–245.

[20] Fornell et al. (2006).

Table 10.2 Global brand equity in the acquisition of Gillette Co. by Procter & Gamble

Business segment	EBITDA ($mn)	Multiple range	Value range ($mn)
Blades and razors	$1,629	19×–24×	$30,951–$39,096
Duracell	$490	9×–12×	$4,410–$5,880
Oral care	$249	13×–15×	$3,237–$3,735
Personal care	$95	13×–15×	$1,235–$1,425
Braun	$95	8×–10×	$760–$950
Total			$40,593–$51,086

Note: Author's calculations based on the acquisition document and Gillette's 2004 annual report

price.[21] Of course, the price premium is not only driven by the equity of the target's brands; the exact contribution of global brand equity to the price premium varies across M&As. However, few doubt that strong global brands—which, after all, represent unique, valuable, intangible and scarce assets difficult to build from scratch—are an important component in acquisition price of any branded business.

In 2005, P&G paid $57.2 billion for Gillette Co., 18% above the market value of $48.5 billion. Merrill Lynch assisted in the transaction. It calculated what Gillette would be worth to P&G, based on earnings per business segment and expected economies of scale and scope. Merrill Lynch estimated the EBITDA (earnings before interest, taxes, depreciation and amortization; this is approximately equal to operating profit) multiple per business segment, based on publicly available information on transaction multiples paid in comparable transactions involving companies in their industry.[22] I use the multiples to calculate the value of each segment and of the company before acquisition synergies kick in (Table 10.2). If we subtract Gillette's book value ($3.2 billion) and account for intangibles like patents, this shows that the approximate value of Gillette's brand portfolio is in the range of $37 billion to $47 billion.[23] So, up to 80% of the amount received by Gillette's shareholders—and approximately $4.4 billion of the

[21] Kengelbach, Jens et al. (2015), "From Buying Growth to Building Value," BCG Report, October.
[22] http://www.sec.gov/Archives/edgar/data/80424/000095012305006039/y06542a2sv4za.htm; accessed March 29, 2016.
[23] Disclaimer: The calculations are mine. I do not imply that Merrill Lynch necessarily agrees with my calculations.

M&A premium—was vested in its global brands, including its namesake brand, Duracell, Oral-B, and Braun.[24]

The Gillette example also shows how marketing executives at privately-held companies such as Cargill or Mars, can calculate the contribution of their global brands to their firm value, based on EBITDA per business segment, the applicable multiplier—obtained using information on transaction multiples paid in their industry—their book value, and intangibles like patents.

In 2008, Anheuser-Busch's Budweiser accepted a $50 billion takeover bid from Belgium-based InBev, forming the world's largest beer maker. This bid represented a premium of 45% over the closing price before InBev first announced its takeover intention. There is little doubt that again, much of the M&A premium of over $15 billion is vested in A-B's brand portfolio, which included Budweiser, the most valuable beer brand in the world. Since the acquisition, AB InBev has successfully grown Budweiser's equity from $10.8 billion in 2008 to $27.9 billion in 2016.

In 2013, Berkshire Hathaway and 3G Capital acquired Heinz for $23 billion, paying a price premium of 20% above Heinz's closing price. Alex Behring, 3G managing partner explained why they were willing to pay an acquisition premium of $4 billion, "Heinz was an appealing acquisition due to the strength of its brands and its global presence."[25] Heinz's namesake brand was worth $7.6 billion at the time of the acquisition. In 2015, Heinz acquired Kraft in a deal worth $45.4 billion. The details of the deal were very complex—Heinz paid a $10 billion dividend to Kraft shareholders—but Kraft's shares rose 36% following the deal announcement.

Many acquisitions of valuable global brands take place in the CPG industry, traditionally an industry with strong consumer brands. Other industries are not exempt. In May 2014, Apple paid $3 billion for Beats Electronic, which includes both Beats Audio hardware and Beats Music, the streaming radio service founded by rapper Dr. Dre and music industry executive Jimmy Iovine. Although Beats Electronic was not publicly

---

[24] Merrill Lynch estimated that P&G could realize cost savings and revenue synergies of around 9% per year and it paid a price premium of 18%. This roughly indicates that half of the price premium is due to its strong global brands as nearly all of Gillette's intangibles are in its brands.

[25] Jargon Julie and Serena Ng (2013), "Heinz Sold as Deals Take Off," *Wall Street Journal*, February 15.

listed, Beats' brand equity was estimated to account for one-third of the takeover price.

Managerial Takeaways

Accountability is a watchword in today's corporations. Senior marketing executives must be able to show how their investments in building strong global brands create shareholder value. The ability to justify marketing expenditures in terms of shareholder value and to present evidence of results gives senior marketing executives a strong voice in the C-suite. Table 10.3 lists the evidence of marketing's effect.

Do not let the CFO usurp your position at the top table because he or she can dazzle board members with hard dollar figures while you have to resort to soft measures of customer attachment and liking. Here is an agenda for marketing executives in board discussions about the need and necessity of investments in global brands:

1. Brush up on your financial knowledge (if necessary). Make sure you are comfortable with financial metrics like market portfolio, Tobin's q, and beta.
2. Present evidence on the effect of global brand equity on various metrics of shareholder value (Table 10.3).
3. Quantify the effects of global brand equity estimates for your brand, including its components like customer equity, on market capitalization, shareholder return, and shareholder risk. Gather time series data and refresh your econometric skills. Business analytics techniques are commonly taught in MBA programs, are available in Excel, and are widespread among colleagues with training in finance or accounting. Work with them to get the results. Get the data from company archives or buy them from brand consultancy agencies. Although quantification requires effort, it is less daunting than it sounds, and it gains you the respect of the C-suite.

Table 10.3 Effect of global brand equity on shareholder value

Shareholder value metric	Global brand equity metric	What do we know?
Market capitalization	Overall GBE ($)	$1 increase in brand equity increases market cap by 25–30 cents 1% increase in brand equity increases the market cap of the firm by 0.22% 1% increase in brand equity translates into 0.25–0.30% increase in market-cap-to-book ratio
	Customer equity	The BAV dimensions have a significant effect on the market cap of firms across different industries. Knowledge and energy are particularly important for industrial firms and nondurable goods firms; differentiation and relevance are especially important for financial, high-tech, and durable goods firms 1% improvement in customer satisfaction increases Tobin's q by 1.6% and market cap by 4.6%
Shareholder return	Overall GBE ($)	1% increase in brand equity increases shareholder return by 0.43% The average monthly return of a portfolio of firms with high-equity brands is 1.15 percentage points higher than the market A portfolio of firms with high-equity brands has an average annual return that is 1.5 times that of the S&P 500 and five times that of the MSCI World Index
	Customer equity	1% increase in customer equity increases shareholder return by 0.75% A portfolio of firms with brands that are high on customer satisfaction has an average annual return that is nearly twice that of Dow Jones Industrial Average and three times that of S&P 500

(continued)

Table 10.3 (continued)

Shareholder value metric	Global brand equity metric	What do we know?
Volatility in shareholder return	Overall GBE ($)	The volatility (beta) of a portfolio of US firms with high-equity brands is 16% lower than the market
	Customer equity	Customer equity reduces stock price volatility; customer equity is particularly helpful in protecting shareholder return during market downturns
		The share price of firms with brands that command high customer equity drops 15% less in a severe bear market than the overall market
		The volatility (beta) of a portfolio of firms with brands that are high on customer satisfaction is 22% lower than the market
Price premium in mergers and acquisitions	Overall GBE ($)	The average premium above a target's pre-acquisition share price is 32%
		The equity of the target firm's brand (portfolio) can easily account for 50% of the price premium paid in an acquisition

4. Use the price premium paid for firms, together with an estimate of the value of their brand(s), which you can obtain from brand valuation agencies to estimate the discount factor the financial markets apply to brands in your industry. Discuss this price premium and the discount factor with the board. If brands are heavily discounted in your industry, this can offer interesting M&A opportunities. If they are not, this further highlights the important assets that you have in your brands and provides crucial information in case your firm is an acquisition target.

11

The Future of Global Brands

The value of the 100 most valuable global brands grew on average 8.8% *per year* over the last ten years, to a staggering $3.4 trillion in 2016.[1] While I am optimistic about the global potential of brands from all corners of the earth, I am not oblivious to the threats that global corporations face.

First, globalization might stall, and possibly even lose ground. Over the last 70 years, brands have gone global with the continued integration of world markets. However, the end of the Cold War has not been the end of animosity between major powers. Hateful ethnocentric sentiments, discriminatory trade policies, and sometimes violent interruptions in the free flow of goods, capital, ideas, and people are threatening channels of commercial discourse, distribution, and economic inclusion.

How likely is this reversal? It is easy to forget but global markets have collapsed three times in world history, none anticipated at the time. Why is the Catholic Church the oldest global organization in the world? Why do Germans drink beer and French wine? Why does much of the world basically have the same legal system? Why are the Spanish and French

---

[1] Millward Brown (2016), *BrandZ Top 100 Most Valuable Global Brands 2016.*

© The Author(s) 2017
J.-B. Steenkamp, *Global Brand Strategy*,
DOI 10.1057/978-1-349-94994-6_11

languages so similar but so different from German or Danish? Why is the hill on which the US Congress building stands called Capitol Hill? Why are US soldiers allowed to retire after 20 years? Why is the downtown city grid of Mainz, Vienna, Belgrade, and Budapest basically the same? Where does the idea of the separation between Church and State come from? What did European leaders invoke when they warned about the consequences of not being able to secure the borders in the midst of the 2015 refugee crisis? Why do you read this book in this alphabet?

The answer to all these and countless other questions is the *Roman Empire*, the most powerful and influential edifice the world has ever seen.[2] In the book of Daniel, the Roman Empire is described as "strong as iron – for iron breaks and smashes everything – and as iron breaks things to pieces, so it will crush and break all the others."[3] Daniel prophesied correctly. The Roman legions swept everything before them, even the vaunted Macedonian phalanx. Rome's trade network reached into India, China, Central Asia, and Africa. Yet, after reigning supreme over much of the known world for 600 years, Rome fell in AD 476 after a protracted period of barbarian invasions, civil war, incompetent leadership, and economic and population decline.[4] Much of the known world plunged into half a millennium of darkness.[5] Intercontinental trade routes were cut off,

---

[2] The separation of Church and State was first developed by St. Augustine in his magnum opus *The City of God* in which he distinguished between the Earthly City (e.g., the Roman Empire) and the Heavenly City (whose portal was the Church). It squashed the idea that Christianity is synonymous to the Roman Empire. People can belong to different temporal polities and still be believers. He wrote this book to explain to a bewildered world why the sack of Rome by the Visigoths in August 24, AD 410 was not the end of the world.

[3] Daniel 2:40, using the New International Version.

[4] Over 200 explanations have been proposed for the fall of the Roman Empire. Important contributions include Gibbon, Edward (1776–1788), *The Decline and Fall of the Roman Empire*, who blamed it largely on Christianity and Luttwak, Edward N. (1976), *The Grand Strategy of the Roman Empire*, Baltimore, MD: Johns Hopkins University Press, who puts much blame on the loss of strategic mobility of the legions. The debate continues to be intense, as exemplified by the sharp disagreement between Heather, Peter (2006), *The Fall of the Roman Empire*, Oxford: Oxford University Press and Goldsworthy, Adrian (2009), *How Rome Fell*, New Haven, CT: Yale University Press.

[5] For an incisive account of the collapse of economic life after the Fall of Rome, see Ward-Perkins, Bryan (2006), *The Fall of Rome: And the End of Civilization*, Oxford: Oxford University Press. On the enduring influence of the Roman Empire on Western thoughts, institutions, and customs, see e.g., Heather, Peter (2013), *The Restoration of Rome*, Oxford: Oxford University Press; Wickham,

and economic complexity declined to pre-Roman levels. Even as late as AD 1700, standard of hygiene in Europe had not reached Roman levels.

The second collapse came with the fall of the Mongol Empire. In the thireenth and fourteenth centuries, international commerce and communication had flourished and hummed along during a period known as the *Pax Mongolica*. The Mongol Empire created a trade zone stretching from Venice to Korea. Among its most famous merchant traders was Marco Polo. Where the Romans had assimilated conquered territories through strong military and cultural presence, the nomadic Mongols were assimilated, and some say domesticated, by their captives. The once massive empire divided into four Mongol khanates, loosely by geography. The bubonic plague swept west from China across the empire, wiping out roughly half the population. Each khanate fell in short order to political dissension, thus ending two hundred years of global progress, trade, and prosperity.[6]

The third global market collapse followed World War I, when Great Britain—exhausted by its war effort where it also had to supply huge amounts of war material to the armies of France and Italy—could no longer act as the linchpin of the global trade and financial system. Tariff barriers went up everywhere and trade (sum of exports and imports) as share of GDP in Britain declined from 60% in 1913 to 29% in 1938, and for the world in total from 30% to 10%.[7]

The global system began to be reconstituted after World War II, now centered on the new superpower, the United States. But of late, our world is again in significant turmoil, with renewed tension in Europe, the Middle East, and Eastern Asia, refugee crises, threats to the Schengen Area (the ID-free travel zone within Europe), and heightened xenophobia. Caution is warranted for B2C and B2B firms alike. Corporations that sell B2B brands to state-owned enterprises and to firms in industries with heavy

---

Chris (2009), *The Inheritance of Rome*, New York: Penguin; Beard, Mary (2015), *SPQR: A History of Ancient Rome*, New York: Liveright.

[6] Morgan, David, and David O. Morgan (2009), "The Decline and Fall of the Mongol Empire," *Journal of the Royal Asiatic Society*, 19 (4), pp. 427–437; Di Cosmo, Nicola (2010), "Black Sea Emporia and the Mongol Empire: A Reassessment of the Pax Mongolica," *Journal of the Economic and Social History of the Orient*, 53 (1/2), pp. 83–108.

[7] http://ourworldindata.org/data/global-interconnections/international-trade/; accessed April 4, 2016.

government presence such as infrastructure, utilities, aerospace, defense, mining, and oil and gas are especially vulnerable. Firms can do something about political factors that might threaten the pace of globalization—e.g., by lobbying for trade agreements like the Trans-Pacific Partnership or the Transatlantic Trade and Investment Partnership. But at the end of the day, their ability to influence geopolitical events is limited

The second threat is a backlash against what critical thinkers call the "McDonaldization of society." These thinkers have lamented the alleged growing homogenization of consumer cultures around "soulless" global brands that do not respect local customs and cultures.[8] They criticize the "standardized, commercialized mass commodities" shilled by global corporations and regard global brands as tools for Western cultural imperialism. They reserve special criticism for the United States: authentic and unique local cultural expressions (e.g., in entertainment, food, or lifestyle) stand no chance against the star power of Hollywood, the ideology of consumerism, the lure of Disney, the ubiquity of McDonald's, and the American dream of rugged individualism. I believe global brands can address these concerns head on—albeit they might want to make their case more forcefully.

First, the implicit idea that global brands homogenize the cultural landscape implicitly assumes that (1) global brands come from a single major cultural and economic power and (2) these brands are big and powerful, sweeping everybody before them. Both assumptions ignore the competitive dynamics in the global marketplace. While it is true that the oldest of modern consumer brands emanate from the United States and Western Europe, increasingly, non-Western countries—first Japan, then South Korea, and currently China, Brazil, and India—are starting to make their mark. Rather than leading to homogenization, global brands increase consumer choice around the world. Moreover, the idea that global brands sweep over everybody else ignores unique opportunities for niche brands to go global through digital channels and communication. Take cashmere company Sand River: it offers a unique combination of

---

[8] See for example Giddens, Anthony (2003), *Runaway World*, New York: Routledge; Ritzer, George (2004), *The McDonaldization of Society*, Thousand Oaks, CA: Pine Forge Press; Ritzer, George (2007), *The Globalization of Nothing 2*, Thousand Oaks, CA: Pine Forge Press; Slater, Don (1997), *Consumer Culture & Modernity*, Cambridge, UK: Polity.

genuine Alashan cashmere and innovative, contemporary designs. For Western consumers, Sand River is an authentic brand that distinguishes them from others when they wear its cashmere. India's Tanishq offers unique jewelry completely different from the cookie-cutter jewelry sold by chains like Kay or Zales. My wife loves Tanishq jewelry more than anything US brands offer.

Second, people buy global brands for a reason. Local brands often do not provide the quality, innovation, and technology of global brands, as anybody who remembers SBR (Belgium) and RCA (USA) televisions, or Simca (France) and AMC (USA) cars can attest. If local brands provide unique value, anchored in the local culture, they can and do thrive. Take beer—despite the tremendous marketing power of global brands like Budweiser, Corona, and Heineken, local brands (which of course includes, say, Budweiser in the eyes of Americans) continue to command a market share well north of 50% in almost any country. Local cultural productions such as Bollywood movies or Korean soap operas command vast and loyal audiences. In 2015, the locally produced movie about the seventeenth-century Dutch Admiral Michiel de Ruyter generated higher box office receipts in the Netherlands than any Hollywood movie, including *Jurassic World*, *Avengers: Age of Ultron*, and *Fast and Furious 7*. However, uninspiring local movies and low-quality local brands lose out to global brands. Not because global brands have a monopoly but because they are better attuned to the needs of local consumers.

Third, many executives are keenly aware that a one-size-fits-all marketing strategy for their global brand simply does not work. Rather than trying to push standardized, mass commodities, they actively look for ways to make their brands relevant for local markets. Those who overstandardize their strategy face the consequences.

Fourth, global brands have dramatically improved the human condition. Thanks to Google, people in Africa have access to information that was the prerogative of well-stocked Western libraries. Cars are safer and burn less fuel than even a decade ago. New medicines eradicate illnesses. Skype and Facebook allow (grand)parents to be closely involved with the lives of their loved ones, even when they are an ocean apart. And so on. In *Atlas Shrugged*, Ayn Rand gives us a glimpse of a world without global brand innovators.[9] It is one of chaos. Companies only invest in R&D if they can legally protect and differentiate their new products. Branding is indispensable for this. Take brands away and there will be no innovation. Companies need to do a better job highlighting the contribution global brands make to the prosperity and well-being of the world.

As small firms start to take their brand global, existing global brands aim to defend and expand their position, and new brands from emerging markets enter the fray, some will succeed, and some will fall by the wayside. My hope is that my book helps executives to make their brand a success on a global scale and, in the process, retain what is good and work against what is bad.

---

[9] Rand, Ayn (1957), *Atlas Shrugged*, New York: Random House.

Appendix: Country Scores on Culture Map Scales

Scores are on a scale from 0 to 100, and are calculated by the author based on Erin Meyer (2014), *Culture Map*, New York: PublicAffairs. The lower the score, the closer the country is to the left-hand pole of the scale, and the higher the score, the closer the country is to the right-hand pole of the scale. For a number of countries, scores are not available on all scales. You can make a reasonable guestimate by using the score of a cultural similar country. For example, for comparing Argentina to the USA, use Brazil's score on scales 4–8 as proxy for Argentina (Table A.1).

© The Author(s) 2017
J.-B. Steenkamp, *Global Brand Strategy*,
DOI 10.1057/978-1-349-94994-6

Table A.1 Country scores on culture map scales

	1. Communicating (low vs. high context)	2. Evaluating (direct vs. indirect negative feedback)	3. Persuading (principles first vs. applications first)	4. Leading (egalitarian vs. hierarchical)	5. Deciding (consensual vs. top-down)	6. Trusting (task-based vs. relationship-based)	7. Disagreeing (confrontational vs. avoiding confrontation)	8. Scheduling (linear time vs. flexible time)
Argentina	54	59	45	20		22	38	
Australia	13		85			82	52	
Brazil	51	63	41	55	62			75
Canada	13	53	80	30				
China	86	75	95	86	87	87	77	81
Denmark	34	25	60	9		15	28	26
Finland	36			30		28		
France	66	24	10	63	65	56	12	55
Germany	24	16	33	53	34	24	17	7
Ghana		80					81	
India	76	72		86	84	90	69	87
Indonesia	91	87					86	
Israel		8		17			7	
Italy	61		10	55	69	64	34	67
Japan	92	98	95	92	6	71	87	16
Kenya	83	72						91
Mexico	59	65	51	71		74	65	72
Netherlands	20	12	68	10	20	12	22	27
Nigeria				100	94	94		94
Peru	62			78			74	

Country								
Poland	44					45		44
Russia	68	10	22	73	80	73	19	65
Saudi Arabia	80	81		78		92	72	92
Singapore	70			82			60	
South Korea	91			92				
Spain	57	82	18	63		61	27	62
Sweden			56	8	12		63	19
Thailand		93				81	85	
Turkey						78		76
UK	34	56	71	45	46	34	50	32
USA	8	50	92	39	57	6	47	27

Index

Note: f refers to citations mentioned in figures
t refers to citations mentioned in tables

© The Author(s) 2017
J.-B. Steenkamp, *Global Brand Strategy*,
DOI 10.1057/978-1-349-94994-6